WHAT A LIFE!

GEORGE GREENING

Author of
Youth in a Permissive Society

MINERVA PRESS
MONTREUX LONDON WASHINGTON

WHAT A LIFE!
Copyright © George Greening 1995

All Rights Reserved

ISBN 1 85863 460 1

First Published 1995 by
MINERVA PRESS
1 Cromwell Place,
London SW7 2JE.

Printed in Great Britain
B.W.D. Ltd., Northolt, Middlesex.

WHAT A LIFE!

PROLOGUE

(With apologies to Shakespeare for a paraphrase in B.)

A.   "One Man in his time plays many parts."

As You Like It, Act II, Scene vii.

B   "Speak of me as I am:
      Nothing extenuate; nor set down
      aught in malice...
      Speak of one that lives
      not always wisely but - still
      rather well."

Othello, Act V, Scene ii.

DEDICATION

I dedicate these stories to the two women above all others who have inspired me throughout a long and eventful life (both with Shakespearean names; though happily having pleasanter connotations). I refer first to my Mother - Cordelia; and secondly to my wife - Kate.

Both have been benign, powerful, long-term stimulating influences, for which I am forever grateful!

CONTENTS

PREFACE

(Apologia: Forewarned is forearmed!)

Most of my stories are about WORK. Only one (or possibly two) about Love. I have often had arguments with relatives, friends and colleagues about the relative values, and importance of these two major human pre-occupations. I recall one colleague in particular, a female teacher of Literature in a Middlesex Polytechnic, insisting that compared to Love and Sex - WORK could never maintain the Reader's interest so long. I argued passionately that the work situation, treated properly, could also hold one's rapt attention.

Apropos: I now call to witness on behalf of my thesis, for example, two of our most famous English writers: Dickens and Hardy, from France I summon up Zola; from Russia, Maxim Gorki; from Italy, Silone and Germanetto; from Germany, Hans Fallada. But perhaps it is America (specifically U.S.A.) which offers the most examples of authors who have used the work situation, and cognate experiences, to illustrate a story often with a didactic purpose. Consider Jack London, Upton Sinclair, Dreiser Sinclair Lewis, Steinbeck, Updike, et al. R.K. Narayan, the fine Indian novelist, is another example supporting my thesis.

Of course, I cannot hope to match these famous talented writers in creative ability and polished style. (I quite realise, like Dogberry, that "comparisons are odorous!") Yet I am bold to boast that I have one advantage over these illustrious authors in the strict context of work experience. I refer to the great variety of jobs I have undertaken in a long and very eventful life. For example, between the ages of 7 and 10 I was a little, but quite active, assistant to a sweet confectioner's (and I still have scars on my fingers - caught in brass rollers - to prove this). Aged 10 to 12, I was a Butcher's boy, and adept on the fast-moving sausage machine. From age 12 to 14 I sold newspapers. Of more significance: at age 14 I entered the coal-mining industry as a Collier boy and remained in this hellish trade until I was 19. After a spell on the dole "I got on my bike" (like Tebbit's Dad) and migrated to London. By vivid contrast with my work as a miner I waited on tables in the "elegant" Devonshire Club, Westminster and at the notorious Café Royal in Piccadilly. Returned to South Wales with another spell of unemployment - I worked, sans wages, as a reporter for the Communist Daily Worker (the most memorable interview I arranged was with Tommy Farr immediately before his challenge to Joe Louis for the Heavy-weight championship fight for the World Crown). After a year as a student in a College of the Second Chance in North Wales, I returned to the dole queue. I was allotted ten weeks work as a navvy (back-breaking work in bitterly cold weather). Then in summer 1938 I got a job in the new Abertaff Cable Works: first as a machinist; later as a crane-driver and "slinger".

In this factory also, I became a Trade Union organiser and Shop-Steward.

Returning to London in War-time (chasing a new, beautiful sweetheart!) I found a job in a paper mill (1941); then in a pencil factory; then in a biscuit factory (three "blind alley" jobs) until I got a highly-paid, semi-skilled position as an "electrolitic parkeriser" of anti-aircraft shell-cases in a munitions works. In the last year of the War (1944-45) I was a Telephoto Lens Polisher.

I started Teacher-Training in autumn 1945. This was a "one year Emergency Course" arranged in a hurry by the Ministry of Education which announced in 1944 that 100,000 new teachers would be needed to fully implement the provisions of the new "Butler Act" of 1944.

So, since 1946 I have been a teacher-cum-lecturer taking all ages of pupils and students from 7 to 70 years of age. In the early days of my teaching in London and being very poorly paid (£5 per week to keep a family of four; £2 rent, etc.), I found a part-time job managing a cafe by night (8p.m. till 2a.m.) for £4 weekly! By the way: I started teaching Juniors, then Senior boys; then after gaining an extra-mural degree (BSc. Econ. London) I moved on and up to Polytechnic work (mainly with foreign coloured students and this was very rewarding intellectually). Later, after achieving an M.A. degree in Sociology and Education (at age 54), I became Tutor-Counsellor with the rapidly expanding Open University (1970-80). I concluded my 35 year teaching career as a Principal of Summer Schools ("English for Foreign Students") at several Oxford University colleges during 1975-83.

So in summary: I can claim with all due modesty, but with clear objectivity that mine has been a life of exceptional varied **WORK** experience, dare I challenge, hard to match!? Most of my stories presented herewith are very closely based on these work experiences. And if I cannot boast, with Shakespeare's Bottom: "All For Your Delight!" I still hope that you will find the tales interesting enough to compel you to read each and every one of them.

Yours truly,

George Greening.

N.B. George Greening and the Glyn Griffiths of stories 8, 9 and 10 are the same person.

HOW I LOST MY FIRST SWEETHEART.

The events embodied in this sad and sordid saga took place in "Abertaff", in Mid-Glamorgan, in 1923 (circa). I was between 7 and 8 years of age, and in Class 2 of Juniors in Ynyslwyd School. There I developed a great passion for my first ever sweetheart: Margaret Hughes. She was exquisitely pretty. She had raven black, crinkly-curly hair. Below her white marble forehead and beautifully arched black eyebrows were large eyes like ripe blackberries. Her rosy cheeks were two pale-red apples with a tinge of strawberry jam (yes, quite right: I could have eaten her!). She had a delightful snub nose, so tilted that I could look right into her nostrils, which, unlike mine, were never sullied with two "candle-grease" runners. Nicest of all, she had cherry-ripe lips that, even at age seven and a half, I longed to kiss (for I was already a film-fan, and had witnessed many tentative meetings of trembling lips on the silent silver screen, albeit in those far-off innocent film days).

Margaret, not yet seven, was one school-class below, but I would contrive to stand or sit next to her in assembly and in the big singing lessons, so well arranged by "Maestro" Idwal Rees for all Juniors. Of course, we would meet in the playground; at least I always tried to ensure that blessed consummation and I was ever proffering Margaret a sweet. For in leisure hours I used to "help" our local Confection-maker, Mr Dan Bray ("Boiled - Mixed: Our Speciality") and he would give me many sweets for my "help". Margaret's firm favourite, as I offered them, was a marzipan bon-bon. Invariably a marzipan bon-bon.

In leisure hours also, especially during the long school holidays, we would meet with many other children in the nearby woods with many spindly trees straggling and struggling for existence on top of ancient coal-tips. One of our favourite games was (as so many of us were film-goers already) Cowboys and Indians, in which I would contrive to be Tom Mix or Hoot Gibson. And I would imagine Margaret (though never telling her!) as Ramona, the beautiful, dusky, Indian maiden. One day when she obliged me to be a "Baddie", I mean a "cattle-rustler", she tied me to a tree with orange rope and as she placed the bonds around my body and pulled them tight, I thrilled madly in an ecstasy of wanton delight! I cannot help wondering - in long-term retrospect - if we had married would Margaret have been a sadist, and I a masochist?

CRISIS!

Margaret lived about a quarter mile away from our school in
bourgeois Hazlewood Terrace. I lived only eight houses from school
in slummy Cardiff Road. I proudly belonged to the "Ynyslwyd
Gang". It was quite natural that, as we all lived within the close
school precincts, we should hang around the school area, especially
outside school hours, and notably, during holidays. We would often
contrive to scale the sharp school yard railings and drop inside to play
ball (albeit a paper or rag one).

Our Gang included: wispy-snake-like, naughty Gordon Jones,
bragging, bullying Lenny Hodge, Doug Wilson "the Creep" and our
"boss" was Windsor Roberts because he was older, bigger and
stronger, and mainly because his papa was an engine-driver whereas
the rest of us only had coal-mining fathers.

A new (almost seismic) phenomenon in our young and tender
lives (circa 1923) was the great Religious Revival which shook South
Wales. It seemed to have its very epicentre in Abertaff. Its main
"Hot Gospel" leader was, in fact, a close neighbour named
Nicodemus Edwards. Every Friday evening between 7:30 and
9:30p.m., the Revivalists (an amalgam of Pentecostals and
Apostolics?) would meet in Classroom 6 on the second floor of our
school and hold their highly emotionally-charged meetings, with
"confession of sins" as the grand climax!

Our Ynyslwyd Gang, if bored with our usual games, would creep
upstairs to Room 6 and, when we were sure that all the Revivalists
were in their seats (say by 8p.m.), we would lurk outside the classroom door and listen to the weird noises within. After a frenzied
(mouth-frothing?) sermon with many loud rhetorical flourishes by
eloquent Pastor Nicodemus, several members of the congregation
would, starting up on their feet, begin shouting such phrases as: "Oh
Yes, Oh Lord - Yes! Yes! Dear Lord God of Hosts: Look at me
with Mercy! Save me, Oh Lord! from Hell-Fire-Damnation. For I
hereby repent all my dreadful sins! Oh, Yes! I have been a Sinner,
Oh Lord! But now I seek thy Bountiful Salvation...!" Then the
members would break into an emotional chant or heated hymn such as
"There is Corn for the Reaper today!" or "He rescued me; He rescued
me: A brand from the Burning, He rescued me!" or another firm

favourite, and even more highly charged and colourful was "There is a Fountain filled with Blood drawn from Emanuel's veins" (and similar Draculian phrases).

Then, the most inspired of the Ecclesia (a "Mystagogue" perhaps?) would lapse into "tongues" i.e. esoteric babblings sounding like "Oh! Adonai! an-ail, Even a barbering-ail! Adonai-an-ail, an-ail Oh! Adonai," etc. Then all the members chanting: "Blood, Oh Yes! The Blood of The Lamb! Blood! Blood! Blood!"

Gordon Jones "the Lizard" (a little bugger!) no "Adonai" he, but he suffered from bad adenoids and bad hearing due to mastoids, thought that "Blood! Blood!" was "Blub! Blub!" and he was soon wont to shout through the keyhole of classroom 6: "Blub! Blubs! Silly old Blub-Blubs!" and we would join the esoteric chorus before racing down the school stone steps.

This caper went on for many weeks, even months. One night, however, in dark November, we even got bored teasing the "Blub-Blubs". So we began to dream up other and more daring pranks. Naughty Gordon Jones stopped halfway down the stairs and stood dramatically by a large smooth facade of stone. And there he boldly challenged us to a kind of feat of bladder and penis control. Specifically: he boasted he could "pee for the highest!", and he quickly demonstrated his *jet d'eau* skills. Then we all had a turn. I went last and made a very special effort, so much so that my spouting urine over topped the vaulting ambitions of the rest!

But suddenly, there came an awful gasp and roar even like the famous 'Pentecostal Wind' on that fateful Day recorded in the Scriptures. This roar soon articulated into a dreadful phrase: "Oh! You dirty little BUGGER!" I whipped around and before I had time to whip my offending Willy decently inside its cuspidol-cover, I saw with awful dread that my urinating comrades had fled and that a mere two steps below me stood Sarah Davies, the 60 year-old school cleaner.

There she was, poor old thing, a bag of bones in a bundle of dirty rags. She stretched out a pitifully skinny arm to grab me but I fled clear, and as quick as a fugitive hare I scampered swiftly upstairs to find the alternative exit on the east side of our school.

I got safely home and brushed aside my tired, long-suffering mother's query "Where have you been so long; so late; and why are you sweating?"

I had a somewhat worried week-end but in the careless rapture of youth I returned to school on the Monday morning hoping, and even expecting, that all the hysteria of Friday night was forgotten.

How wrong I was! Before I had properly settled in my class-room seat after Assembly, a message came that Head-Master Bleddyn Stevens wanted to see me. I hurried to his Study with thumping heart and wobbly knees. Sure enough, there he stood - like an Avenging Angel (or so he thought - perhaps though, I saw him more as Lucifer!). In his right hand he held an evil-looking long, wispy, bamboo 'gansen' cane, the usual instrument of punishment for school misdemeanours in those days.

"Are you going to deny what our poor hard-working school cleaner told me about your conduct on last Friday evening?" Stevens asked.

"N-n-n-no!" I faltered.

"Very well," he boomed. "You deserve this punishment! Hold out your hand! No! Your right hand! No, hold it straight out!"

And he administered what used to be called "Six of the Best" (To me they were six of the worst! And the last was the unkindest cut of all, for it caught me on the knuckle of the wrist! Ouch!).

I bore it all with true stoicism and fortitude. But alas, there was worse to come. Not physical but emotional torture!

For stern Stevens marched me around the School starting at Room 6 and working downwards, reciting my wicked deeds to everyone and threatening any imitating culprits with similar swift corporal justice.

At last, horror of horrors, he came to class 2, and then...! And there in the front row alas, sat my (self-proclaimed) sweetheart, Margaret! I couldn't help noticing the utter horror on her face; the deep blushes which suffused the lovely cheeks as she listened to Mr Stevens recount in awful detail my dreadful misdemeanour.

Later that day, and I waited until the afternoon play break to let things simmer down hoping that Christian mercy which we so often sang about would prevail, I strolled over in mock nonchalance to where Margaret was standing (actually she had just emerged from the outside toilets). I decided to confront her boldly and bravely. I reached into my cleanest pocket, and tentatively proffered my usual marzipan bon-bon.

Her response was a look of the utmost scorn. Her lovely snub nose rose up high in the air.

"I don't want your marzipan bon-bon!" she shrieked, "Or any other kind of sweet from you ever again! You wee-weed on our lovely school stairs. I'll never speak to you again - EVER!"

And so alas, I lost my first sweetheart.

MY THREEPENNY PIECE AND MY EASTER EGG

It was Easter 1923. The Great Studt's Fair was at Abertaff for two weeks. There were great roundabouts and swings and chair-o-planes, the Ghost Train, the Helter Skelter, many coconut-shy stalls, stalls for throwing rubber rings to win "wonderful prizes", booths for amateur boxers to take on "Studt Sloggers", for "Jack Lemme: the Strongest Man in the World!" "The Bearded Lady", "The Sultry Snake Charmers of old Baghdad". All this and much more, and all to a background of powerful hurdy-gurdy music. Great fun for everybody especially if you had plenty of money, a commodity not over lavish in the Abertaff of 1923.

The Ynyslwyd Gang of which I was an ardent member, had very little money. So we didn't go to the fabulous Studt Fair very often.

Instead, as it was the school holiday period, we hung about the school precincts. Our Leader (two years older and a head taller) whose father was a Railwayman and a bit better off than the average miner, had a small rubber ball. So, as we all lived along the main Cardiff Road with much traffic, we clambered over the school railings (avoiding the nasty spikes) to have our own peculiar version of football. It was a bit tricky to play our kind of game with a small rubber ball on a stony playground, for the asphalted yard could be cruel to knees in short trousers if one fell!

There we were, the usual five or six of us - Windsor Roberts, the eldest; Lenny Hodge, the bragging bully; Doug Wilson, "the Creep"; Gordon Jones, "the Lizard" who could wriggle into any aperture however small (especially into Danny Bray's Sweet Factory by night, for Gordon lived next door!); and, of course, there was myself: the youngest and easily the most simple as I can soon show, but I was only eight years old.

During a hectic scramble for the little rubber ball Windsor Roberts kicked it high and awkwardly and it simply flew through a wide open window of a class-room. There was no argument as to the chosen Houdini who might be able to recover the ball. Gordon, the "Lizard", hoisted up on Windsor's big shoulders, slithered through the window. However, he was quite some time in returning and we all began earnestly to speculate on the reason for this. No-one else would volunteer to follow the "Lizard", not even bragging, bullying Lenny Hodge. ("What if Gordon had been captured by old scraggy Mrs Davies, the main school cleaner?") After what seemed a year, probably ten minutes duration, the rubber ball was thrown back to us.

Then Gordon's rosy, cheeky face appeared with a most mischievous grin on it!

"Wait till you see what I have found!" he prophesied.

Eventually, helped down by Windsor, Gordon, who somehow looked as if padded-up for a war of American football, began to unbosom himself, verbally and physically.

"Look!" he demanded as he pulled lots of paper money and coins, in separate little loads out of pockets and under his jersey and shirt.

Of course, it soon dawned upon us that it was not real money. It was "School money", used to teach young children to be ready for the great world of Commerce (significantly, in Abertaff schools nothing above a £1 note was used even in mock money). But ten year-old Windsor Roberts, eldest and most sophisticated of our Gang, mused awhile, stroked his chin, and then said, slowly and very deliberately,

"Ah! This may be only school money but some of it may have possibilities...!"

We wondered what he meant but with growing and awesome suspicions.

"These are of no use," he said, as he quickly passed the £1 and ten shilling notes back to the disappointed Gordon, or to others of us who had rarely seen this paper wealth (for in 1923 two pounds sterling was almost the average weekly wage of coal-miners, and cautious parents would seldom pass such precious notes to young kiddies when sending them on shopping errands). So, Windsor came down (like a budding Chancellor of Exchequer) step by disappointing step to the coins.

"These half crowns are too big and obviously made of cardboard. So no use! We simply cannot pass these in any shop!"

Now it began to dawn on us younger and more innocent kids what the wily "Fagin" Roberts had in mind...! And we looked at each other with a wild surmise, silent upon a school-yard in Aberdaria!

At last, Windsor, with a wicked smile and an evil gleam in his hazel eyes, said hoarsely, "But... This should pass!" and with triumph he held up, but with digit difficulty, a cardboard threepenny piece. In those (1923) days the threepenny "bit" was a very tiny silver coin. We called them "ticky bits". "Now," said Windsor, rather more quietly, and looking around with caution and getting us to huddle closer, "NOW we have to try it out!"

"What do you mean?" we queried, though even I, a veritable Oliver Twist simpleton, was beginning to divine "Fagin's" intentions.

"We will go to the nearest shop," said Windsor, "I mean the nearest sweet shop. And one of us will try to pass this ticky bit."

"Oooh!" we all murmured in awe.

"Dare we do it?" asked Dougie Wilson, the "Creep".

"Yes, of course we can!" said bragging, bullying Lenny Hodge.

"O.K. then, let's go!" said our Al Capone, as we clambered over the school railings.

We walked up Cardiff Road. We seemed to know, almost instinctively, in which direction to go. We saw Danny Bray's Sweet Factory, but we realised that he only sold his confectionery wholesale, and in any case he would always be on the look-out for Gordon the "Lizard". No! We had all guessed the name of the sweet shop we were going to plunder, (No Protection Racket involved; it was called Salmon's and kept by an old woman of that name. She came from a distant rural village in West Wales. She was very short and very fat, like a little tub. My mother always called her (without malice) "a Country Bumpkin"; or was it "Pumpkin"? There was always a distinct clatter as she entered her shop for she wore clogs. Some of the local folk, in fact, called her "Dutchy Salmon". Actually, her son Monty was in the same school class as myself and he always smelt of Pear Drops when he spoke to you.

Now, why had Windsor chosen Mrs Salmon as our prey? Well... he quickly and cleverly pointed out that she was "short-sighted, nearly deaf, and too fat to chase us if she spotted the false coin". His arguments were irrefutable.

As we approached the shop (not a Curiosity to us), I noticed that our cunning Gang Leader, Windsor, was stopping and stooping every two minutes and picking up some spent matches from the gutter. We all wondered what he was up to and why - a little later he put five or six of these old matches in his big fist as if to crumple them. Soon we realised his strategic plan (or was it merely a tactical ploy?).

"Now!" he commanded. "The one who picks the longest match stick will go in to Mrs Salmon's Shop, and ask for one of those penny

Easter eggs you can see there in the window, then offer her the mock ticky bit, wait for the egg, get tuppence change, and then RUN LIKE HELL!"

Need I tell you that I - Simple Simon - chose the longest match-stick. I gulped hard and, no doubt, was sweating like the Devil, but to please my own Captain Courageous, Windsor, I hurried in to the shop and soon heard the familiar sound of Mrs Salmon's clogs. She smiled benignly, poor old soul, for she knew my mother well as a good honest customer though might have thought it rather odd that I had a whole ticky-bit to spend!

But answering my bold request she gave me the silver wrapped, penny chocolate Easter egg, and even the tuppence (real money!) change. I rushed out of the shop like a whirl-wind and shouted, "I've got it, and the tuppence change!"

Windsor ordered a lightning-quick strategic retreat!

As we sped ever so rapidly up the Cardiff Road towards the Taff Vale Railway Station, we shared and ravenously devoured the little chocolate egg and I'll swear I saw Dougie Wilson eat the silver paper as well, for he was always hungry.

Windsor, ever our "Boss", said, "Don't let us go back to the school yard because we will have to pass Mrs Salmon's shop again, and she might have spotted our ticky bit trick. Let's go to Studt's Fair and we can get some extra fun out of the tuppence change," he said, without asking me but Fagin's Law held sway in our Gang (and there is honour, even among thieves!).

Alas! The choice of things we could do with our two pence was strictly limited. The Ghost Train per person cost sixpence, a ride on the Chair-o-Planes threepence. To see the Bearded Lady or the Snake Charmers of Old Baghdad or the Strongest Man in the World also threepence (or was it fourpence?) So now we had the embarrassment of SMALL riches! At last, Windsor, as usual, had a brilliant idea,

"Try your luck..." he coaxed, or was it ordered "...on that stall that shows those grand things. Don't bother with the beads and bracelets, they are sissy things. Go for the gold watches and if you win they'll give you the "Double Albert Guard", that's what my eldest brother says, anyway!"

"Yes!" chimed in bullying, bragging Lenny Hodge, "Show Big!"

The others agreed. So despite serious reservations as to my skill in throwing the rubber rings to capture a gold watch, I decided that I couldn't chicken out! The cost of the rings was tuppence for four and when I stood at the stall perimeter I thought how far, far away the coveted prize looked. But summoning up my utmost courage and raising my self to my maximum (four foot and a fart) height (I was known in the family as "shorty"), I threw three of my four rings. No luck! In mounting despair and trepidation I turned to Windsor. After all, apart from being the Leader of our Gang, he was at least a head and shoulders taller. He took the last ring, screwed his hazel eyes up tight, or at least one of them, and I saw him bite his lower lip and I winced in dire tension. He threw and the ring caught the base of the gold watch stand, it twirled with promise. The stall-holder snatched it away shouting, "OH! Bad luck son!" There was no adult there to challenge him.

So now our tuppence was gone. The Fair had suddenly lost its glamour. We walked around the area for about ten minutes more and then strolled home, I arrived home at about 8:30p.m. It was getting quite dark. When I got to the kitchen, crossing the plain (uncarpeted) sanded floor, my poor half-starved skinny mother, Cordelia, always cheerful, ever kindly, asked, "Where on earth have you been? You've been out a long time! Aren't you hungry?"

"Only been to see Studt's Fair with Windsor Roberts and some other pals. Yes! I am hungry."

"Studt's Fair?" asked Mother, "But you haven't any money. It couldn't have been much fun... anyway as you are hungry I have a special treat for your supper!"

"Supper?" I asked. "Special treat?"

I looked at Mother with a wild surmise. I noticed that she seemed to have a strange fiery gleam in her blackberry eyes, "Sit at the table," ordered Mother. "You can even sit on your Dad's armchair. Don't worry, he's out in the Full Moon pub as usual, and he won't be home 'till Stop-Tap."

So I settled in my father's arm-chair and felt important for a little while.

"Are you sitting comfortably?" asked Mother.

"Ye... ye... yes," I faltered.

"Then watch me conjure your special supper."

And with a great flourish she put an egg-cup in front of me and declaiming "Behold!" she popped an Easter egg into the cup. It was a perfect copy of the one I had got dishonestly from old Mrs Salmon!

"Yes, son," Mother said very calmly, and without malice, "I can afford a penny chocolate Easter egg although we are poor. You don't have to steal one."

FIRE

The summer of 1929 seemed to me to be long, warm, sunny and altogether lovely! Perhaps that was mainly because it was my last summer of freedom. For in mid-September I was due - by father's stern decree - to start work; not merely to start work but to begin as a collier-boy in a very deep coal-mine. (After all, I was fourteen now and he - Dad - had started as a collier-boy aged ten).

Of course I was worried, for, at the start of the long school holiday in late July, as our depleted Ynyslwyd Gang played in the open space between the corner of Wind Street and Cardiff Road, a loudly clanging, speeding ambulance had driven us frantically out of its dusty path. We saw it tearing up the wide leafy lane that led to the nearest local pit we called Blaengwawr.

"Come on," said bullying, bragging Lenny Hodge, "let us follow it!"

We did so and soon saw the ambulance at the pit head.

Strangely, no one stopped us kids approaching the area. Apart from the sharp but subdued bark of orders from the colliery overman and the main ambulance man, all was deathly quiet. Even the huge colliery wheel spinning and lifting the cage, seemed slower and more quiet than usual. Soon we saw the lift cage and observed its steel frame door open. Two miners in front staggered out followed by a stretcher, borne from the rear by two other colliers.

We kids couldn't help noticing with awe a prone figure on the stretcher crudely covered with a coarse grey woollen cloth. We then distinctly saw the top of a bloodstained head. We heard low voices mutter in solemn agreement, "Oh, yes! It's Cliff Coles alright. Yes, the poor bugger's had it. He's dead for sure."

Dougie Wilson, "the Creep", I noticed had turned a ghastly pale and looked quite sick. We turned away and as we quit the morbid scene Dougie confided, "I'm supposed to start working there, yes that same bloody pit, next month! I'll never go down under now. I'd rather die first!"

And Dougie never did go down. Before he was fifteen he migrated to London to find safer work and as far as I was concerned, he drifted into oblivion.

I suppose that the death scene we witnessed (though they were fairly common in Abertaff in 1929) helped to make that summer really, and strangely, a halcyon one for me. That morbid incident seemed to WILL me to enjoy the season to the full! In spite of poverty, a small income, an over-crowded house, and my parents' constant marital bickering, I was a pretty happy boy at fourteen years of age. I had lots of interests and a real zest for Life

I loved playing in the many fields of Abertaff. I delighted in climbing the many tall trees and especially our high mountains that bordered our broad valley. Even the many filthy coal tips were exciting. For we boys (and sometimes girl "tom-boys" like sister Ann) would delight in acquiring a shovel cut down from a collier's spade, climb to the top of a steep slag tip and slither down as fast as possible pretending we were astride a super fast motor-bike (such as we would never own!) like an A.J.S., or a Norton or a Rudge.

The huge Blaengwawr slag tip - accumulating for well over 50 years - was our favourite ski-slope! One side of the tip, however, and its adjacent land, was forbidden territory (or so the Colliery overmen thought!), for it led, circuitously, into a Level or Drift mine cut into the Graig Mountain. From this busy coal-mine, at regular intervals, emerged a train of ton-laden coal trams. On a parallel set of lines rattled into the mine a train of empty trams. Not far from the entrance of the mine was a dire notice: "TRESPASSERS WILL BE PROSECUTED!"; and a little way beyond on a small brick building fenced around with spiked railings, was another even more dire notice: "DANGER! DYNAMITE!"

The rest of the large hill bordering the big slag tip was a picturesque area with bracken and golden gorse. Of course, in late summer the gorse had turned brown and grizzly.

I revert to my moods and games and hobbies, within or outside our Gang that late and lovely summer. Apart from playing shovel-slides on slag-tips we had occasional games of football, albeit with a very small rubber ball, with two large stones for goal-posts. Lenny Hodge and Dougie Wilson and a few others (Gordon Jones "the Lizard" had left with family to seek work in Coventry) would improvise a game of cricket with home-made bat, twice as wide as a regulation M.C.C. one, and wickets painted on any handy wall. Only Jackie Nichols whose father was a railway driver, had a real, though small, cricket set, but he was very discriminating in his choice of team. Another favourite hobby of mine was reading. I couldn't afford to buy books but we had a good library a mile walk away. It boasted "many volumes", but the librarian, haughty Mrs Sturdey, would not let kids pass her "barrier"; a strong door with a very small open window aloft. She would stand on guard and wait for us kids to ask for "a book". She would then choose one suitable for Christian children (*Pilgrim's Progress* and even Dante's *Inferno* in a prose version!).

Another pastime I had, but in a somewhat alien sphere. I would visit the Aberaman Gang from time to time in their favourite haunt, The Garth meadow. Somehow they would welcome me as a kind of "Guest Star". Their Leader was a bright and handsome boy named Willy Landry who was often pursued by a beautiful girl named Beatrice Mosley, with whom I fell madly in love that summer.

Strange that with all these hobbies, games and pursuits I should have landed myself in such a desperately dire situation that September! The fact is I found a full box of matches! I had never had one to myself before. I seemed to go berserk!

I found the "Lucifers" in the area of Blaengwawr, close to the slag tip. It was about 3 to 3:30p.m. Strangely, there was no one about. I started striking match after match.

After a time I was disappointed that I could see no great conflagration. I found an old, discarded, local newspaper (very thin in those days). I started twisting it into a kind of candelabra. I made it into a small torch and then threw it into a clump of bracken. I saw, with momentary delight - like a Mountain Mephistopheles - that the tinder-dry bracken started burning brightly. Beginning as a mere wisp of blue smoke the nearby gorse caught fire.

Suddenly, to my extreme horror, I saw a thin lick of orange light burst into long menacing tongues of flame.

"Oh my God!" I almost screamed. "What in Hell's name have I done?"

I realised it was useless for me even to attempt to stamp it out and there was no water! The fire was spreading all too rapidly. I fled in panic. But upon retreating ever so rapidly I was constrained to look back over my shoulder from time to time but only to see the fire spreading quickly and extensively.

I quickly quit the Blaengwawr area. I soon passed the corner of Wind Street and Cardiff Road. Now I was ever so near my home but I felt I dare not enter.

I simply had to get as far away as possible and as rapidly as possible from the scene of my terrible arson crime!

I bolted fearfully, down the Cardiff Road, past no. 20, my home and soon I passed no. 60! Then I made a quick (strategic?) diversion. I raced down the back tracks towards my second favourite play area - the Garth. Inside the large Garth field, a sizeable, fenced-off area with a palisade of steel railings made a playground for young children. I sat on a swing but couldn't help looking back towards the Graig mountain, trying to focus my gaze on the big coal tip.

Alas my worst fears were being realised: the fire was raging and seeming to spread. Alternately I would look on to the playground before me, then compulsively at the slag-tip and the awful fire. I was sick at heart and terribly fearful. What had I done? Surely I would be detected, arrested and imprisoned!?

While musing morosely and morbidly in this way, suddenly I was aware of someone standing at my side. I was terribly scared: a policeman I wondered? But soon I realized, with great relief, that the person was an old school chum. His name was Henry Butlin. He was the same age as myself, a near neighbour, and was due to start work in the same coal-mine on the very same day. We also attended the same (Christadelphian) chapel. Henry was very intelligent, quick on the uptake.

"Helloh!" he greeted. "How long have you been here? By the way, have you looked up to the Graig area in the past few minutes? I mean, to the area of the big slag-tip?"

"N... n... no!" I faltered.

"Well look NOW!" shouted Henry. "I'll swear there's a fire raging! LOOK!"

I pretended to look intensely. "NO! NO! I don't think so. It seems to be the sharp rays of the setting sun."

"I don't think it's that," curtly observed clever Henry. "The sun's rays, if showing, always point to Mountain Ash at this time of the year. Anyway I'm going to investigate. Are you coming?"

"No, no," I apologised, "I have to go on an errand for my Uncle."

"What now? Why on earth are you sitting here then? Can't be important."

"Oh! Oh, it is; my Uncle lives on the Aberaman side of the Garth. It's a long way so I'm taking a little rest."

Henry looked at me dubiously and said, "Oh, very well. But I'm going to investigate anyway. So long."

I now found even the Garth playground too uncomfortable for my peace of mind for I could still see the fire burning and spreading. So I walked away out of the area and into the lower Cardiff Road - possibly two miles from home. In the main shopping precinct near Lewis Street, I bumped into another old chum. It was the lively Willy Landry.

"Helloh!" he hailed. "What are you doing in our neighbourhood? Slumming?"

"NO. I'm going to call on my Uncle," I lied. "Are you going my way, perhaps?"

"No," he replied "I have to get home soon, no later than 5p.m. for Dad wants me to look after the shop."

Willy's father was bourgeois. In fact, he owned the only Radio & Gramophone Shop in Aberaman. By my poor standards Willy was rich, and I often wondered if it was this fact that made him more attractive to girls than I.

After leaving Willy, determined not to go home in the daylight while the awful fire might be still fiercely burning, I wandered ever so slowly back to the Garth playground. Focusing my gaze into the darkening sky and more narrowly towards the Graig and slag-tip, I thought that I discerned more smoke than fire now and was, to that extent, somewhat heartened.

Still, I waited a while longer, perhaps for an hour, until I thought I was possibly the last person in the playground.

Then I began slowly to walk towards home. I had to cross a small iron bridge strung across the River Cynon. Half way across I almost stopped in horror. Coming straight towards me I saw the huge figure of burly, bullying Police Sergeant Williams.

"Oh, my God!" I thought. "I am detected, he is going to arrest me!"

I determined to look down until I could only see his bloody big boots. He stopped right in front of me. "This is it," I thought.

"Look where you are going, son, for Christ's sake!" he barked.

I looked up at his huge, red, beefy face. (On an earlier occasion I had good reason to remember, in 1926, when I was only 11 years old, I had encountered him on this very spot, also at dusk. He had then stopped me in my tracks and hit me hard behind the right ear shouting, "Bugger off home, kid!"; and I have often wondered if his nasty blow caused premature deafness.)

I felt myself cringe now in an attitude of self-defence. This time, however, P.S. Williams only asked, "Where are you off to, kid, Not looking where you are going?"

"H... h... home!" I stammered.

"That's it, lad!" he rejoined. "That's it. Don't hang about, bugger off home!"

I heaved a mighty sigh of relief and hurried on. What an ESCAPE! Oh Gee!

After a pause I strolled home, but only very, very slowly. I arrived in the long passage to our poor kitchen at about 9p.m. Unusually, not only my mother, but my five sisters (two or three already married) were grouped around the small kitchen and were having an animated conversation.

"Helloh!" said Mother as she, at last, noticed me. "You're out late... Still, be a working MAN soon won't you?" Before I could offer any answer, she continued, "Anyway, you've missed all the excitement. Or have you? Perhaps you know all about it."

"Excitement?" I said as calmly as possible, but guessing the worst. "Excitement? I've been for a long walk down the Garth and Aberaman and met Will Landry."

"D'ye mean to say you missed all the excitement? Didn't you know about the BIG Fire!?" Looking around the room she appealed for corroboration to my sisters who all spoke excitedly, all together.

"Great big fire on the slag tip, a HUGE FIRE! Biggest Fire in the History of Abertaff! Even threatened the Blaengwawr DYNAMITE HOUSE. Three Fire-Brigades called. Many hours there!"

"If that DYNAMITE HOUSE had caught fire and exploded," said sister Alice, "God alone knows how many people would have been killed."

Very quietly and cautiously, I asked, "Wh... wh... who started the fire...?"

"Why should ANYONE have wanted to start it?" demanded eldest sister Elinor, giving me a stern stare which made me blush.

Ever-wise Mother summarised, "Oh, some collier, careless with a spent cigarette, perhaps. I cannot imagine anyone deliberately trying to start such a dangerous fire. Yes, a fag-end still lit, I guess. Anyway, the bracken and the gorse is so tinder dry after this hot summer, it was almost ready for spontaneous combustion!"

Feeling guilty and very uncomfortable I soon went to bed.

For the next week or so I remained in a state of anxious excitement and nervous tension, wondering if someone had witnessed my dire-fire incendiaryism. This secret witness would be waiting for a suitable moment to tell all! The police would then act swiftly and remorselessly. Arrest and jail would inevitably follow, not to mention lasting disgrace!

In fact, eight days later I began working as a collier-boy deep underground and 'my fire' only seemed to be a kind of horrible presentiment of a far, far greater, but kindred, disaster. For on my second day in the coal mine, a haulier with pit pony came to my "Butty's" (master) work-place to collect a full tram and told him in great excitement, alas but in Welsh, of a crisis. My "Butty" then informed me that news was filtering through of a terrible fire still raging in Abertaff General Hospital (I realised with horror that my sister Alice worked there), and that so far three firemen had died.

Later that day the awful news was confirmed, but my sister was safe.

WORK APACE, APACE.

Work apace, apace, apace,
Honest labour can make a dirty face.
But we must make MONEY! MONEY! MONEY!

With apologies to Thomas Dekker, c.1600

I started work in my first coal mine in mid-September, 1929. Three weeks later the "Great Crash", presaging the Great Economic Depression, occurred. I believe I can claim, with little fear of contradiction, that there was no connection between the two events.

I had now turned 14 years of age, and my "dear" father decreed that I must follow his trade as coal miner. My mother was worried and argued with him. Though I was tubby and looked strong, I was not healthy. I was a "War-baby", (1915), and had hardly ever tasted real butter. And after the long miner's stoppage (seven months in 1926) I had developed a nasty wracking cough. My mother knew, though she never dwelt on it, that I was suspect T.B. There were no medical examinations in those days to determine physical fitness for miners.

My last school teacher, Tom Richards, had begged mother to keep me in school a while longer because I was "his best student with a real flair for journalism". However, weak in Maths, I had failed the Eleven Plus one day scholarship exam by five marks. So Dad could argue with Mam, "He can't be all that brilliant! Anyway, he is 14 now, and looks a strong lad. And after all, I was in the pit at 10!" His final, clinching, ever so logical summary was overwhelming. "After all, son, you are going to keep me in my old age!" Incidentally, Dad always bemoaned his parental bad luck - five daughters and only two sons!

So, in mid-September 1929, I had my rude awakening. Up at 5a.m. instead of a leisurely 8. And I saw, for the first time, my poor, skinny mother (a bag of bones) struggling to light a coal fire with wet sticks, brewing "smokey" tea and boiling an egg each for her three colliers: Dad, Eddie and the "new man" - ME! As she worked, Mam coughed terribly all the while. Dad worked in local Blaengwawr,

Eddie in the two feet seam in a Drift mine called Wimber, five miles distant. Strangely, Dad had found me a lovely place (!) in Bwllfa no. 1 (sometimes called Nantmelyn) four miles away. So I was to catch the same Colliers Train as brother Ed. However, he did not wait for me for I had promised to call on my pal Henry Butlin who lived ten doors further up the Cardiff Road, nearer the station. Henry was also starting to work in the same seam, in the same deep mine, on the same day.

Rigged out in very crude colliers clothes (no special safety gear in those days), my first long, tough trousers, old jacket passed down from elder brother, cloth cap (never a helmet), with tin grub box and tin drinking "jack" holding cold water, I walked up Cardiff Road to call on Henry. If I was apprehensive about the new life, Henry was dead scared! Henry was a terribly weedy boy. He was the last but one of a long family of boys. (My Dad often moaned, "Will Butlin was bloody lucky to have seven boys, and only one girl!") Henry was dreadfully skinny with spindly legs that made him fall victim to constant spills in games. His skin was the colour of white chalk. His mother, like mine, had begged his father not to put him underground. But tough old Will had used much the same unanswerable logic as mine in insisting on Henry's future: "I was only 10 going underground. He is 14!". So Henry and I started out on our new life, after a brief kiss and swift embrace from his mother. I had had no kiss, for like the Joads, "we were never a kissing family!"

Henry and I walked briskly up the Cardiff Road to the Taff Vale Station and boarded the Colliers' Train. This would travel four or five miles on a narrow valley with two or three stops near various coal mines on the way. There were about six mines in this valley, more than forty in the valleys of Abertaff.

In our railway carriage, which held about ten or more miners (including my brother), we were soon exposed to cheeky comments and crude ribaldry by the older and seasoned miners. We had to endure - chapel boys notwithstanding - the sound of our first really bad swear words. And in a little while, one of the colliers named Will Thomas, gifted with a strong, sweet tenor voice, started a ribald song which had an obscene chorus which all the others joined in with great gusto. Henry looked at me with a scowl of distaste.

We arrived at our destination just before 6a.m. (After the Miners lost their "Lock-Out" in 1926, their working day was extended by one hour to eight, for a shilling less per day in pay). Our day would start at 6a.m. and end at 2p.m. We were met at the pit-head by two men aged, I guessed, about forty-five or so. They would be our "Masters", though the usual designation was "Butties". Mine proved to be a kindly man named Evan Davies (though I noted that most miners called him "Eevan"). Henry's Butty introduced himself as Dai Thomas.

They now took us to the Lamp Room. Here we were given a metal disk. It was explained that this disk was important in case of crisis such as fall of rock, explosion and so on. The disk had the same number as the lamp we now received.

We boys were warned that these were "OIL lamps" and had to be "handled with great care!" For if they were tilted at too sharp an angle the oil would run on the wick and extinguish the light and could spell disaster! I noticed that most of the Butties collected electric lamps and I would often wonder, in months and years ahead, why the apprentice boys were given the poorest lamps!

We were now escorted by our Butties to the top of the pit, and I gazed with new awe at the huge pit-head gear. It was a very deep coal mine. I had been told that it was about 2,000 feet deep. We approached the pit cage (Henry and I) with obvious apprehension. After waiting a while for other men to be taken down the shaft we two boys, with trembling and wobbly knees, stepped into the lift-cage built to hold ten men at a time. I looked up with some patent trepidation at the steel cable from which the lift-cage was suspended. One of our Butties, with traditional words of cynical solace consoled, "Don't worry boy-bach, that rope you are looking at is made to last one year, and the year isn't up till tomorrow!"

I was quite surprised to note that before the lift-cage went down it seemed to rise high in the air then it suddenly plunged into the deep shaft. I had a sickening feeling in the pit of my stomach and I must have groaned audibly, for my Butty, Evan Davies, put a paternal hand on the tip of my shoulder and said, "Nasty feeling first time isn't it? But you'll get used to it lad!"

After a descent which seemed endless, we arrived at pit bottom with a light bump. As we left the lift-cage I was agreeably surprised by the well-walled and well-arched surroundings, and how brilliantly lit it all was. I also noticed with growing optimism that everything looked clean and spacious, more like a fine factory than a dirty coal mine. How cruelly deceptive my first impressions were!

Now," said Evan, my Butty, "prepare, boys, for a long, long walk to the coal-face."

"How long?" I asked.

"Oh! About one mile at least."

There were about a dozen of us walking on till we came to a division in the roadway, then two miners with a "Cheerio!" turned off on to a new gallery. These gallery divisions were called, in fact, Headings.

"We are now in the Graig district," I heard Dai Thomas tell Henry.

Now I was obliged to note that though still well timbered, our heading space was obviously shrinking. Whereas at pit bottom the height was at least twenty feet, it was now down to less than ten and at about every twenty yards falling rapidly. Quite soon the height had fallen to eight, or possibly seven feet.

Meanwhile, on advice from our Butties, we had put our oil lamps to hang on the front of our belts so as to have our hands free because we were warned, "There's a lot of water ahead and you will have to hold on to a wire rope so as not to get feet wet!" We found that this wire rope ran from pit bottom to infinity.

Soon there was a general cry, "Here it is. The damn DWR. The bloody DWR!" (DWR means water.) Presently we saw a long, long sheet of it looming up. "Now boys, you new lads, put your left up and grab the wire rope and prepare to do a trapeze act!" A man in front demonstrated like a Blondin on wire over Niagara Falls. He raised his left hand to the rope and went shuffling across the left side rail of the narrow gauge tram railway at our feet: one foot carefully following the other on the one rail. We all followed carefully in turn. Henry was the last in the pit procession. As we all thought we were all safely over, DISASTER struck! There was a kind of muted soft splash: for below our feet was not only water but soft mud the miners called 'slurry' (i.e. water and small coal). Henry had fallen into it! Not on his knees but full length face down, his oil lamp beneath him.

Instead of expressing sorrow and sympathy, Dai Thomas groaned aloud, "Oh! Oh! What a stupid little bugger! And on his first day. A fine bloody start, Henry! And now I'll have to get his oil lamp re-lit at the next Locking-hole!"

Two men fished Henry out of the soft muck. He looked a sorry sight! He was covered head to foot in the slurry, face and all!

"Oh! Oh!" he wailed. "I want to go home! Now, PLEASE, let me go home, PLEASE!" Instead of getting words of comfort, all the miners roared with laughter.

Dai Thomas shouted: "HOME? Henry bach, HOME? No, no boyo. You're down here for eight hours and you won't see HOME nor your lovely Mammy till about three o'clock! In any case," Dai concluded with dismal summary, "it's just as well that you've had your baptism now. For you're going to be in water all day long!" Of course I was alarmed at this dire prediction. It was all too true!

When we arrived at the coal face about twenty minutes later, I found water dripping from the fissure in the rocky roof and resembling a rainy day. The mine was being worked on the Pillar and Stall method, so that large pillars of coal and rock were being left behind. Each miner had a place (stall) of about ten yards running either way from his main gallery. I soon noticed an empty ton tram on the tram rails running right to the coal face. But soon I was alarmed to find that the actual coal seam was less than three feet high so that one had to crawl on hands and knees to get to the coal.

Butty Evan now apologised: "Sorry lad but you are now going to get very wet! I hope your father warned you!"

"No!" I replied. "He said he was finding me a nice place underground."

Evan snorted scornfully and said, "Oh well. We'll have to make the best of it. Take your jacket off and hang it on that large nail on that post." There were T posts everywhere, supporting the rock-roof.

"Make sure your grub box is shut quite, quite tight, oh and your water-jack well corked for there are lots of rats about and they are thieving little buggers!" I obeyed with great care.

"Now," advised Evan, "before we can cut and fill the coal we have to bale the water out down by that pillar. Can you see it, and the hole above it?"

"Yes," I answered innocently, "but isn't there a steam pump to do that?" (I had learned so much in school about Newcommen's Pump, invented 1710 AD). Evan laughed, but rather sombrely I thought, and he handed me what looked like a large biscuit tin. In the light of a lamp I noted that it was a "Lovell's Toffee REX" tin.

"Look after your toffee tin," said Evan. "It's your steam pump. Now, there's no two ways about it. You've got to crawl to that end of the face. You'll have to lie in that water for a while and start baling the water out through that hole in that pillar of coal into the next place! There's a slope you see. Oh! And you might like to know that your pal, Harry, will be baling it out to the next stall down below him!" I did as I was told and found the water very cold, but started baling out.

After about half an hour of this miserable work the water had dispersed, and Evan started cutting the coal with his mandrill (a miner's pick). He then shovelled the cut coal behind him. My job now was to gather the coal into a large scoop, called a curling box and, on my hands and knees, take it back to the tram where I could stand up to tumble the load in.

This work went on for about six hours, with one break of twenty minutes or so for grub which we ate with pit-props behind us to rest our backs. I had the traditional grub for miners, as recommended by Dad: bread and cheese, washed down, alas, not by beer, but by cold water.

Just after 1:30p.m., Evan called a halt after completing two trams. "That's enough for today," he said. "Anyway, you probably know our eight hour shift is bank to bank. Cage down; cage up; and we've got a long walk back!"

We arrived back on the pit top just after 2p.m. and I waited around for Henry. There were no pit-head baths in those days; the bath was a tub in front of fire at home.

Soon Henry arrived and he looked the utmost picture of misery! He seemed to be caked in mud.

"What did you think of our first day under?" I asked.

"Oh! Oh! Oh!" he shuddered. "It was dreadful! A terrible nightmare! I'll not stick it! I'm going to beg my father to get me out of it as soon as possible!"

We caught the Colliers' Train and suffered again the coarse comments of the miners. They noticed we were wet, especially Henry, but no sympathy was forthcoming.

"Did you have a nice swim?" one asked.

Another enquired, "Nice bathing in the Graig District?"

And then Will Thomas regaled his audience with songs about swimming and bathing in exotic places.

I got home about 2:45p.m. Mother had the bath water warming in a huge tin boiler on the large open fire. The constant routine was: bath in wooden tub before the fire in two halves, top half with Mum or Sis to scrub the back, alternating bathing positions with Dad and Eddie. Dinner to follow.

After Mam's salutation, "Well, bach, how did it go?", she asked me to strip off ready for bathing. When she saw my shirt and vest she almost howled in dismay. "What the hell have you been doing?"

"Working in water," I replied. "There was no escaping it. It runs through the rock-roof like rain. It gathers in pools and we have to bale it out!"

Mam turned to Dad with a sharp admonitory air. "I thought you were finding him a LOVELY WORK PLACE! Just look at the state of his shirt and vest! Soaking!"

Dad merely scowled and then said, "Tut, tut, woman! I've been in a worse state many times. And don't forget, I started at 10 years. He's 14. And you'll find his 12/6d per week very handy!" The stern logic silenced Mother.

Three weeks later in Sunday chapel, Henry approached me with a sly smile.

"I shan't be seeing you tomorrow," he said. "I've finished in the Pit for good, thank God!" (Henry was a far more devout Christadelphian than I was.) "I've got a lovely new job in the Co-op Bakery!"

When I told my mother later, she sighed and smiled, in her stoical manner. "Oh!" she summarised, "Emma has worked it nicely." (Emma was Henry's mother).

"What do you mean, Mam?" I asked.

"Well, didn't you know that Emma Butlin is the Chairperson of the Co-operative Womens' Guild? She has obviously pulled strings and got Henry a nice, clean, safe job!" We were both silent for a while, then Mother said, "I am sorry, my son, I have no strings to pull for you!"

And so I endured six more months working in the water in the deep mine, with five more hard slogging mining years to follow.

ACCIDENT; AND ALL ALONE IN THE COAL MINE.

In the autumn of 1932, aged 17, I was already working in my third Abertaff pit. This was the deep coal mine called Powell's Pit (known otherwise to keen Welsh-speaking people, as "Bwllfa no. 3").

There was no water in this mine; on the contrary, it was in most working parts, very hot and dusty. My boss or Butty was named Evan Llewellyn.

He was a very tall, skinny man of about 40-45 years of age. By nature his was a kindly soul. I use the word soul advisedly for he was very religious, a chapel deacon who never swore, well never worse than, "Oh, bother!", or "tut-tut", or "Oh the Devil!", or "drat it!". In his social life he was very popular for he was gifted in music: he played the piano and the church organ. He had recently founded a choir called "Cor-y-Glyn" (the "Valley Choir").

Alas! As a coal miner Evan was a poor specimen. To begin with he seemed far too weak for the rigours of hard mining. He was also very accident prone. And the trouble for me was that, unless I was very alert, he could easily lead me to injury. I recount now one of the accidents that nearly cost me my life.

In spite of Evan's frailty and incompetence, there were no examinations nor inspections for fitness for coal-mining. He had been given the hard and important task of driving a heading (a main roadway) to link up with another driving towards us, to create an airway.

It seemed to me that nearly every time Evan put up a large post from ground level to rock ceiling in order to hold a special hand-wound drill, the post would wriggle free and dangerously jump out of hold! Evan would sweat like hell, and "tut-tut!" and sometimes give vent to an un-chapel-like blasphemy, such as "Oh! Gosh-darn it!" Although our main job was to get our heading driven to meet the other, we also cut and filled coal from a rather rich seam. It was, however, a three-feet six-inch seam so we had to kneel to work it.

This seam was made up of what old miners called "face-slips" This coal strata was more difficult and dangerous to mine than "back-slips". For after digging out the "butts", large lumps of coal would be left hanging over the men. Some of these overhanging lumps could be as large as small tables and the good/careful miner would prop them up with T-shaped timber posts and very carefully wedge them down with a crowbar at the desired moment. Evan was lax in taking these precautions!

One day Evan said to me, "Get your curling box (a large iron scoop) and collect those little lumps on the far side of the face - there." I looked apprehensively at a huge slab of unprotected coal looming over my low passage.

I asked, in worried tones, "What about that big face-slip piece hanging there without a prop?"

"It's all right," consoled Evan. "I've tested it with my mandrill. It is as solid as the Rock of Ages!"

Very reluctantly, I moved forward on hands and knees with my curling box towards the top end of the face. As I did so, was it nervous instinct, or was it a real sound (?), anyway, I thought I heard a low crunching noise, and as I did so I leapt backwards only just in time, for the huge slab of coal came crashing down, and pinned my right foot and ankle underneath it. I felt a dreadful sickening pain and cried out in agony. I tried but could not move. Evan rushed to my side. "Get your foot out!" he shouted. I tried again.

"It's no use," I said. "I can't move."

Evan then got a long crowbar, and as he eased the slab of coal up I snatched my foot away.

"Stand up!" Evan demanded. I tried.

"It's useless," I replied: "I'm afraid I've broken my ankle!"

Eventually, Evan gave me a drink of water and, no doubt ridden by guilt, begged, "Please don't tell anyone how it happened, will you? PLEASE?"

Reluctantly, I agreed.

What followed that day turned near tragedy into farce. For, had that big slab of coal landed on my body I would have been badly injured or even killed. Evan now kept asking me to try to stand. I found it impossible. "I'll have to try to carry you back to the corner of our heading," he said, "and find a haulier (with pit pony and tram) to take you back to pit bottom and then out to the Ambulance Room." He started to carry me on his skinny, bony shoulders, and immediately collapsed.

"We'll have to wait for Tom Jones to call on his rounds," he moaned. An hour later Tom arrived. I was then lifted by both men and put inside his empty tram. Then for the first and only time, I had a ride to pit bottom. Arrived on top, I was taken to the Ambulance Room. An 'expert' ambulance attendant then said, "I'd better not take your boot off or your foot will swell so much that you will not be able to get the boot back on. It's better to have your foot attended to by a doctor in his surgery!"

So this 'expert' bound up my boot and lower leg with an enormous white bandage. At the same time the Colliery Manager, quite fortuitously, looked in. He was Fred Forey, and happened to be a second cousin to my mother. When realising who I was he took more than a passing interest.

"Sorry, but you'll have to wait for the next ambulance to arrive back here," he said. (Colliery ambulances were always busy in Abertaff, as in all mining areas).

"Oh, no!" I said. "I don't want an ambulance. I don't want to scare my mother."

"That's a sensible boy!" Forey concluded. "But we've got to get you home."

The eventual result of the deliberations of Forey and others was that I was lifted and put astride a rather large pit pony, guided by a haulier, and led by a sooty black collier-boy, with huge white bandage on foot and leg all the way (three miles) home. As we passed through the main shopping streets of Abertaff, I seemed to be the cynosure, and extreme comic spectacle of all the eyes of the towns-folk. And when my mother answered the door to the haulier's knock; as she wiped her eyes with her canvas apron she couldn't help laughing.

I turn now to more academic matters. Despite the continuance of the Great Economic Depression and the long drawn out crisis in the coal industry with pits closing regularly, my brother Ed had persuaded me to join him in attendance at evening technical classes. The long-term aim of our studies was to obtain an M.E., a Mining Engineering Certificate. Two nights a week we trudged to the night school over a mile away. Our main teacher, who had also been a coal miner, was William Davies, M.E. He was a good and kindly tutor. However, I made little progress for I was poor in Maths and Science. In fact, the only lessons I really liked were those in Basic English and even then because the English also gave the reading of extracts from Pritchard's English Literature Selections. These contained select passages from Milton's *Paradise Lost* and the ones I liked best, *Samson Agonistes*. From time to time Davies asked us to write essays and on one occasion on returning my essay he said, "You may not become an M.E., but you'd make a good journalist."

I revert now to my work as a collier-boy. After three week's rest to restore my ankle and foot to tolerable working, I returned to Powell's Pit (for weekly compensation only amounted to 8 shillings as compared to my weekly wage of 15/ld).

One day, within an hour of quitting, our regular haulier, Tom Jones, arrived. By the way, he had the delightful nickname of "Twm Royal" because in 1912, King George V and Queen Mary had called at his miner's cottage (it was a typical miner's home and the declared epicentre of Abertaff) and had even stayed to tea! As he collected our full tram of coal, Tom said to me, "Will you do me a big favour, lad, and work on a bit late to raise a pair of rails?"

"Oh," I burst in, "I can't! You see I've got miners' night school tonight."

"What time is night school for criisssake?" asked Tom.

"Oh, 6:30," I replied.

"6:30!" shouted Tom, "Good God, boy, I only want you for half an hour to pick up some rails in old workings and you'll earn half-a-crown extra in your pay next Friday." Two and sixpence on top of fifteen shillings was an inducement I could not possibly resist!

At about 1:45p.m., colliers began to leave the mine and start their trek home. I now waited for "Twm Royal". Evan, my Butty, as he left me alone, bade me: "Good luck in the old workings!" Suddenly it sounded rather sinister and frightening, for now I realised I had never been in old workings before! Soon Tom arrived with his pit pony - "Billy" - and tram.

"O.K." Tom said. "Let's go! I'll be riding on the front hitching plate as usual (behind the pony's rump), you will ride on the rear hitching plate and please hold on tight to the pair of rails on return!"

The ride to the old workings was like a trip on a Fairground Ghost Train with this vital difference: one knew that the Ghost Train was unreal and ended safely. This pit ride was for real and safety could not be guaranteed.

As we left our main heading, we started to climb slowly into the old workings. The first thing I was bound to notice was that the geological squeeze had pressed the rocky ceiling down in a menacing fashion. Then, I was only too well aware that the timber supports, whether arches or scores of T-posts, had, with age and some dampness, gathered a grizzly white mould. I was also very conscious of huge sinister, clinging spiders webs and of the frequent squeal of many rats. It was altogether a very eerie experience.

However, we made a rickety journey safely to our destination. The end of the narrow gauge railway track.

"Now," ordered Tom, "off you get, lad, and help me raise a pair of rails!" He had a mandrill and lifted two rails with little effort. Now he needed my help to lift them onto the tram for they were twelve feet long and very heavy. "Now," Tom advised, "hang your lamp on the front of your belt for safety so that you can hold the rails steady as we make our way down back to your place. Remember, we are going downhill so hold on tight!"

We started quite well and covered a couple of hundred yards when, suddenly, with no warning, there was a big bump, a loud bang, a piercing cry from the pony, the rear end of the tram leapt in the air and I realised with horror that I had lost my grip of the rails! It all happened so fantastically fast and my escape from injury was incredible. I sometimes wonder if I am blessed with E.S.P. for I had managed to leap off my hitching plate perch, landing safely on *terra firma*, and with my dubious oil lamp still lit!

Gradually coming to my senses, I realised that our tram was off the rails, that the pony had broken free and bolted, and that Tom in front was groaning and apparently in the dark! Eventually I managed to crawl around to the front of the tram to find Tom partly underneath it. He had ceased moaning and this made me extremely anxious that he might be dead.

I waited awhile in some dread. At last, to my immense relief, Tom revived and sat up. I noticed with marked concern, that the glass in his lamp was shattered. After a long pause Tom said, "We're in deep trouble, lad!" Another pause and he continued, "Our bloody Billy has bolted. I hope that instinct will send him back to pit bottom and will alert them there. I HOPE. But meanwhile my poor bloody lamp has had it! There's nothing else for it now. I must take your lamp and walk back to the nearest locking hole to get another and hope to find my pony!"

I have often wondered many times since that awful day if Twm Royal was making the best decision, leaving me in old workings, in deep mine and totally in the dark! And what would have happened if both lamps were broken? I did not argue with that old, experienced, miner. How could I, a 17 year old novice, contest his 'logic'?

So there I was, in total darkness, sitting and waiting, and hoping that Tom would return quickly. While awaiting his longed-for reappearance, I went through a gamut of emotive and perplexing thoughts: what if Tom was really badly injured and had now collapsed during his walk back? Deep in old workings, would I ever be found? I could hear the rats squealing and remembered with horror a story my father would recount from time to time. He would recall how a young collier-boy went missing in old workings. When found many days later, there was evidence that he had tried to keep himself alive by eating candles and failed, and his corpse was partly devoured by rats! Naturally I shuddered as I recalled the grisly story.

From time to time I tried to focus my eyes into the distance, of course it was useless. I couldn't help recalling those lines from Milton's poem *Samson Agonistes*, which had much moved me when reading the work in night school: "Eyeless in Gaza... Oh! Dark, dark, dark: amid the blaze of Noon! Irrecoverably dark; Total Eclipse: without all hope of Day! Oh Let there be LIGHT!..."

Occasionally, as I peered anxiously and hopefully into the Stygian blackness, I thought I could see a spark of light. But no! It was illusion. The minutes seemed to be hours, perhaps days? I began to lose all logical sense of time. Had I been here a couple of days already? Were my worst fears now realised: had Tom collapsed and died?

At last, once more I thought I saw a spark of light, then I surmised I saw two sparks and both bobbing up and down and growing bigger. A devout chapel boy, I started to murmur the pregnant lines of a famous hymn: "Lead kindly Light, amid the encircling gloom: lead Thou me on, the night is dark, and I am far from home; lead Thou me on!..."

As if in answer to my prayerful Hymn, I soon discerned the silhouette of dear old Tom at last, carrying two oil lamps. But there was no pony Billy, no pony at all.

All Tom said was: "I couldn't find our bloody Billy. Anyway, I've had enough for one day, have you? Let's get to hell out of it!"

I arrived home after a three mile walk down the valley, about two and a half hours later than usual. My mother, well used to colliery accidents and cognate crises, asked quite calmly, "Where have you been so long? Why so late? I've had a bit of a struggle to keep your dinner warm and I've had to take your hot water for your bath off the fire several times!"

I then recounted the story of my misadventure as recorded here.

My Mother's only comment was, "Oh! So you were working with Twm Royal. Fancy that! A bit of an honour, don't you know? Did you know that he had the King and Queen to tea in his house in Bute Street in 1912?"

MY LAST YEAR AS COAL MINER

My last year as a collier-boy was full of incident: tragic and comic; bizarre and hilarious; and at the close of the period, pregnant with foreboding and yet with a promise of better prospects.

I begin my narrative in the autumn of 1933. Abroad, this year heralded the menacing rise of fascism in Germany. At home in Britain, and especially in Wales, unemployment continued to be the major problem with many coal mines closing in South Wales, and "hunger marches" beginning. Both my father and brother Ed were now on the dole, with Ed supporting the hunger marchers.

At last, after three years of fitful attendance at evening classes in a vain attempt to gain the M.E. "degree", brother Ed, in morose but militant mood opined, "It's no use going on with our old studies, it seems that the coal industry is doomed! So let's try something else, something more realistic!"

So in the September/October of 1933 he persuaded me to join him in an evening class in the same building as before (the Abertaff/Glam. County School) but in a totally different subject. This was "Economics and Social Science". In fact, Ed had started the course some time before. The peripatetic tutor, based in Cardiff, was one Harold Watkins BSc., Econ. (incidentally, a brother of Sir Percy Watkins, Welsh Education Secretary). Watkins proved to be a very friendly, humane man, with a nice sense of humour and a very fine clear style of teaching. He had returned from a tour of the U.S.A. where, he was proud to proclaim, he had met Upton Sinclair, the famous author and politician. And like Sinclair, Watkins was a dedicated Socialist.

I remind my readers that my brother Ed was five years older than I and was by 1933, a very active Atheist and Communist. He was a great and rapid talker, very unwilling to let anyone else get a word in edgeways in argument. His favourite clinching summary was: "For criissake! Go and read more and be better informed!" He had also become an incorrigible writer of radical letters to local and regional newspapers. He treated me as a silent worshipper and devoted disciple which I was decidedly NOT! He would always ask me to verify his biased left wing opinions but before receiving my uncertain mumbled answers he would silence me with his imperative command, "For criissake read more, brother! You are still ill-educated!"

I well remember the first night I accompanied him to Watkins's Economics evening class. Ed advised (albeit "ordered"), "Now, listen carefully, brother. I'm briefing you carefully about our tactics and strategy for tonight's class and what I say will hold good for many weeks to come. Watkins divides his class time into two equal halves. In the first hour he lectures without interruption. In the second hour he invites discussion. Now, you surely recognise by this time that I tend to shine in debate discussion. So you will not participate in discussion in the first or even the second term. You need more experience, backed up of course, by a lot more intensive and extensive reading. So I suggest that you will simply listen to me making my strong and shrewd dialectical points, and simply nod in agreement and occasionally say 'Hear! Hear!', O.K.?"

Somewhat strange to relate perhaps, I observed Ed's instructions to the letter!

I turn now to the work situation. I had changed my coal mine yet again! This was my fourth pit in as many years. However, this new one was not a deep mine. On the contrary, it was a drift mine, i.e. a long tunnel boring into the mountain side. It was called River Level Drift and it ran into the upper slopes of what we called Merthyr Mountain, above the village of Abernant. It also ran, for the most part, over the Abertaff golf links. As we miners toiled below, the soon-to-be-famous Dai Rees was learning his golfing skills above. River Level Drift was the craziest coal mine I ever worked in, and I would challenge any old miner to describe a crazier one. I must stress that these were the days of almost unbridled privatisation, *laissez-faire* carried to extremes. The basic fact was that the geological strata was full of "faults" and "folds", which meant that one day we would be working a rather good three feet six inch seam of good steam coal, but the next day we would be hammering or boring into hard Quartz rock. (Dai and Shoni "Quarr" would then have to get busy with their Flopman power drills. Of Dai, more anon, alas!)

The frantic, yes, frenetic search for the precious coal in the Drift - completely unregulated it seemed - meant that the entire mountain-side above Abernant was riddled with a maze of tunnels. And sometimes these tunnels burrowed out into the surface. Some miners claimed that they had even found golf balls in their workplace though I never saw any. One of the worst features of this honeycomb of seams running so close to the surface was that two or three streets of houses in the area started slowly but surely to collapse; Richmond Terrace in particular! Whether householders were ever compensated I cannot say. The worst part of working so near the surface for us miners was that we felt under constant pressure of roof collapse, as grit rumbled on our support-lagging incessantly!

I deem it important to record that my new mining Butty was my cousin Aneurin Jefferies. He was about six years older than me (I was now 18). I should also mention the recent tragedy in his family that affected me deeply. His brother Jesse, the same age as myself, had recently been killed in the River Level deep Pit, which was situated very near the Town centre. Jesse, a school-mate of mine, given a decent chance, was a great prospect as an athlete, a wonderful runner, high and long jumper.

I have to remind the reader that in those days we miners wore no protective clothing; notably no safety helmets. The grim report of Jesse's sudden death recorded that there had been a "top-hole", i.e. a shot-firing by dynamite to blast the top rocks down so that the trams could be brought in to the coal face. The deputy, or "fireman", one Dai Sam Davies, had fired the shot at a safe distance (about thirty yards back) with Jesse and his Butty safely behind him. The Butty reported at the inquest that Dai Sam went to inspect and that the ever eager Jesse hurried on also. As they did so two lumps of rock not much bigger than a football, fell and utterly crushed the unprotected heads of both unlucky miners!

One might have thought that Jesse's untimely end, which affected me greatly, would have made Aneurin, his eldest brother, sad and morose for many months. But not so! For Aneurin was what some people call "A broth of a boy!", what some others designate "One helluva lad!" He was a charming rogue. He could make impromptu little speeches and spin lovely canards (tales one can hardly believe), and he had an unfailing repertoire of jokes and stories that would make his ever willing audience rock with laughter. Their reactions would be: "Oh, that's a tall one, Nye!" or "Pull the other one, Aneurin!" or "Tell that one to the marines!" Yet they would howl with glee. I knew, however, as all members of my family knew, that

Nye was a fibber and a petty sneak-thief. He had, in fact, spent two or three years in a Reform School in Quaker's Yard.

However, for me, in the six months I worked with him, he was a joy! He never exploited me as some other Butties had and he always kept me in a cheerful mood. He was so popular with the other miners working close to us that they would seek him out at grub time in our work place just to listen to his jokes and enjoy his stories, true or tall! And Nye was ever-ready to play to the gallery.

On one occasion he sported a huge pair of boots which his father (my uncle Arthur) had found on Abertaff's main rubbish tip and had "repaired".

"Good God, Nye!" exclaimed Dai "Quarr". "Those are bloody big boots you've got on! What size are they for criissake?"

"Oh, twelves!" replied Nye proudly. "D'ye know, when I stand up I can even turn around in them! Inside them!"

On another occasion Nye was struggling with a new set of false teeth. All our mining pals sympathised for most of us had suffered likewise. At last, after a noisy munching Aneurin took the new teeth from his mouth and popped them into his grub box shouting, "Do it yourselves, you horrible bloody gnashers!"

A fortnight before Christmas, when we all looked forward to two days (unpaid!) holidays, Nye ran a raffle; 2d per ticket. It ran for two weeks and knowing what a rogue Aneurin was, those who had bought tickets (I had one) started interrogating Nye but only in a light-hearted teasing way, "When are we going to have the result of the Raffle, Nye, or is it just another bloody swindle?"

"No, no!" Nye would quickly rejoin. "Just be patient for a little while longer and you'll gave a pleasant surprise. There will be three prizes, especially for any hungry buggers waiting up for Santa Claus!"

Sceptical men scoffed, "Oh! That will be the bloody day, Nye, you scheming bugger!"

However, on Christmas Eve on the night shift as the colliers gathered round to test Nye's (raffling) sincerity, from somewhere, even I knew not where, Nye, like a professional conjuror-magician brought forth three large packages, albeit wrapped in old newspapers.

"Now for the GREAT RAFFLE PRIZES! BEHOLD!" Nye bellowed. He called out a number and Shoni "Quarr' ('hard ground' John), who had bought ten tickets, responded. "Here you are, Shoni, open it now if you like," offered Nye with a mischievous smile as he handed Shoni a large package. Shoni was naturally suspicious. "Go on!" urged Nye. "It won't bite you!"

"Yes!" some shouted. "Go on, open it, Shoni. See what the sly bugger is up to. Test him!"

Slowly and very furtively, Shoni unwrapped the package while we others winced hard with bated breath. At last, after a lot of wheezing and tutting, Shoni now displayed to our astonishment, a large and scrumptious looking side of beef! We all gasped with unrestrained delight. We paused awhile, then Nye called out another number. This time Dai "Quarr", who had bought six tickets was the winner. Another newspaper parcel was unwrapped, this time with more confidence and speed. A nice leg of pork was proudly revealed. More cries of wonder and delight. The third prize was gained by Sid Saunders, who had "lashed out" on four tickets. This proved to be the *piece* (or was it string?) *de resistance*! Sid began to unroll before our incredulous eyes a very long string of sausages, so long was it that Sid and Nye pretended to measure the coal face, in grand imitation of the "yardage chain" used by deputies for assessing hard-ground men's claims for bonuses, all this to a great howl of laughter.

Naturally we were all convulsed for many minutes. But eventually a modicum of common sense prevailed and interrogation of Nye began, "Where the bloody hell did you get all the lovely, luscious meat from, Nye?" and "We're pretty certain you didn't BUY IT!" and "Which poor bloody Abertaff butcher is busy looking for his beef and pork and his mile of sausages?"

Nye said never a word but smiled and guffawed with Mephistophelian mirth.

"Anyway," summarised one phlegmatic non-recipient, "some of you lucky buggers are going to have a sumptuous Christmas!"

"Hear, hear!" we agreed.

Another Aneurin-style event is worth recording. It was on the nightshift, Nye and I were trying in vain to extract some thin coal out of a face which had dwindled into hard, brassy rock. After a couple of hours of hard pounding with a blunted pick and an inadequate chisel, Nye called a halt.

"It's no use, boy-bach," he said to me, "this rocky face is like the Hobs of Hell (whatever that phrase meant.) Let's leave it awhile and have our grub!"

Twenty minutes later when I hinted that we might re-start Nye said, "Oh! It is no use, let's have a short kip," and he produced as if from nowhere, or like a conjuror's cape, a large tarpaulin sheet. We lay down on the coal-dusty floor and Nye pulled the sheet over us. Some time later (I had lost all sense of the time-span) we felt a sharp prod in our sides. Starting up we saw Fred Stevens, the under-manager of the mine, with his walking-stick. He was on his twice-nightly rounds.

"What the hell are you doing down on this dirty floor, Aneurin? Are you, in fact, sleeping? You're not being paid for sleeping you know!"

"No! No!" lied Aneurin. "We've only just finished our grub. Isn't that so?" turning to me for compliant corroboration.

"I doubt it," growled Stevens. "Anyway, get back on the job, *pronto*!" (Stevens travelled abroad and he liked to show off his linguistic skills).

We carried on hammering at the brassy rock face for about thirty minutes more when Nye threw his blunted pick down with a curse saying: "It's no bloody use! The Hobs of Hell boyo, let's lie down and have another bloody kip!"

I cannot say how much longer we lay there but it must have two or three hours for Stevens came around again and caught us - literally - napping! Again he prodded us with his stick but this time more sharply and angrily he shouted, "What the bloody hell is the matter with you, Aneurin? Are you bone idle or are you going to pretend that you are still having your grub? I warn you, Aneurin, that we can't go on paying you for skiving! If you go on like this Nye, I promise you the end is nigh!"

Yes, Stevens was witty, in a sarcastic way.

"Yes," Stevens went on, showing off again (this time in French), "If you go on like this Aneurin, it will be the *coup de grace* for *vous*!"

"Cows grass?" spluttered Nye. "What on earth do you mean, Mr Stevens?"

"I'll give it to you in plain, basic English, Nye, you will get the SACK!"

"Oh, but really, Mr Stevens..," pleaded Nye. "I'm not really lazy; this rock-face is like the Hobs of Hell and in any case, I'm ill very ill!"

"Ill?" barked Stevens. "What is the illness this time, Aneurin?"

"It's very serious, and terminal!" said Nye in his most sombre tones. "It has been diagnosed as Brights Disease!"

Stevens was evidently unimpressed. "Bollocks!" he replied, "If you go on like this, you will certainly face the sack! *Vous vous fini!*"

Aneurin's discharge was superfluous: a week later he was lodged in Cardiff Jail for theft - at least three Abertaff butchers gave much evidence.

Nye might have derived some ironic pleasure from the news that Fred Stevens was discharged by his own beloved Coal Company for being found asleep in the lamp-room when he should have been in the Drift mine on his rounds.

I was now transferred to yet another new Butty. He couldn't have been more different from Nye. His name was Ben Phillips. He was nearly 60 years of age, a very skilful miner but a dour, hard man without a jot of humour. After working with him in the River Level Drift for about two months we were put on short time because the coal kept disappearing and the hard ground seemed to get harder. (Incidentally, Dai was killed in a most dramatic and even hideous manner. He was trying to bore into the Quartz rocks with his very noisy Flopman drill, when a few loose trams crashed into his back and drove the drill right through him).

Meanwhile, one of the deacons of my chapel who managed the local screens where the coal was sorted and "cleaned", thought he was doing me a big favour by offering me some work there during the slack time in the mine. Actually, from my point of view, it was no favour. In stark fact, it was 'Hell upon Earth'! Almost as bad as anything Dante imagined in his *Inferno*. For at least once a week, I was obliged, with another "favoured" lad, to go down and clean out the Duff Box. This was the chamber which held all the fine, fine dust which filtered through from the coal conveyor belt. My pal kept a sister's silk stocking around his mouth and nose as we shovelled out the fine dust which clogged our nostrils, earholes and mouths. We were never given face masks. I did not borrow a sister's silk stocking, but prayed for early deliverance.

I turn to academic matters if only for light relief.

I continued to attend the evening Economics class every Monday, with brother Ed. I still obeyed his injunction to be silent while he did the talking for both of us! However, whereas Ed continued to steep himself in Marxist classics, with only Balzac for light relief, I assiduously studied the set books prescribed by Tutor Watkins on Social and Industrial Psychology, the main ones by Myers and McDougall, though I also got very interested in Alfred Adler and even Freud and Jung. We were asked to hand in a fortnightly essay. I was always on time. Ed, though unemployed, was casual, for Marx and Balzac were his top reading priorities. He "could easily cope with exam subjects in plenty of time later". The exam was due just before the Easter break.

"The ten best students per exam," promised Watkins, would be chosen to join others from his various Glamorgan evening classes to attend a summer school for three weeks (digs; subsistence allowances; etc. guaranteed!) at the prestigious Swansea University College by the sea.

Ed assured me with great confidence, "I'll certainly be in the top three, with luck you should scrape in!"

When Watkins read out the list of "winners" in late April, he placed me first of the ten successful students. Brother Ed was not on the list. In his verbal summaries, Watkins said of Ed's work, "In answer to the topic 'Heredity and Environment - which is the greater influence?', the lives of Marx and Balzac, however brilliant, were hardly relevant."

I revert to the work situation. In May (1934) our River Level Drift Mine was finally closed and we, Ben Phillips and I, were transferred to its sister coal mine. This was called River Level Pit, very near the town centre. This was a very deep pit. One day in July, in the busy throes of coal-face work, my ever-so-careful Butty, Ben, said, "Go back down the road a little way where the timber is and cut a post this length and a lid." (This would make a T-post for supporting the roof.) Ben added cautiously, "I don't like the look of this part of our roof!"

I went back as Ben ordered me and started to cut the post and lid but I was immediately assailed by a strange, maybe a unique feeling. I wasn't sure whether I could hear or sense a dribbling or a rumbling but I quickly had goose pimples. I hurried back to the coal-face. Ben looked around to see me empty-handed.

"Where is that post and lid?" he demanded sharply.

"I - I - ca - can't do it, Ben," I stammered.

"Get me that bloody prop quick!" he bawled.

I went back to try again but I seemed paralysed by fright. I felt the hair on my head and the back of my neck bristling. I hurried back to the coal-face and shouted, "No use. I don't like it, Ben!"

"O.K.! 'Nuff said! Let's grab the tools and get to hell out of it!" he shouted. We scrambled back frantically - albeit with heavy tools - for some fifty yards and as we did so, with a portentous roar or rumble, the entire coal face collapsed!

I have often thought it strange that after my E.S.P. (?) experience which saved Ben and me in River Level Pit, why he never bothered even to mention it? Was he such a dry old stick or did he not want to give me credit or praise. Or was it simply for him, a miner for fifty years, a fairly common experience?

In fact, the fall in our place that day was generally so extensive and heavy that the whole District never opened again. I can't remember if any miners were killed or injured that day. In any case, we took coal mine casualties very much for granted. (Well over 1,500 miners were killed in U.K. pits in 1934.)

Our Gadlys District never opened again, and I found myself on the dole for the first time in my life and, in fact, my life as a coal-miner was quite finished. If I had gone on as a collier boy, for another two months, I would have completed five years.

My dole money was only 17 shillings per week, soon to be cut to 10/-. My main compensation was that I was now free to attend the summer school at Swansea University College which included a 30/- per week bonus! So, for three weeks I lived like the Prince of Wales!

Moreover, I gained first prize for an essay award devised by our tutor in International Relations, one Dr. I. David. And calling me aside to tell me, quietly and in advance, that I had gained the coveted prize with my essay on Imperialism, he kindly asked me about my life and aspirations. On learning that I was an unemployed miner, he advised, "I really think you could do quite well in an academic sphere. Think hard about it, will you?"

So, the end of a turbulent year as a collier boy held out some promising prospects beyond the pit!

RAYMOND

(A Weird Tale! Was it E.S.P.?)

I first met Raymond Bolton in, or about, 1927. We became school-mates, and I believe our original encounter was when I rescued him from a playground bully. I was not very healthy but I was physically strong. Short and tubby with strong arms and legs. I would develop into a useful boxer and by age 10 I was a very clever wrestler. I could easily pull down a boy twice my height by throwing myself to my knees and pulling the other boy down by his knees.

Raymond was a weakling, very small and awfully thin. A "weed". His main colouring was a ginger-brown. He had thin brown hair, bright brown eyes and a little face speckled with a multitude of brown freckles. Though a victim of school bullies he was a merry, chirpy little chap.

After my Raymond rescue act, however, I came to have ambivalent emotions about my "heroism", for thereafter Raymond latched on to me like a limpet. He would follow me about like one of Christ's Disciples. Unlike Peter, I am sure that he would never have even ONCE let alone thrice, betrayed me!

Eventually, I mentioned the name of Raymond Bolton to my mother. She was a wiseacre who seemed to know everybody and everything about them, in Cardiff Road, Abertaff.

"Where does he live?" asked Mother.

"Sunnybank Street," I replied.

"Oh!" observed Mam. "His is a sad case then!"

I was surprised. "Why?"

"Oh! Don't ever tell or ask him but his father, Roger Bolton, was once an important and prosperous man. He had one of the best employment positions in all Abertaff. He was the Head of the Co-operative Furniture Department with a very big salary. He always dressed beautifully and was always a leading light in big Abertaff functions. Now the poor devil is on the dole!"

"But why?" I asked.

"Oh!" Mother explained, with sadness in her voice. "The poor chap was too fond of the booze - rather like your Dad - but Roger had an insatiable craving for the more expensive tipple: SPIRITS! Be warned, son! Ah, yes! Mr Bolton began to neglect his work and the rumour was that he had started dipping deeply into the Co-op's Petty Cash and other firms moneys. So he got dismissed!"

"How long ago?" I asked.

"Oh, it must have been - let me see - at least two years ago. His poor delicate wife took it very badly. She avoided meetings and even stopped seeing old friends. You must have seen Roger Bolton passing this way down our main road from time to time, he's always immaculately dressed: pin-stripe suit and bowler hat but his clothes are beginning to look a bit shabby now. Well, well, so Raymond, his son, is a friend of yours? Don't tell him what I've just told you will you?"

In September 1928 I had to transfer to a new school. Raymond also. For we were two of those who had failed the dreaded one-day Eleven Plus exam; I by only 5 marks, due to inadequate mastery of Maths.

The new school, Town Council Board was, by contrast with easily reached Ynyslwyd Juniors, a full mile away. But we never took a school bus or tram; rain or shine we always walked it. In my last two or three years in Junior school I was a star pupil, always top in the exams because I was good in every subject except Maths. I soon made my academic mark in the new school and I soon became the special (without any fawning on my part) pet of our main class-room teacher, Mr Tom Richards. I was quickly made his Prefect and he often read, or got me to read, my essays to the class. He strongly advised me to become a journalist. He told many boys over subsequent years that I was a model student! But Raymond would often mock me about my special relationship with Richards.

Meanwhile however, I was beginning to find my friendship with Raymond rather cloying. He followed me everywhere like a love-sick calf! Other boys who sought my company for games and wrestling bouts were beginning to make caustic comments. Poor Raymond was too weak to join in the rough and tumble of hard sports and strenuous games! So, somewhat reluctantly, I began to avoid him. I believe, however, that he noticed my cool responses and I think he started a strategy of wooing my friendship anew. One day, perhaps during school holidays, there was a light knock on the door and my younger sister reported that Alun Bolton, Raymond's young brother, wanted to see me. I responded in surprise and with a little alarm.

"We want you to come to tea," said Alun.

I expressed surprise and some embarrassment.

"Oh! Mum and Dad especially want you to come. You see Raymond has passed his big Music Exam and Mum and Dad are preparing a special tea to celebrate and they want you especially to celebrate with us!"

Mother heard all this and nudged me meaningfully, and whispered, "It's quite an honour. Do go!"

So I presented myself at the Bolton House in Sunnybank Street, a substantial one, much better than ours. Mam had dug out a better jersey (assuming I had more than one?!) and had made me comb my hair.

Alas! It was all a mistake! It seems that the party and invitation story had been concocted by the young brothers. I had to share the acute embarrassment with Mr and Mrs Bolton.

"Anyway!" said Mrs Bolton coyly. "Now that you are here and we are meeting Raymond's hero at last, you must stay to tea and hear Raymond play." Poor Mrs Bolton continued awkwardly, "I didn't know until a few minutes ago that you were coming to tea. I haven't been out shopping so far this week," she said, "otherwise we would be having a nice Dundee cake." (I had never tasted one, anyway.) "Anyhow, we will do our best!"

The special "celebratory tea" promised by Alun, consisted of some brown bread and butter, very spicy blackcurrant jam, and a banana (no, half a banana).

Then Mr Bolton asked Raymond to play on the rather handsome piano. Raymond started sorting out his many music sheets.

"Play some Chopin and Liszt and I'm sure you would like to show your friend how well you can play Rachmaninov's *Prelude No 1* since you tell me you are both fascinated by it!" (I ought to explain that Tom Richards, a great lover of classical music, had played a gramophone record of a rendering of the *Prelude No 1* by the great Paderewski in a Musical Appreciation lesson recently. Richards had also offered us his own interpretation of the piece. It was vivid and very morbid. He said, "The music depicts a disaster. It tries to show a man buried alive and knocking desperately to get someone to save him." Raymond and I often discussed this macabre tale later. Was it some weird kind of dire prediction?)

Anyway, Raymond played several piano pieces for me, turning around between each effort to see if I was duly impressed and indeed I honestly was!

I hurry on to 1929: in the meantime my relationship with Raymond had become more fitful! I had many more pre-occupations. But suddenly, in July, we were brought together more intimately. The fact was that certain South Welsh councils, especially those run by the Labour Party, started various schemes for the alleviation of the plight of the unemployed. One idea was to provide at least one good holiday for the children of those men on the dole. As it happened, Raymond qualified and so did I. So we were told by Tom Richards that we were entitled to have a fortnight's holiday at Pendine "New School Camp"! Furthermore, we could be rigged out in a new suit of clothes, free of cost! My Mother was delighted, Dad gave his grudging approval and Brother Ed, still working as a collier-boy, growled, "Lucky bugger!" My mother insisted on being with me to choose my new suit. Alas! She made a huge strategic blunder from my point of view.

I was now 14 years of age but admittedly, still a "short-arse". But I longed for my first long-trousered suit. But Mother was adamant! I was still "her little boy", and she deliberately chose a royal blue, blazer-type suit with swanky breast-pocket-badge and shiny brass buttons and, alas, short-short trousers. On meeting Raymond a few days later, I was dismayed and acutely embarrassed to find that, though he was a "spilk" and much smaller than I was, he was proudly sporting his first long-trousered suit!

In mid-July, Raymond and I and quite a number of Abertaff school-boys met at the High Level Station for making the rather long journey to Pendine, via Swansea.

The holiday - my first ever - proved wonderful! We had lovely weather. We were housed in neat wooden huts. As I had only known life in a poor miner's house, I considered the accommodation almost palatial. Yes, fit enough to house the Prince of Wales!

We had twice daily trips to Pendine sands: seven miles of glorious beach. In a mound in the flat sands only half buried, was the wreck of the famous Parry Thomas's racing car, with a sign-board embedded beside it bearing the poignant legend: "Here Lies Poor BABS!" BABS was the famous racing car in which Thomas had been killed outright while breaking the land speed record (175 m.p.h.). As Raymond and I stood beside the wreck of BABS - although so young - we became philosophical. I had read much about the 1927 disaster and opined, "Apparently it was a very violent death, it must have been horrible!"

"Oh, I don't know about that," observed Raymond. "Perhaps it was a very sudden death, like a lightning flash. With no suffering. Better that than growing ill and old!"

I have thought so many times since, how shrewd and meaningful that sentiment was for one so young.

On these same Pendine sands our camp teachers would arrange games and races for us boys and when I finished first (but in a breathless state of collapse) in a Marathon, Raymond was obviously thrilled. On another occasion I was chosen to represent our hut (containing thirty boys), in a boxing championship. I fought a draw and Raymond was hugely delighted.

Alas! All good/nice things come to an end. On August 1st our School Camp Holiday terminated. Meanwhile, a couple of days before, Raymond had received a very important message. He was not to return to his Abertaff home. He was to go to a new home in a new town - Maesteg. It seems that his father had been economically and socially rehabilitated. The Co-operative organisation had forgiven him and was reinstating him but at a slightly lower level. He was now to be under-manager of Co-op Furnishings at Maesteg. (My omniscient mother explained all this to me later.)

Raymond was, rather naturally, ambivalent about the news: glad for his father's sake, but sad and apprehensive about moving to a new home in a strange town. When he told me his news I was also ambivalent in my emotions; of course I liked Raymond for certain qualities and talents he had but he had also become a bit of a millstone or clinging vine. As we said goodbye I was acutely embarrassed to see tears in his eyes

"We must surely meet again?" he pleaded.

"Of course," I politely replied. We never did (or did we?).

When I say Raymond and I never met again I mean in the flesh, as to the Spirit, I am not so sure.

I hurry on to the strange - even quite bizarre - *denouement*.

Some years passed. Six weeks after bidding Raymond goodbye I became a collier-boy. My life as a coal-miner lasted five years.

After two or three months on the dole I went to London and after a short crash course training, I became a steward/waiter, first in the posh Devonshire Club, later in the famous, or notorious, Cafe Royal. Two years of near-slavish conditions in this job drove me back home to Abertaff, where I had wangled myself back on the unemployment register to qualify for dole money.

My brother Ed was now a very active Communist, and - incidentally - had acquired a newspaper round, selling the Daily Worker. He was being paid 5 shillings per week for this. He soon induced me to do likewise, and 5 shillings to augment only 10 shillings dole allowance was not to be sniffed at. We both had old, second-hand bikes (mine with no mud-guards, dicey brakes and certainly no lights, front or rear). At Ed's suggestion I accepted the longer delivery round: Rhigos, Hirwaun and the upper Abertaff valleys.

One evening, having finished my round, and riding home fast to beat lighting-up time, I passed along-side the Abertaff cemetery, which is about a quarter of a mile long. As I cautiously glanced to the left side I could see, between many dark-green yew trees, several gravestones including, I knew, some of my forebears. Suddenly I had a very strange sensation, which evokes goose-pimples, and seemed to make my hair bristle. I could have sworn that my school pal, Raymond Bolton, was cycling along-side me on the left-hand - cemetery - side. This bizarre sensation lasted until I reached the end of the cemetery. I was in a kind of daze which I tried to shake off, mumbling, "stuff and nonsense" to myself. However, as I cycled through Abertaff's Cannon Street I saw, again on my left-hand side, a new publicity hoarding, in very bright colours announcing the new film to be shown (in the Palladium Cinema). It read *Stolen Heaven* with star Gene Raymond. Again I had that queer sensation.

When I got home only Mother was there in the kitchen, with the omnipresent teapot on the hob. As we sipped tea together I said to Mam, "Do you remember Raymond Bolton who was my school-pal for a time, the son of Roger Bolton?"

"Of course!" answered Wiseacre Mother. "But why do you ask?"

"Oh! I had a funny feeling a little while ago."

"Funny feeling?" Mam cut in, "funny feeling? Why, what do you mean?"

I was rapidly on my guard for I knew Mother was very inclined to be psychic which made all of us children, especially "Marxist" Ed scoff.

"No! No! I didn't mean 'funny feeling'. It's just that I suddenly remembered him and I wonder how he made out?"

"Well, as a matter of fact," said Mother, "Raymond came here one day not so long ago, but you were in London. He was, of course, hoping to see you. He was very disappointed to have missed you."

"Oh," I rejoined. "Did he happen to tell you what he is doing these days?"

"Oh yes! He is working underground, in a Maesteg pit."

"Working UNDERGROUND!" I gasped. "In a coal mine? That is absurd. It's bloody incredible! He was such a delicate boy. How can he possibly stand the strain? It's ridiculous!"

"Oh don't go on so, son. He is driving a little engine, and he says he likes it. After all, he is not working at the coal-face, nor lying in water, as you used to do... Furthermore, you might like to know that he is keeping up with his music, in fact he is the main organist in his local church."

"Oh, I see," I responded. "You have relieved me now. I'm glad if he is well and happy."

A few days later on returning from my newspaper round, my mother warned, "Be prepared for a shock, son!... Mrs Gibbons called - you know her, Olwen Gibbon's mother, you used to be in Olwen's class in school, remember? Well, in case you didn't know, she's Mrs Bolton's sister, Raymond's aunt. Well..."

I was impatient, knowing my mother's irrepressible tendency to elaborate any story.

"Well," I broke in. "So what! What is the shocking news, for God's sake?"

"Please don't blaspheme, son. It's too serious and tragic. Mrs Gibbon was a bearer of very sad news. She has received a message from Mrs Bolton. Raymond was killed in a huge fall of rock in Maesteg's P.D. no.1 pit last week!"

After a long pause, Mother who had known so many pit disasters, including the biggest ones like Cilfynydd (1894 with 260 killed) and Senghenydd (1913, 439 killed) but could still empathise with the single/one family loss, moaned, "Mrs Gibbons said it was a very heavy fall. Poor Raymond might have been buried alive. But I hope he didn't suffer long."

"Yes," I rejoined, "I hope it was like a lightning flash!"

STRUGGLE FOR THE DOLE

My story starts in the town of Abertaff in industrial South Wales, in the mid 1930's. This was a place and time of industrial depression, mass unemployment and massive migration, especially of the younger workers. It was a time of hunger marches from the depressed areas to London; it was also a time of intense political agitation especially against poverty and fascism and incipient war. Or so the pundits say!

The Griffiths family of Cardiff Road, Abertaff, were caught up in this maelstrom and came, willy-nilly, to play a significant part in the storms and stresses of this period. The Griffiths family was a large one and a poor one. There were: Mam and Dad, Cordelia (yes, Cordelia!) and Will and eight kids, Uncle Edward (a lodger); and a hundred yards down the road and very much dependent on the Griffiths', was Uncle Gomer, a dwarfed and crippled cobbler (shoe-maker *manque*) and a bachelor.

Will Griffiths, now 55, had been a coal-miner since the age of 10 and very proud of it. But getting old, steadily more radical and a Union activist, found himself on the dole in 1931. His eldest son "Young Ted", also a miner and even more radical than his father - Atheist and Stalinist at 21 - joined his father on the dole in 1933. Glyn the younger son, idealist, sentimentalist and Seventh-Day Adventist, would-be intellectual and "litterateur", five years a miner, also joined the ranks of the "ragged army" in spring '34.

Things were getting grim, especially when unemployment benefits were threatened with savage cuts in early autumn 1934. The single man's dole allowance was to be cut from 17 shillings to ten bob a week. However, Cordelia - incorrigible romantic and optimist - remained sanguine. "We shall manage," she would maintain. "In any case things can't get worse."

The two eldest daughters were married. Helen, the eldest of all, was also married to a coal-miner and he joined the dole queue in 1934. Gwenno was luckier, being married to a railwayman who continued working for £2 8s 0d per week throughout the depression. Young Ted described him as "bloody bourgeois". Agnes, the third daughter, was a probationer nurse at Abertaff General Hospital, and Ann the fourth girl, was in service (very much Downstairs) in London. Olwen the youngest, delicate and blonde, "the scraping of the ovary-pot" as mother subtly put it - was still in school. (The eldest son was dying in a sanatorium.)

As the Depression deepened between 1930 and 1934, the National Government put the financial squeeze on to economise, the going got tougher. There was a feeling in upper-class circles that the unemployed men were beginning to accommodate to the situation, were even beginning to enjoy it. After all, they were having their bread with jam, and the dog-tracks and the three penny cinema provided the circuses. So in autumn 1934 came the cuts. The squeeze on the unemployed was on. Development Areas lay in the future, the immediate policy was to get the malingerers off the dole-queue and into new, more prosperous, areas. Men like Will Griffiths were offered £50 removal expenses to hit the "Oregon trail" to Coventry, Rugby or London or similar El Doradoes. But Will Gee was 55 and was very sentimental about Abertaff and his old Powell's Pit which he felt certain would reopen.

Ted Griffiths's dole was to be cut to ten shillings but he would not move except to join the hunger marches and radical activists. He would not be driven out to become cheap labour in Birmingham or Slough, this would be playing into the hands of the Capitalists and neo-fascists. He would stay and fight. "After all," (he would insist repeatedly) "Capitalism can't last much longer!"

Young Glyn was apolitical, more romantic and more adventurous. When his dole allowance was threatened in the October he accepted the alternative: railway-fare to London and "rehabilitation" in a Training Centre at Park Royal, Acton. God knows why but he commenced training as an hotel waiter in the first week of November 1934. What a transformation - from coal-miner to hotel waiter within five months! But he learned so fast that he was actually chosen to wait on Lady Astor when she visited the Training Centre in January '35; the very same Lady Astor who had slandered the unemployed by calling them "that horrible Ragged Army". Had his brother, Ted, known that Glyn was waiting upon her at table he would have "bloody well throttled him and he would have strangled that upper-class tart, Astor, with Glyn's entrails" (à la Arouet[*]). But Glyn thought her charming, especially when she silently and subtly slipped a silver sixpence into his shaking hand.

---

[*] Arouet = 'Voltaire'.

But the day of reckoning came. On March 1st, after a crash-course in very refined hotel-waiting, complete with the *hors d'oeuvres* of French conversation, Glyn was thrown out of the cosy comfort of the Training Centre Ivory Tower and cast to the wolves of London's West End.

His first job was as a Steward in the Junior Imperial, Westminster. But he had to live out and share a squalid flat in the Albany with a dozen other commis-waiters. It was so overcrowded that the young lads had to sleep three in a bed on two shifts, the bed never empty. It was rather gruesome, for apart from a lifetime of claustrophobia, Glyn feared for his virginity. You know what waiters are!

There were other features of his life at the Junior Imperial he detested. First there was the bloody "monkey suit" complete with long tails. The white wing collar cut into his fat neck and the large white bow tie tickled his nostrils when he bent down to serve. Then there was the stupid gold braid and brass buttons on the uniform. When he espied himself in a long mirror he looked a perfect Wodehouse twit. A jelly-baby Jeeves. What would his old collier buddies say if they saw him? And more than once he had seen unemployed miners come down Piccadilly and St James Street singing Welsh hymns. And if his brother's posse of hunger marchers found him in this suit they'd bloody well slaughter him as a minion of the aristocracy or as a boy-bastion of the bloody bourgeoisie. (Lynch the bugger!)

Again, the discipline at the Imperial was strict as laid down by the Club Secretary, Colonel Quentin Knatchbull-Hugheson Jnr., one-time Equerry to the brave Duke of Devonshire V.C. etc., etc. One must be on duty sharp at 7:30 - ready to serve breakfast - and one must be collar perfect, spic and span, and with the French menu memorised and word perfect. Remember to serve sherry, pale or dark, with the Pwoisson (not poison!) and remember it's a silent P (as in fish) for Ptarmigan. And be sure it's the "Sauce Cardinal" with the turbot, and the most appropriate dessert after Chicken Maryland is Omellette Souffle Surprise; etcetera etcetera. Oh, but the food below stairs was quite different: hard boiled eggs and cold toast for breakfast, and lentil soup or stale fish for dinner. At last, the waiters started a Round Robin to improve their lot and somehow contrived to get Taffy Griffiths to appear to sign first. Within hours he was

summoned to the imperious presence of Colonel Quentin Knatchbull
(or was it "Scratchball"-Hugheson as some waiters said) and Glyn
received a terrible bollocking!

Glyn was tired of the Imperial anyway and put up a feeble
defence and within a week or so he transferred to the famous Hotel
Royale. Yes, Hotel Royale - even the name sounds romantic! It had
a French flavour, a Napoleonic crest, and was the Mecca of all the *fin
de siècle* intellectuals. The notorious Oscar Wilde had been a regular
diner there. Wasn't it in the red-plush room that the pugnacious
Marquis of Salisbury had taken the whip to poor Oscar, and called
him "sodomist"?

Glyn was an omnivorous reader in his spare time and had, as we
said earlier, academic pretensions. He had started serious reading in
his five months unemployment in Abertaff and had discovered a huge
dust-covered library of elegantly bound books in the study of the
Junior Imperial. And he found also that he could see it open often
and discovered he could rifle the shelves. One day, to his delight, he
had hit upon the complete works of Plato in B. Jowett's translation
and was amazed to find that though they were in the 1880 Edition, the
pages remained uncut. (Evidently Sir Hugh and his cronies were not
readers. More for music maybe.)

Glyn hoped that the atmosphere in and around the Hotel Royale
would be freer than was the case at the Junior Imperial. After all, the
name itself was redolent of the Quartier Latin, Montmartre and Place
Pigalle. "A permissive society?" Sure enough, the waiters did not
have to wear flunkeys uniform, only simple black dress with white
shirt-front and black bow tie. That was reasonable enough. But alas,
within days, Glyn realised that he had jumped from the elegant frying-
pan of the Imperial into the fire of the notorious Hotel Royale. Hours
were longer and the food was even worse. At the Imperial, waiters
could filch the best food because it was served from silver dishes
which were frequently returned to the sideboard half-full. Also wine
bottles could be returned half full. In fact, Glyn had tasted his first
champagne (half a magnum of Medoc) towards the end of the Royal
Jubilee banquet (June '35). Now these perks were impossible in the
Hotel Royale, and the favourite lunch and dinner for the waiters
seemed, almost inevitably, to be stale cod washed down by weak pale
ale, and with a garniture of hard rolls. Also, Glyn was no longer a
steward waiting directly on the tables but merely a commis running

loaded up with dishes from a hot steamy kitchen through dangerous swing doors to a sideboard where an old waiter was in attendance. There was a "tronc system" operating, that is a tip pool, a collectors sealed box into which all tips were supposed to be placed and shared out at the end of the week. But the most that Glyn ever got from it was 1/9d. And the hours of work were inordinately long, starting at 10a.m. for late breakfast, on through lunch, then three hours off from 3 till 6, then on for dinners, from 6p.m. until 2a.m., this including late suppers. And oh, how the feet ached and throbbed and even bled after all those hours of standing and running; and all for 25/- per week! The glamour of the famous Royale soon wore thin despite the cantering ghost of dear Oscar hovering over the red plush room, and the actual presence of artistic worthies like Ivor Novello, Matheson Lang, Hitchcock, and even the gorgeous Ramon Novarro and his many boys!

Soon Glyn came to hate the place with a passionate intensity. His digs were in faraway Bloomsbury (and crummy lodgings they were) and at 2a.m. he had to walk to his digs. It was all so much bloody slavery!

There was only one redeeming feature in his life now, or so it seemed to him then: the Hotel Royale was only a stone's throw from Leicester Square and in the corner of the Square was Orange Street with its excellent Middlesex Central Library. He found it quite by chance one day and thereafter he frequented it regularly. He was eventually allowed to borrow books and he would religiously lug the treasured volumes into Leicester Square and, portentously, under the statue of Shakespeare on a hard bench, he would read and read until he would be "quite sicklied oe'r with the pale cast of thought".

He now began to read intensely and omnivorously in classical literature. In his last three years in elementary school he had begun to develop into a scholar, or so his teachers said. He became particularly adept at geography and history, but above all in Literature. He however, remained hopeless in maths, and in any case, he developed too late to win the coveted Grammar Scholarship (the awesome Eleven Plus) and so had been obliged to quit school at 14 and to work in the coal-mines.

The five month period of unemployment had given him a chance to read again and he began to revive his old interests in Social History and World Literature. Now, strangely perhaps, in view of his inimical environment, working over twelve hours a day in a soul destroying trade, the urge to culture and academic pursuits surged up again and stronger than ever. In those precious three hours of free time he began to read voraciously. By chance he got hold of *The Outline Of Literature* edited by John Drinkwater. This opened up countless avenues into Chinese, Greek, Roman, French and Italian culture. Soon he wanted to know more about Li Po and Tzu-Fu; about Homer, Hesiod, Euripides; about Juvenal, Petronius; Ronsard, Villon, Dante, Petrarch. Then he got two chunky volumes by the American Will Durant entitled: *The Story Of Philosophy* and *Mansions Of Philosophy*, and this stimulated his intellectual curiosity. He would not be happy until he knew a great deal about every major philosopher from Plato to Russell.

Meanwhile he had received three letters from home: one from Mam, one from brother Ted and one from sister Olwen (now 14). They all attested the fact that a new evening class had opened in Abertaff Grammar School which was free to the unemployed people. Two new lecturers were opening new classes; one 33 weeks in "Literature and Society" and the other 33 weeks in the "History of Philosophy". Ted Griffiths had joined both and they were excellent he said. Furthermore, attendance for the whole course plus an exam in May, gave anyone of reasonable ability a chance to win a modest scholarship to Swansea University Summer Schools (a three weeks' session, all paid, in August). And who knew what might follow?

This made Glyn doubly frustrated. Here he was with a new and overwhelming zest for learning, chained to "a juggernaut of slavish toil", on a terrible treadmill, (or like Sisyphus in the Greek story), working twelve to fourteen hours a day, with only three hours of real leisure. The rest was a case of bed to work; and all for 25 bob a week.

Thus he brooded miserably on his park-bench. Back to reality at 6p.m., he was running from the steaming kitchen with piles of dishes stacked high under metal-covers, pushing precariously through those dangerous double swing-doors with head waiters shouting in a cosmopolitan babel of tongues: "Allez-allez! Toute suite!", or "Pronto garcon, molto-pronto, bambino!", or "Come on lad; quick!" etc.

And often the Maitre d'Hôtel - Ferrario from Florence, a tubby, swarthy, moustachioed, fussy-but-kindly man, would catch him gently by the arm and whisper, "Good boy! Bravo bambino!, you runna tente-vita; plenty quick, eh? You are a a fasta-commis, no? You maka da gooda waiter, maybe a Heada Waiter? You works da wells and maybe I promota you, eh? How youa likea dat, yes/no?"

And Glyn would be mumblingly ambivalent in answering what appeared to his melancholy mind to be a vague and doubtful proposition.

For however good a commis-waiter he was shaping into, he had come to loathe the servile and soul-destroying work. Walking "home" at 2a.m., falling exhausted into bed in a tiny, seedy lodgings in the slummiest part of Bloomsbury (with never a La Bohème touch to cheer him; only the occasional poxy prostitute to salute him on his weary way). Then up again at 9a.m. and after a hurried and inadequate breakfast, hastening by bus or tube-train to Piccadilly to be on duty to serve late breakfasts (and who, by the way, were the bloody parasites who wanted late breakfasts?) by 10a.m. Then laying up for lunch, then helping in the steamy kitchen to wash up filthy dishes after lunch. Then back on at 6 to lay up and fold those serviettes (Napoleon style) for Dinner. Then wash up and dry again ready for suppers and on till 2a.m. Then walking home because of lack of transport, stopping at that all night coffee stall for a quick cuppa and a Melbury pork pie which invariably gave him the gripes next day.

What a life! He made up his mind that if he stuck it much longer he would vegetate and wither and die. He had been diagnosed as partial T.B. in 1933, after an X-ray test for persistent bronchitis.

And now he yearned for intellectual pursuits: to read literature, poetry, drama, philosophy. To become a journalist, a short-story writer (!), or a lecturer in Liberal Studies, or something akin.

He was getting more desperate daily. He must get his discharge. But he would have to be dismissed. Get the sack "toute suite!" "pronto!" He could dodge the column, malinger, but this went against his nature, and would take too long. He must have a bold plan to achieve an immediate dismissal. Otherwise he could not qualify for the dole. He had written a skilful letter of enquiry to Councillor Trevor of Abertaff and the latter had assured him that he must get the "D.C.O." (the dirty kick out), the sack, to qualify for benefit. He wracked his brains for a solution to his dilemma. Then one day, sitting in Leicester Square under the Shakespeare statue, trying to concentrate on Li Po's poem *On Solitude, Its Compensations* (Waley's translation), a wonderful opportunity came. Or so he thought.

A shabby youth was busily, frenetically giving out leaflets. He hurried from bench to bench in an embarrassed fashion, thrusting the leaflets into willing and apathetic hands. He gave one to Glyn. It bore the headline:

"AGAINST FASCISM"

"Rally to Red Lion Square and Conway Hall on Sunday evening to protest against Mussolini's invasion of Abyssinia. Down with the Fascists and their Neo-Fascist backers in Britain!
Down with the War Mongers!
All out on Sunday!" etc.

It came to Glyn in an inspired flash, this was his way out! He ran after the youth who was moving south rapidly and said, "Can I have a bundle of those leaflets?" The youth looked dumb, then suspicious.

"Wor for?" he asked.

"I believe...," stammered Glyn. "I agree with the leaflet. I'd like to give some out."

"O.K. chum," said the youth, slowly smiling, and he thrust a bundle into Glyn's hand. Glyn sat down and counted them - 31. That was enough. This should do the trick. These leaflets were, in the words of the political wiseacres, 'inflammatory material', maybe 'seditious'! They were against fascists and neo-fascists and Italians. At least a third of the waiters in the Hotel Royal were Italians. Maybe some were fascists. In any case, the average diner was a rich man and *ipso facto* a Tory, possibly a neo-fascist. He would distribute the leaflets around the tables on the Balcony. He would put them under the Napoleon serviettes as he laid up tonight. Then he would wait upon events. Doubtless there'd be a row. Inevitably an enquiry. He would confess, and then - hey presto - the sack! He treasured the leaflets back to the Hotel.

With some doubts and anguish, heart thumping against his ribs, he carefully, silently, placed a leaflet folded once only, under each serviette he laid up. This was at 6:30 precisely. At 7 o'clock the first early diners would appear. By 8:30 the Balcony would be full, then the balloon would go up! The period between 6:30 and 7 went slowly by, agonizingly slowly. He began to be assailed by new doubts. He was going too far, too drastic. There'd be a riot maybe? He might land up in court, jail even. He could hear the Tory judge passing sentence: "You wicked Radical! You shocking Red!" etc. etc. *ad nauseam.* There was still time to whip around to recover the fatal leaflets. But NO, too late! - the table waiters were already coming into the main room to man their side-stations. And Maitre d'Hôtel, Ferrario, was on his rounds of inspection, bustling and beaming and twirling his waxed moustaches between his chubby fingers.

He came alongside Glyn, much to the latter's fear and shame. He whispered kindly, "*Buono sera!* How are you, me boya? You worka molte-vita, plenty quicka tonight, eh? We have a speciala party ona numero ninea so you runna *tente* fasta no?" and so on.

Glyn was smitten with awful guilt for a moment. "But," he rationalized, "No! It's got to be. The die is cast. I've simply got to get out of this shocking place. I've got to think of my future, preferably an academic one." Then he ran to the kitchen, already sweating, but more from psychological strain than any physical effort.

The night's work got into swing, and as he came through those awful swing doors with piles of food-dishes for the third time he noticed an altercation starting on Table One between a gesticulating diner all alone and a perplexed waiter (an Italian named Melandrone, as melancholic as his name). So the balloon was going up. The rows increased and by 9 o'clock there was pandemonium. The 31 leaflets had now been discovered and on the "special party" table (no. 9, which coincidentally included one Tory M.P. and a film director) there was hell to pay! Two of the diners were calling for the Manager, shouting "Outrageous!" "Vile Propaganda!" "Communist Waiters!" "A typical Red plot!" "Disgusting," etc. etc.

And at 10 o'clock, as the dinners ebbed away and tables were relaid for suppers the Manager, Allen, the Maitre d'Hôtel, Ferrario, and some head waiters were in the corridor in earnest discussion, and inspired rumours said that a full enquiry would be held before 11 o'clock. Passing through on a mock errand fifteen minutes later, Glyn could hear a row developing. In the centre of a group of Inquisitors (most of the Italians with suitable names like Il Papa and Cardinali) stood Jock McGurn, the only Scotsman on the staff.

He had come to London as a hunger marcher and had stayed on as an indifferent kitchen hand. He was a well known radical,

frequently to be seen reading the Daily Worker. As Glyn, who had
now got so frightened he determined to say nothing, passed by he
heard Jock shout through red and purple cheeks, "Och Na! I didna do
it, I tell ye. Aye! I agree with the sentiments alricht but I didna do
it." But Jock McGurn was on the rack, hard pressed, and the
bastinado would squeeze tighter very soon.

It was too much for Glyn. He boldly marched up to the group
and, though very nervous, he plucked Ferrario by the sleeve.

"Can I have a word with you in private, Signor - I mean Mr
Ferrario - sir? It's terribly important. No in private, please."

Ferrario looked deadly serious, he put his hand gently on Glyn's
quivering shoulder, walked him quietly down to his office, and on
entering asked, "What is it, mio bambino, I mean my gooda boya?"

Glyn answered, tremulously, "I did it!"

"Whata you meana, ma boy?" asked the incredulous Ferrario.

"I did it!" persisted the trembling, sweating Glyn, "I got the
leaflets and I put them under the serviettes!"

Ferrario blinked and stared and seemed ready to "exploda" like
Mussolini on the Piazza Venezia on hearing bad news from Ethiopia.

Then he suddenly went calm and said, "But why, ma boy?" he
moaned. "You! My favourite commis. You ara ma besta boya. My
finesta worka. Buta why? Oh Mama mia, why?"

"Because," said Glyn stoutly, "because I am an Anti-Fascist and a
Pacifist. I am against all wars, against Mussolini's war in Africa!"

"But," protested the kindly Ferrario, and Glyn noticed with
mixed feelings, that the Maitre d'Hôtel was not angry but merely sad,
"But my boya. I am also Anti-Fascisti, and I am mucha Pacifista!
And I say to Mussolini and his Blackshirts, 'Poof, Poof!' You see I
agree with you my bambino, but please-a do not make-a da molte
propaganda here-a, not on the Balcony-a, not here in the-a Hotela. If
you musta speak outa, you please-a go to the Trafalgar Square ora to
Hyda Parka Spouter's Corner. Yes? But nota here-a. Please?"

Glyn hung his head, a tumult of ambivalent emotions. "So," he
ventured at last, "aren't you going to sack me? Aren't I going to be
dismissed?"

Ferrario beamed a kindly little sad smile. "No, no, mia
bambino," he said softly. "Mama-Mia, you make-a da bigga mistaka,
that's-a all-a, you are-a misled-a. You-a been-a used-a by older
avanti popolo. I can-a see it all-a. You go back-a to work-a. Forget-

a the propaganda, eh? You worka da harder. I promota you some-a day-a, eh?" And he turned wearily away and indicated that the Inquisition was over. And Glyn, unlike Galileo, realised that nothing had moved. He had lost. He could not get the sack. He was back to Square One, and a horrible square-bashing prison square, it was!

EPILOGUE

But this was not the end of the affair. Glyn sank back into his awful work-a-day groove. The "Leaflet Incident" proved less than a nine days wonder. In fact, he became a pseudo-hero. But he waited and wondered, and dreamed and schemed for another inspiration. A better one.

It was Christmas week and homesickness was intense. He wrote himself a pathetic letter with his left hand. And signed it with his youngest sister's name. It was addressed (by him) from Cardiff Road, Abertaff. The sombre message said that Mother was very, very ill and that Father was still a drunkard and a wife-beater. Mam and two daughters were at the mercy of a brutal father. They needed protection, would Glyn consider returning home? And soon!

Glyn took it to the Manager of the Hotel. Allen proved a kindly and sympathetic man.

"Well," he said at length, "I suppose you'd better go home."

"Yes," said Glyn sadly. "Perhaps I'd better but you see if I leave voluntarily, I'll not get unemployment benefit."

Manager Allen mused awhile, looked at his watch and inkstand and then at Glyn (who was feeling awful). Then Allen smiled coyly and said at length, "I see - then I'll give you your discharge, and to put it nicely, say we're overstaffed at present."

"Thanks awfully," said the shamefaced Glyn.

Allen signed the necessary paper and on saying goodbye pushed £1 note into Glyn's sweating hand. "There," he said. "And buy a nice present for Mother."

PUBLIC HERO NUMBER ONE!

Glyn Griffiths returned home to South Wales after his troubled exile as a London hotel-waiter, in the February of 1936. He had tried for over a year to earn his living in hotels in the Metropolis but had rebelled against the "hellish slavish" conditions: working a twelve plus-hour-day for a pittance of about £1 per week.

Meanwhile the threatened dole cuts of 1934-35 had been postponed due to political demonstrations and riots in the depressed areas, so the dole for single men still amounted to 17 shillings per week. So what was the point of slaving for £1? So Glyn Griffiths, like millions of other unemployed, reasoned.

He found that his father, Will, idle since autumn 1931, was still on the dole and, Micawber-like, rooted in Abertaff, and waiting for something to turn up!

His brother, Ted, was also still unemployed. He was more rebellious than ever and had played a leading role in the organising of the famous unemployed demonstrations and semi-riots of Glamorgan (1935-36). In fact, Ted had now joined the N.U.W.M. and a local branch of the Communist Party; he was an activist and an agitator much in demand. The local Tories (not many in number) called him a "squalid nuisance, and a bloody little Trotsky!" (Stalin they should have said.) He thought of himself as a latterday Gracchus - "a true Tribune of the People". He tried hard to get young Glyn to join up as a C.P. member and as a dog's-body to himself. But Glyn, formerly a Seventh-Day Adventist Christian, with academic aspirations, resisted the siren call of the Stalinists. Being by nature a rebel, he did compromise to the extent of joining the little, but active, branch of the I.L.P.'s Youth Section.

The brothers also joined the local W.E.A. and attended regular and well organised lectures on Political Science, Economics and History. Also Ted persuaded Glyn to enlist, albeit belatedly, in the Evening Class run at the local Grammar School, the course being Literature and a very good one. So all in all, although the brothers were officially unemployed and drawing dole, they were never idle. They kept fit in a local gym and both had a side-line newspaper round (8a.m. to 3), one The Daily Herald and the other The Daily Worker. Then there were the cultural activities by night which were soon extended, in the spring of 1936, by the advent of the rapidly expanding Left Book Club. The Griffiths' brothers were among the first hundred to join in South Wales. And soon there was an active and intense L.B.C. Study Circle meeting in the Workmen's Institute every Wednesday evening. An added attraction appeared soon in the shape of two nubile sisters: Dora and Doris Davies. Soon the Griffiths brothers and these sisters were a foursome avidly discussing the book of the month (L.B.C.), and arranging hikes over the plentiful hills of Glamorgan with a little petting on the side. Years later, in retrospect, Glyn and Ted reminisced nostalgically over those happy halcyon days. (Those were the days, my friend! Pity they came to an end!)

Meanwhile the eldest Griffiths sister, Helen, was hard pressed. Her ambitious husband, Billy, was still on the dole and had sublimated his undoubted histrionic gifts into local operetta. But he was also in great demand as a Jolson Jongleur and a Joplin plebs-pianist in local public bars. Thus he was hardly ever at home. He was also a Roman Catholic and, true to faith and to form, he had begot five children in quick succession. In the middle of the depression, Helen had opened a sweet-shop, because she had a business flair, but when this flopped in 1933, not heeding the warnings of the legions of financial pundits national and local, she had put her rapidly dwindling assets (all of £10!) into a fish and chip shop, and that had turned vinegary too. So Helen was weighed down by the shop and five young children but still battling on.

Thus Cordelia Griffiths, who lived right opposite her hard-pressed daughter, would do her best to render all aid possible. In particular, during 1935, when Glyn was working in London and young Ted remained on the dole in Abertaff, Mrs Griffiths would urge and beg Ted to try to relieve his sister Helen by taking one or two of the kids for walks. Ted resolutely refused to trundle a pram on push-chair, it being too sissy. But he did consent, from time to time, to carry one on his strong shoulders up to the Abertaff Park (about a quarter-mile up the broad valley). This was a beautiful park with a large boating lake and a charming duck pond. Three year old Geraldine became his favourite: she was dark and vividly pretty with a demanding voice and a precocious personality. She came gradually, to present herself at the Griffiths' door every sunny morning demanding, "Uncle Ted, are you going to take us to the Park? I want to see the boats - I want to feed the ducks. Let's go up the Park, Uncle Teddy!"

Meanwhile a romance, or two maybe, was budding between the Davies sisters of Mountain Grove and the Griffiths brothers.

These halcyon days were shattered in the summer and autumn of that year by events abroad; strange to relate. In mid-July 1936, the Spanish Civil War erupted. A traumatic event that was profoundly to affect the lives, not only of many millions of Spaniards, but also of countless thousands far beyond the Iberian peninsula; Wales not excepted. As the War dragged on and became more violent and ideologically orientated, on the one hand neighbouring Fascist powers like Italy and Germany intervened with arms and troops. As a kind of military counter-balance, whereas the elected Republican Government failed to get arms from abroad in any substantial quantities, its beleaguered plight aroused the passionate sympathy of "progressives" all over the world. Young radicals everywhere rallied to the cause of Republican Spain and soon the International Brigades, "to fight for the freedom of Spain", were formed.

The first International Brigadier to leave Abertaff for Spain was one Howell Jones-Thomas, actually a mild, middle-aged, intellectual ex-miner. Coincidentally he was a close friend of Ted Griffiths. This acted like an inspiration amounting to an electric shock to young Ted and he, galvanised into action, vowed he would emulate Thomas. Long and anxious arguments, sometimes intense and bitter, now took place in the Griffiths household. Ted was adamant that it was his bounden duty "to join up and defend the Cause." His mother and father and sisters urged him not to be so soft! Not to be a bloody sentimental idealist, not to be a martyr to a clouded cause. In any case, they agreed, "he could serve the cause of progressives and the working classes better among the unemployed and the deserving-poor at home". "Let others be Public Hero No.1!" etc. etc. So the arguments raged throughout the autumn and winter of 1936.

And actually and surprisingly, it was Glyn Griffiths who answered the call from Republican Spain first. He was in a meeting of the Youth Section of the I.L.P. one night when Fenner Brockway, M.P., turned up and made an eloquent and impassioned speech on the need for aid for Spain. He announced that his bosom friend and fellow M.P., Bob Edwards, had just left for Spain, and he vaguely hoped that others would emulate him. Before the night was out four young men, including Glyn, had determined to go. Glyn had been thinking of it for a long time but now his thoughts and will crystalised into a firm decision. But he knew that his family would try to break his will so he left that night for Cardiff and stayed with a friend, having first sent a message home that he would be "staying overnight with a friend and not to worry!"

The next day Glyn and two pals (one had changed his mind!) went to a rendezvous in Cardiff. They were not absolutely sure that it was a Trade Union H.Q., it might have been the C.P. headquarters. No matter. There they were questioned carefully on their backgrounds and present intentions, then given the rail-fare to London with another address where they would get further briefings.

On the journey to London the three volunteers from Abertaff were joined by others, one from Neath, two from "Red" Rhondda. The man from Neath - Scourfield - a bid blonde chap, was very talkative and rather boastful and crude. He kept saying he was pretty sure he'd fail to return from Spain but that if he could have a "bit of Spanish stuff" before the end he'd die happy! "Always fancied a bit of Spanish stuff. Very passionate they tell me," and so on. Glyn, a Puritan at heart, was disgusted.

When the volunteers got to London, after a quick meal in a seedy caff around Paddington, they went by arrangement, to 16 King Street, Covent Garden and were there briefed by a nice, cheery, comfortable, rosy-cheeked, titian-haired woman by the name of Marjorie Pollitt (Harry's missus?). The briefing included the intelligence that they, the volunteers, were to pretend they were going for a weekend to Paris. A special weekend rail and sea ticket would be provided. Passports were not really necessary. In Paris, from the Gare du Nord, they would walk a couple of blocks and find Rue Blondin and at no. 216 they would meet a mysterious lady named "Rita" (rumour had it she was J.B.S. Haldane's wife!) who would give them further data to work on.

Glyn by now was thoroughly excited. For he had never been abroad before - let alone to notorious Paree, and to have a rendezvous with a Rita (could she be Rio-Rita, a *Senõrita*?) and be briefed by some "Mata-Hari" about a secret mission to Spain - well, this was tremendous.

But Glyn's elation was very much subdued by the journey from Victoria to Newhaven, for the pork and beans he had eaten in Paddington were now proving disagreeable and it was getting late. Worse still, they boarded the Newhaven - Dieppe ferry after midnight and the crossing was ghastly and Glyn was as sick as a dog.

When they landed at the Dieppe - "Douane" sheds, in the very early hours of the morning, all the voyageurs were feeling pretty rough, but Glyn was half-dead. He felt terrible. He wished he was at home. Suddenly the five or six volunteers (for the I.B.) were whisked away by Customs officials and thoroughly searched, then approached by Gendarmes plus a very good interpreter and closely interrogated. They were, in fact, strongly challenged that they were going to Spain to fight against Franco's forces. They all stoutly denied this. They insisted they were going to Paris for a weekend ("a dirty weekend I hope," sniggered the sexy Scourfield). But no doubt Glyn's shabby clothes and lack of cash aroused suspicions about their story. Finally they were all asked to prove their identity. They all succeeded with paper work, in doing this, except Glyn. He was duly segregated from the others who moved on to keep their date with "Rita". Glyn was taken to some kind of jail in Dieppe, lodged there for his dirty weekend, and then sent back to Newhaven on the Monday.

Frankly, Glyn was relieved. He made his way to south-east London and stayed for a week with a sister and had a pleasant time on strictly limited cash. He couldn't afford to go to his old haunt, the Hotel Royale, for a meal, not even tea. But while in London he read that a ship called the Barcelona, out of Marseilles and heading for the Spanish port had been torpedoed, probably by an Italian submarine, with a substantial loss of life. Several victims were believed to be volunteers for the International Brigade. On reading this sad and dramatic news Glyn, ex-Seventh-Day Adventist, was convinced that he had been saved by some *Deus Ex Machina* (some esoteric Providential interference?). Perhaps the "Divine Master" was saving him for destiny; choosing his for some great future (perhaps he would yet become a journalist, a teacher, a short-story writer?). True enough, his new compatriots had sailed on the S.S. Barcelona and two had been drowned, one of the latter being the blonde, sexy, boastful Scourfield. (So he didn't get "the Spanish bit of stuff" after all!)

Another week and Glyn was safely back in the bosom of his family at Abertaff. His mother and sisters were greatly relieved, but

Ted and his party comrades asked Glyn some awkward questions. Had he ratted at the first distant whiff of grapeshot? In fact, a kind of Communist cloud of doubt, if not unknowing, hung over Glyn and his brother for some time until one day, was it July 1937? (Was it the exact first Anniversary of the outbreak of the War?) Suddenly Ted disappeared and the family and Abertaff learned in a few days that he had volunteered for the International Brigade.

After a long pause, actually some months or more, a first letter arrived from Spain. It was headed on the top right-hand-corner: c/o S.R.I. 161, Plaza de Altazana, Albacete. It read:

"Dear Mam and All,
This is my fifth week in Spain. Not to worry - I am well. In fact in great shape physically, and in good spirits.

Would you believe it, last week I met my good friend Howell Jones-Thomas, who has been here a long time? In fact we are now billeted together.

We have now left our former base and are quartered in a new billet undergoing intensive training. We are all anxious to have a go at the Fascist enemy, we are all convinced that the policy of non-intervention will soon cease and that plentiful arms will pour into this, the legitimate Government of Spain and that we will then be on equal terms with an intrinsically inferior enemy.

You will be surprised and delighted to know, Mam, that our company commander is one "Taffy" James-Evans, a nephew of the Vicar of Abertaff! Also in our company is Esmond Romilly, an apparent nephew of none other than Winston Churchill. I wonder what Tory Winnie is thinking? Another of our number is Ralph Fox, the famous writer. Stephen Spender, the poet is also due out here soon. So you see, we're in good company! I have also met Lewis Clive (who claims to be a direct descendant of Clive of India). I have had some interesting discussions with him.

Meanwhile I hope everything is well with you at home. I've written to Dora Davies, but no reply as yet."

All in all, it was an inspiring letter. And there were many other courageous and elevating missives from Ted to follow.

But as the months went by the news from Spain got steadily more sombre, and by the early winter of 1938 it began to appear all too clearly that the Republican forces were losing. Madrid, under siege for two and a half years, was beginning to crumble, and in spite of the Government victory on the Ebro, Franco's forces, backed by the might of Nazi Germany and Mussolini's Italy, were winning.

Only Catalonia might be relatively safe, and there now one saw internecine strife erupting and spreading like volcanic fire, as Communists attacked Liberals, and they in turn were in dire conflict with Socialists and Anarchists, and they assailed by Trotskyists, the P.O.U.M. and innumerable splinter groups, *ad nauseam*.

Ted was in the middle of the great battle of the Ebro, and though he thrilled to the victory, he was shocked and saddened to find the shattered body of budding young Lewis Clive on the battlefield. Then before he could indulge his grief, Ted and his hard-pressed comrades were besieged on hill-top "421", on a rugged exposed ridge on the Sierra Pandoles, where the British Battalion suffered terribly, where Ted had to bury the mangled body of his best pal, H.J. Thomas.

Then came the news that the I.B. was being disbanded and sent home including the British Battalion.

One day came a telegram from Newhaven that Ted was on his way home and expected to arrive at the Taff Station, Abertaff on the afternoon of December 15th (1938).

"God be praised!" said Mrs Griffiths. "That St. Christopher chain I put around his neck a few days before he left - despite his protests - has brought him back safely." (However four others from Abertaff, one a Catholic and two ardent chapel-goers did not return, and Ted was an Atheist!)

The Abertaff Silver Band was alerted and half of them turned out and the news spread among the Radical Faithful that Ted Griffiths, "brave International Brigadier" was returning next day.

A huge crowd (well, two hundred anyway) turned up to the station yard and the Silver Band (well half of them, at any rate) played the *Red Flag* and *Comrades In Arms*. And the crowd sang - rather fitfully - some of the *Internationale*. (The words were uncertain but the tune sounded thrilling). And Ted made a fine impromptu fighting speech, ending with the tocsin cry, "The last fight let us face, and unite the human race." As the roars of applause died away, the proud red-faced Ted, helped down by his brother Glyn, whispered in the latter's' ear, "Jesus Christ! I'm Public Hero No. 1!

I never expected this crowd, this welcome, wonder what Dora Davies will say? By the way, how is she?"

Glyn dare not tell him there and then that school-teacher Dora had recently married a wealthy C. of E. curate, soon to be a Vicar, and had moved to a beautiful rectory - Winterbourne, near Bristol.

"Yes, Glyn bach," repeated the exultant Ted, "I'm Public Hero No. 1. I'm bloody glad I went - despite all the miseries!"

They marched the remaining five hundred yards from the station yard to the homestead, where a lovely ham tea, and Mam and the family were expectantly and proudly waiting. Ted could still hear the strains of the Silver Band's *Internationale* or *Red Flag* and the cheers of the faithful "Good old Ted! Long live International Socialism!" etc., ringing in his ears. ("Public Hero No. 1 in Abertaff anyway.")

As he rounded the corner with only ten yards to his front door, he saw his favourite niece, Geraldine, now 5 years old, racing across the street to greet him.

"Helloh," he said, "remember me? Who am I, Geraldine?"

The dark pretty little vivacious face beamed up at him but there was a note of reproach in the eyes.

"Hulloh, Uncle Ted," she lisped. "Where you been? Up the Park...? Why didn't you take me?"

"Jesus Christ!" Ted gasped, and turning to Glyn he said, "Would you believe it? I hope I get a more intelligent appreciation from my Dora Davies." (Glyn dared not tell him then.)

WHAT HAPPENED TO 'MY SUPER SUIT'?

The Griffiths Family, I stress and reiterate, was very poor, especially in 1930's.

"Poor, but always proud!" Cordelia proclaimed always.

Depressed in the Great Depression maybe, but never downhearted for long! Unemployed perhaps, but certainly never idle! In fact "So busy!" insisted Ed quite frequently, that "we never really have the time to look for work". Most members of this large family fairly hummed with intellectual curiosity, especially the two adult sons, who were seeking political and/or academic "glory"!

Incidentally, as noted elsewhere, their uncle Gomer, living about three hundred yards down the Cardiff Road, was a "Pierian Spring" of knowledge, ever ready to be tapped by any eager member of the Griffiths family.

"Dear old Gomer" was a hopeless cripple in body, but he had a razor-sharp mind. Physically he was a Caliban but intellectually and spiritually, an Ariel; a dwarf, maybe, but with the mind of a Titan, albeit a polymath, and a constant inspiration to those members of the Griffiths clan who wished "to sit at his feet". He would constantly enjoin them to, "read, mark, learn and inwardly digest!" He seemed to have all the books, gramophone records and piano sheet-music for his ancient piano, to encourage them to fulfil any cultural ambitions.

Cordelia, the mother (incidentally, so named by her romantic and literarily disposed mother in 1878) was also a very fine mentor to her children. She was always gay, talkative, interesting, and ever keen to learn herself. She had only received six years of formal schooling, and those precious few thanks to the 1870 Forster Education Act. Her parents had never received any education (both at work from the age of eight!). Yet Cordelia's mother had taught her father to read. Cordelia had her schooling from age 5 to 11 years. Even so, her headmistress vowed that at age 11 she had mastered all that was available for her in that place: the National School, Abertaff. Apart from her ample knowledge of English Literature, History, Geography, Art, Nature Study, etc. she had also achieved a wonderful style of copper-plate handwriting. She frequently showed off her calligraphic skill to her children.

"No pen handy?" she would ask. "Give me that wooden skewer, that will do nicely." She always challenged a family story that lasted many years, as apocryphal: that when she sent our little sister, Olwen, with a note to Woolworths store, when it was truly a 3d and 6d shop, in answer to her request for a loofah, the manager had replied "Sorry, Madam, there are no teapots at 6d!

After Cordelia's schooling, she was obliged to start work at Abertaff's main laundry, enduring twelve hour shifts in a torrid, steamy room, all for 10/- a week. She married (possibly as a relief or was she pregnant?) in 1899 aged 21. She would frequently say: "We got married in a winter blizzard, and it has been a blizzard ever since!", laughing as she said it.

Cordelia had borne eight kids in quick succession, or was it nine? The first son died of tuberculosis in a Welsh sanatorium in 1923. A mighty blow to Will Griffiths who only wanted sons to keep him in his old age. (I often wonder what Cordelia saw in Will, she was so bright and witty, he so dull.)

It is very important to record for a main motive of this story that she had always shown the most tender regard for her elder and crippled brother, Gomer.

In any case she had promised her dying mother to care for him always. She often told her children how Gomer became the victim of a tragic accident in his very early youth (aged three?). He seemed to be doomed to an abject life of dependency and failure. "But just like Toulouse Lautrec," Cordelia would rhapsodise, "he overcame his bad luck; and has made a success of his life. Consider his accomplishments!" These in cool, objective terms were that he had trained as a shoemaker (really a cobbler, for no-one in Abertaff could have afforded his boots or shoes); he had a small talent for sketching; he could play passable tunes on his ancient piano (keys so old that you could pick up a tune on the multi-coloured white keys!); above all he had provided himself with a very fine library. He had a vast store of good books supplemented with a set of Encyclopaedia Britannica (1911 Edition) and a set of Harmsworth Self-Educators, also a very prized copy of G.H. Lewes' *History of Philosophy*. Cordelia and Gomer had deliberately contrived to live near each other and she supplied him with all possible culinary comforts, especially a cooked dinner daily (or every other day). In return, Gomer provided

Cordelia and the children who sought it, plentiful intellectual and cultural nourishment.

Perhaps Gomer, maimed and crippled for life from infancy, could be excused by sincere Christians, if and when he became a militant agnostic. In fact, he was, early on, a staunch Atheist. He religiously (sorry) regularly took Bradlaugh's (or was it Chapman Cohen's?) *Freethinker* and persuaded young Ed to become a "disciple". One of Ed's treasured memories of Uncle Gomer was when attending a relative's funeral and standing at the graveside in a gale and pouring rain. The officiating preacher was one of those fundamentalist Bible Thumpers so prevalent in old Wales.

"A spell-binder from way back," moaned Gomer to Ted under his breath, until he could stand it no longer and he boldly walked up to the preacher (who was three times his height) and shouted, "Do you mind cutting it short, Your Worship, I mean dear Reverend? We're all getting soaking bloody wet and I doubt if that poor sod down there (pointing to the coffin) can hear or understand a bloody word you are uttering. He only understood Welsh! Anyway he doesn't deserve your lavish praise! He was a BLOODY CROOK!"

Brother Ed was convulsed with hysterical mirth by Uncle Gomer's grave-side impromptu "sermon", and was full of gladsome compliments later that day. Gomer cut him short with a very serious plea, "Promise me, Teddy, that you will not allow any bloody preacher, Welsh or English, renowned or obscure, to mouth a lot of religious cant and holy twaddle over my corpse! In fact you can bury me! Oh yes, don't be alarmed. It is quite simple. Just recite the Atheist's "Mass". Don't you know it yet? It runs: "Dearly beloved Brethren. We are gathered together here today to pay our last respects to Brother Gomer (or Mr X). Nature bore him and to her/his bosom he returns!" That's all! Lovely isn't it?... You can, for good measure if you are in a poetic mood, recite some lines from *Afterwards* by Thomas Hardy,

'When the Present has latched its postern behind my tremulous stay,

And the May month flaps its glad green leaves like wings; etc.'

I'll show you the poem in good time. All right? Will you promise to do this service for me?"

"Yes. I Promise faithfully," said Ed, fervently.

All through those so-called months and years of Depression 1930 - 1937, the Griffiths brothers were never really idle. In particular they were sitting at the feet of their Gamaliel Uncle Gomer, ceaselessly imbibing culture in Gomer's side room as he hammered away on the customers' shoes, or occasionally for light relief, hammering out a tune while he hummed it on the old piano.

When Glyn Griffiths returned from London at Christmas time in 1936, he was fired with a burning ambition for an academic future (a school or college post or even successful authorship!). So he resumed his private studies in his Uncle Gomer's side room where he was given unrestricted access to Harmworth's Self Educators, Encyclopaedia, and hundreds of books. He also attended evening classes in Economics and Social Studies in Abertaff's old Grammar School. His studies were never ending.

One day, a very auspicious one for Glyn, a man somewhat below middle age, balding, be-spectacled, short but bouncy, walked in with a pair of shoes to mend. Glyn could not help hearing some of the rather intellectual conversation the stranger was having with his uncle. Eventually the old cobbler called out to Glyn, "Come here! This gentleman might have some interesting and promising news for you. You must hear what he has to say!"

The stranger who introduced himself as David John Evans then repeated something of what he had told Gomer. He had almost worn out his shoes on the mountains of North Wales, on and around Snowdon especially. He had just returned, he confided, after ten to twelve months intensive study at the residential college called Port Meirion. The College was unique he claimed, for it threw open its doors to disadvantaged men (especially the unemployed) who were keen on seeking further education. The aspirants should be over 22 years of age and preferably under 55, and especially those who had missed the chance of a Grammar school education through failing that notoriously unfair Eleven Plus, one day exam. In fact, this Port Meirion Academy was also called The College of the Second Chance. It had originally been the palatial home of a rather cranky American millionaire. But he had been persuaded by famous Socialist intellectuals (including Bernard Shaw, R.H. Tawney and the Webbs) to bequeath it to the new Council for Social Services for a worthwhile Social purpose. Hence the college!

Glyn was all ears! "What do I have to do to get in?" he brusquely interrupted. "What exams do I have to pass! What academic standards do I have to reach? Do I have to show any certificates, any testimonials?"

Evans smiled omnisciently and with a benign air, "Hold on!" he said. "Easy does it! Don't fret. All you have to do is send for application forms to the Warden - T.T. Bowen, M.A., c/o The College. And when you return the completed forms, you also submit an essay of about a thousand words on the title *My Life And Aspirations*.

Before the day was out Glyn had sent for the required papers and within the same week he had sent them back with the desired essay. Gomer had vetted the composition and, with a correction or two and a suggested phrase here or there, he deemed it "very good!"

A long and irritating delay followed and in the interval, Glyn even tried to enlist in the International Brigade (volunteering to fight for Republican Spain). He failed to get through and on receiving a good reply from Port Meirion College, Glyn even thought that Divine Providence had saved him from death in Iberian war, choosing now a higher destiny!

Yes, Glyn had been accepted for a full year's residential course at this increasingly prestigious college, situated in a beautiful place facing Cardigan Bay with towering, scenic Snowdon in the background. He was to study, on discussing with the Warden, T.T. Bowen, and three tutors: Economics, History, and Literature.

Glyn left Abertaff for the College in early October and had a wonderful journey through mid-Wales in glorious autumnal, sunny, colourful weather. As he approached the splendid gates of the building and saw its massive oaken door, the motto above gates and door in Medieval Welsh seemed to say: "Abandon All Ignorance: Ye that enter Herein!"

And how he thrilled to those expanding days, (aye and nights!) of college life!

How he enjoyed the stimulus of the wonderfully new and varied cultural activities! changing daily from the dismal science, Economics (as Carlyle dubbed it) to the romance of History and then climbing the never-ending "Alps" (Pope) of Literature! (And withal, what a lovely contrast with his former life as collier boy and hotel waiter. This was Dante's *Paradiso*!). Then again, in the Great Hall some afternoons, and especially in the evenings: musical appreciation with acoustically perfect large gramophone and with splendid verbal interpretations by expert teacher Graham Thomas, Mus'Bach! Then again, not to be overlooked, a dance every Saturday evening (with gramophone records) with local girls invited (all thirty of the village belles - some old and rusty and not ringing tunefully), with a chance to date one or t'other!

Another pleasant feature of College life was that of making new and intelligent and stimulating acquaintances, some to become life-long friends. There were forty five full-time students in all and about ten of these came from overseas: one from Canada, two from France, two from Germany, three from Denmark, an Austrian and a Jew (from Palestine, he said; some cynics thought Stepney).

Glyn was pleased and excited to find that one of his room-mates (out of three) was a young Frenchman, exactly his own age and size and physique (many declared they could have been twins from a short distance!). He was named Paul Govinian, a handsome young man and from the deep south, Arles, not far from the Pyrenees (shades of Bizet, *Carmen* and *Provençal Song*, Glyn considered in his romantic way). Paul had raven-black hair, and blackberry eyes and, unlike Glyn, he had his own natural teeth! He could easily have passed as a Spaniard. Many said (especially the girls at our dances) that Paul looked like a younger version of Charles Boyer, matinée idol of the time. "Oh! But Paul was much handsomer!" Actually Paul was already well educated; in fact, he had gained a first class degree from the Sorbonne in Literature and the Humanities. He explained that he was only taking this course in this obscure Welsh college "to improve his English" ("In a Welsh accent!?" one comic asked). But, *sotto voce*, some opined that Paul was dodging military service.

Glyn and Paul became very good friends, to mutual advantage: Glyn could help Paul with his English (albeit with a Welsh accent) but he gained most because Paul was able to extend Glyn's nodding acquaintance with the French classics, notably: Rabelais, Voltaire, Stendhal and Balzac.

However Paul, with his good looks, Gallic charisma and Chevalier accent dominated the sparse sexual relationships between the students and the very few local girls! Paul had the power to date any one of the thirty available.

Glyn told me: "Paul had another big advantage over the rest of us in attracting the girls, especially over me. He was easily the best dressed man in Port Meirion. After all, most of the British students were unemployed proletarians; some of us had been on the dole for years with few, if any, changes of clothes to boast of. Paul, we noticed, by contrast, had at least five excellent suits to wear for various occasions. There was even a persistent rumour that he had a family relationship with the famous Ovaltines! I, alas, was probably the poorest dressed student of all in my year. My entire wardrobe was what I stood up in!" So Glyn reported.

This could easily prove to be an embarrassment. And it did! One day Paul and Glyn were strolling in the village and met two pretty girls, strangers to those parts. They had "come across the border", they said, and "were holidaying in Port Meirion". The four spent the afternoon together and made great progress! They arranged to meet again that evening but on the way back to College they were caught in a heavy rain storm and were soaked to the skin. After tea Paul asked Glyn if he was ready for the romantic assignment, but Glyn's only suit, albeit a very shabby and threadbare one, was now hanging in an airing cupboard, put there to dry. And now Glyn sat rather sadly in an obscure corner, dressed in a very ragged pullover and a pair of khaki shorts, borrowed from another room-mate. Glyn did not explain his sartorial predicament to Paul, and the latter was too well mannered to comment. So, after brief awkward moments, Glyn excused himself from the date, and Paul went alone. (However, I believe Paul had noticed Glyn's plight, as the ongoing narrative strongly suggests.)

Some months later the students were busy packing their bags to return home on completing their year's course. Glyn had packed his pathetic little suitcase in record time for nearly all he owned, mainly books, were inside the case or otherwise on his body. Paul, by contrast, was still filling three large, elegant cases: two marked "luggage in advance". He now, probably pretending, seemed to have a great struggle closing his last case and probably feigning exasperation, turned to Glyn and coyly said, "I say, old man, are you willing to do me a favour? I simply can't get this extra suit into this case. In any event, I have already packed four or five other suits and this one is getting too tight for me anyway. Do you think you could use it or get rid of it for me or something? You know the porters and chambermaids (this last with a sly wink) here better than I do, can you help me?"

Glyn tried hard to hide his excitement, but avidly grabbed the suit! For despite Paul's (feigned?) denigration, it was a splendid suit; a SUPER SUIT! It was obviously a very expensive suit, at least £7, possibly £8, when the average price of a decent copy of this one was about £3. Glyn had never paid more than 30/- for his. The one he stood up in now was, in fact, thirty bob, bought four years ago and in its present, threadbare condition resembled the words of the song about June busting out all over!

On subsequent inspection (when Paul had gone), the French suit, a kind of grey pepper/salt, was "pinched in" by elastic at the waist and so flattering the tubby figure (which applied to Glyn as well as to Paul). Glyn noticed, when inspecting the lovely jacket, the real silk lining and behold, a legend on the inside pocket in gold braid and crimson which proclaimed the maker's name: "Jules Freres, NIMES". This maker's badge or legend, when whispered softly seemed to breathe affluence! (Try it, if you please.)

A couple of weeks later back home in Abertaff, Glyn decided to go to a Three-penny Hop (a dance) at the local Memorial Hall. Shyly and somewhat furtively, he donned the French, Govinian suit. It immediately caused a great stir in the entire extended Griffiths family. Explanations were rapidly called for! How could Glyn have possibly afforded to buy such a suit on very precious dole-money in College? Had he stolen these wonderful garments? Glyn then recounted his rather unlikely story to a very sceptical audience. So he had to try to prove the veracity of his tale. He drew their attention to the gorgeous trade-name legend on the inside breast pocket. Everyone then meticulously examined the beautiful badge. Under instructions from Glyn imitating Paul Govinian whispering in awe, "Jules Freres, Nimes"!

"Oh, there's posh!" said Mam.

"Shades of Charles Boyer," observed Ann, who had been film-struck for many years. Then, by way of further corroboration of his sincerity, Glyn produced a small passport photo of Paul he had found left in the trouser fob pocket.

"Fair enough!" said Ed, looking rather enviously at the jacket. Then everyone waxed eloquent and unanimously declared the suit to be SUPER!

Over the ensuing months it came to be hailed in the Griffiths family as "the posh French suit" or "the Paul Govinian clothes" or even the "Charles Boyer garb" but most regularly as "the SUPER SUIT!" Uncle Gomer, a self-styled sartorial connoisseur (though he rarely went out into Abertaff) was particularly impressed, calling it: "elegant, stylish and decidedly *à la mode*".

One need hardly emphasise that Glyn was a great sartorial success in the Memorial Hall dances (though he was no great shakes as a ballroom dancer!).

Glyn now sometimes wondered: do clothes, after all, make the gentleman? Though as a long-term poor fellow and badly clothed, he always hated the saying. The most sartorially minded person in the extended family was, in fact, brother-in-law Billy, married to sister Elinor. He always tried to be a natty dresser but now unemployed for years his suit(s) was/were starting to look shabby. And it was he, in fact, who cast envious eyes on the French suit, not Ed. For the latter was far away in Spain in 1937-38 trying to stop the triumph of Fascism there.

However, time passes inexorably, and in the late summer of 1938, Glyn got a job in the new Cable Works just opened in Abertaff (as a matter of fact he nearly fainted when told by a Communist pal that a Green Card offering him a position in the new works awaited his collection at the Labour Exchange). It would be his first job in Abertaff for four years. The new job paid the princely sum of £2 11/- for an eight hour shift, but for eighty hours per week ("Overtime compulsory! If you don't want it there are plenty waiting who do!"), Glyn could earn £5 per week! Money even beyond the avaricious dreams of a Shylock or Scrooge! So within the year, Glyn was able to buy another suit for £2, a double-breasted, navy blue, and later, heralding the spring, he lashed out on yet another, clerical-grey for Sundays! His sweet heart, Doris Davis, now declared that he was the best dressed young man in all Abertaff.

Meanwhile, as recorded elsewhere, Ted Griffiths returned from Spain but only after the cruel defeat of the Republicans he had supported. Despite his hero's welcome rally in Abertaff Station and temporary ebullience, he soon sank into a mood (quite uncharacteristic for him) of deep depression. His chosen sweetheart, sister of Doris Davis, had married another, and his Mother had commented that she had "captured a 'cop' " (a nice well-off chap), contrasting with unemployed Ed, now idle for nearly six years! So at last, Ed decided that Marx and Lenin might have been wrong after all and Capitalism could last a few more bitter years, that he'd better accommodate to the *laissez faire* situation and get a job. However, he was convinced that he was truly black-listed in Abertaff and he had better move out. And so in early December, much to the unhappiness of Mother, Ed departed. He told everyone he was going to distant Carlisle, actually he moved just across the Welsh border.

On Christmas Day, 1939, Mrs Griffiths, as usual, sent a special dinner down the road to dear old Uncle Gomer. Olwen, the youngest, took it and she reported that Uncle looked quite well but was unusually quiet.

But when Glyn next day went to retrieve the dishes, he was very disturbed to find Gomer slumped over his kitchen table with his grey-haired head lying in the uneaten Christmas dinner. Glyn, increasingly alarmed, stealthily approached his Uncle, calling his name repeatedly. He tried to shake him gently by the shoulder. But Gomer felt icy cold and rigid. Glyn also observed with distaste amounting to nausea, that Uncle's head was covered in cold gravy and mashed potatoes. Glyn had never witnessed such a sordid sight and quickly quit the kitchen and house.

"Well?" asked his quick-witted mother, "where are the dishes?... What's wrong, Glyn? I fear something bad!"

Glyn told her what he had seen. Cordelia Griffiths rapidly donned her coat and hat, and hurried down the Cardiff Road, furthermore, she insisted on going alone. She did not return for several hours.

Naturally, all the Griffiths clan, less the migrant Ed, gathered in the main room (the kitchen) of their natal household and eagerly awaited the return of mother. She arrived three or four hours later. She confirmed Glyn's worst fears.

"Oh yes! Gomer's dead! No need to call a doctor. I've laid him out very nicely on the big sofa. No trouble at all. The poor chap is so small!"

Cordelia was quite calm; there were no tears. She never did cry; she had known too much sadness and premature deaths in her time. Abertaff being a coal mining town, disasters were prevalent. Two of her brothers were killed underground. Her eldest son had died of T.B. at the age of 22.

"After all," she summarised philosophically, "I've expected Gomer's passing for many years. It's something of a miracle that with his poor little physique he has lived so long. After all he is, or was, 75. Longer than the average man, I doubt if your father or I will have such an innings!"

At last, after almost an hour of Cordelia's calm obituary, including impromptu tributes to Gomer "who was so courageous, so talented, just like Toulouse-Lautrec", etc, Elinor, the eldest daughter, who had a "flair for commerce" but who had come a cropper with a shop she had opened during the Slump, but still had commercial ambitions, had the temerity to ask her mother, "What about Uncle Gomer's money, Mam? He was so busy with his cobbler's work in the shop all day that he seldom went out, and lived so frugally... why ... he must have left a tidy little sum!"

Others observed, "Yes Mam, and perhaps not so little either!" Elinor summarised. "After all you did for him, all over the years you are, surely, the sole heir or heiress!?"

"Well," said Cordelia, "I will tell you what I intend to do but after I, or shall I say WE, have given Gomer a decent Christian funeral. Then I will go back to the house, look for his will and thoroughly investigate, alright?"

"Hold on a moment, Mam," said Glyn. "You spoke of a Christian funeral for Uncle Gomer. That would be a mockery. Sheer hypocrisy! You know very well he was a dedicated and a life-long, vociferous Atheist!"

"Oh! Don't be so old-fashioned, Glyn," complained his Mother.

"Old-fashioned!" retorted Glyn. "It's you who is old-fashioned, Mam! I belong to the Modern Age, like Ed,... aye... and Gomer. Despite his 75 years, he belonged to the 20th Century. Sorry Mam, but your outlook is Medieval, you're a mass of ancient, religious superstitions. If you insist on giving Our Gomer a 'Churchy' funeral, I won't be there! You surely know that he asked brother Ed to officiate at his grave-side. He even asked him to deliver the sermon: *The Atheist's Mass* he called it."

"Then it's just as well that Ed is far away, so I shan't send for him!"

"Oh," responded Glyn, "I also know *The Atheists Mass* and the Thomas Hardy poem *Afterwards*. I learned it in school, when Hardy died. I'll say it!"

"Don't be so daft!" said Mother. "What will the neighbours say? Why, you'll have the whole town talking! I'll never be able to go to Church again. I'm adamant that my beloved brother, Gomer, gets a decent Christian burial!"

Glyn gradually realised it was useless to argue with Cordelia in this mood. And it was tacitly agreed that an "armistice" was the best idea that day.

A week or so later, after the decent funeral, the Mother returned for the promised inspection of old Gomer's house. She was away over an hour, meanwhile all the children gathered with "Great Expectations!" Were they to be blessed and suddenly become the *nouveaux riches* of Abertaff; and being willing to forsake Christ and Communism for the delectable delights of the *dolce vita*?

As she entered the main room in her home and witnessed the upturned, expectant faces, Cordelia was clinically bland, "Abandon all Hope, ye who enter Uncle Gomer's house! Thus sayeth the Lord! There's NO MONEY!"

"WHAT!" they all gasped. "Surely Mam, you must be joking! Tell us truly."

"Honest to God! And you all know I will never take the Lord's name in vain."

"Have you searched thoroughly?" one asked.

"What about the will?" queried another.

"There is no WILL," replied the Mother, "and the only money I can find in the entire house is - wait for it and believe me - it's 14 shillings and 9d!"

"WHAT? 14 and 9d! Never! Surely you are joking, Mam!"

But she wasn't!

"What the hell did he then do with the money? He was always working cobbling so many shoes, never going out, living so abstemiously, it doesn't make any sense!" Ann said.

"God only knows!" Mother summarised, but more like Seneca than St. Mark! After a long pause someone suggested that that scoundrel Cousin Albert (the clever bloody thief!), he with the mark of the hangman's rope around his neck, had nipped into Gomer's house and swiped the will and all the money. Anyway, the tragic Mystery continued indefinitely.

Glyn hurried home from work one evening and had a specially good bath, albeit in the old wooden tub in front of the fire. He then had a better than average shave. He put on to his shirt a new neat collar, and a flashy tie, then smeared an ounce of scented Vaseline on his hair.

"Where the heck are you going?" asked his mother. "All dressed up like a dog's dinner and face polished like a pig's bum in the butcher's?"

"It's the annual Cable Works Dance, didn't I tell you? And there's a pretty new girl in the office and..."

"Oh-ho! Courting is it?" she teased. "Special occasion, eh! so special clothes, eh?" As she blurted out the last phrase she put her skinny fingers up to her thin lips, and perceptibly winced.

As if given a signal Glyn said, "Yes. Good idea!" and he dashed upstairs. He searched the old, dark oak, creaky (totally inadequate) wardrobe propped up by a wooden wedge in one base corner). He searched in vain for his special suit.

He rushed back downstairs. "Hey, Mam!" he challenged, "what's happened now to my best suit?"

His mother looked a trifle uncomfortable but only for a moment. Then in a firm and steady voice asked, "What best suit? Oh, you mean the clerical grey. Oh yes, I know now!"

"No! No! You remember. My very best suit... the 'SUPER SUIT'."

"The 'Super Suit'?" his mother asked in a very vague and vacant way.

"Yes, silly! The 'Charles Boyer'; I mean really the 'Paul Govinian'. I simply can't find it. Have you moved it? I'll go and have another look. I'm determined that's my suit tonight. I want to make a good impression on a certain girl."

"No, Glyn," observed his mother sternly, and even apocalyptically, and she could even out-do Isaiah and Jeremiah combined whenever necessary. "Don't go back upstairs, Glyn bach, you won't find that suit. It's... GONE!"

"GONE!" he shrieked. "What the hell do you mean, Mam? GONE! You know very well that it's my very best, my SUPER GOVINIAN SUIT! GONE! Gone where, for CRIISSAKE?"

"Please don't swear, Glyn. Don't blaspheme," urged his mother, with a tender, cautious, restraining hand on her son's arm. "Yes, GONE forever! Thus saith the Good Lord!"

"Gone Forever!" he bellowed. "Are you out of your mind, Mam? Or are you trying to drive me flaming mad? GONE FOREVER! Jesus Christ Almighty!"

"Oh! Please don't go on blaspheming, Glyn bach. It's no joke! the 'Super Suit' is gone forever. The ways of the Lord are mysterious; inscrutable..."

"Look, Mam!" her son moaned, "stop quoting stupid, sentimental, sickly scripture! I have to warn you now, Mam, I'll search this bloody house room by room, yes, room by room: stone by stone if necessary!"

"No use. You'll not find it here," summarised his mother.

Suddenly, Glyn stopped dead in his tracks. "I've got it!" he said, "It's bloody Billy, our dandy brother-in-law. He told me recently that he could do with a decent suit to attend an Operetta Reunion of the Desert Song Troupe! Yes, that's it! The best dressed man in Abertaff; the Adolphe Menjou of the Valleys! I'll give him *Desert Song*, by damn I'll chase his *Red Shadow* all the way to Morocco!" He started to make his way across the road to his brother-in-law's house.

His Mother now barred his path with a passionate gesture. "NO, Glyn, PLEASE! You are making a terrible mistake! Billy has NOT got your super suit! Your Govinian Super Suit is wrapped around your Uncle Gomer's corpse in his beautiful red plush coffin. No, No, hear me out: your Special Suit is with dear Gomer six feet deep in our Abertaff cemetery. Dig him up if you dare, but know you will have to get an exhumation order from a coroner first!"

"Good God!" exclaimed Glyn. "Can this be really true or is one of us MAD?"

"It's all too true. I told you: Gomer was going to have a decent Christian funeral. You said you wanted him to have what Ed called an Atheist's Mass. I simply couldn't allow that. Remember, Glyn bach, Gomer had very little joy in this life, a Vale of Tears for him. And he really fancied that suit! You know he did! Alright, he was an

Atheist, I can admit it. But we were both brought up as good Christians. So I decided to compromise. I decided not to bury him in a holy shroud so I dressed him in your 'Super Suit'. In fact I hoped that you would be pleased and even proud?"

Glyn was suddenly, psychologically and spiritually, exhausted. He slumped into the nearest chair, not noticing that it was his father's special, taboo chair.

"OK, MAM!" he groaned, "YOU WIN! Yes - You BLOODY WELL WIN!"

Only many years later, long after his mother Cordelia was also dead, did Glyn come to question, even suspect (God forbid!) the veracity of his mother's bizarre/grotesque story.

And I now ask you, readers all: what really did become of that 'SUPER SUIT'? What is your opinion? Please reply to George Greening...

CABLE WORKS

You could have knocked me down with the proverbial feather when I was told that I had a green card for a job in the Abertaff Cable Works. The Works was very newly opened: the first factory ever to be founded in Abertaff (July 1938). It was also the first response to the chronic state of unemployment in our distressed valley which amounted to over 60% of the work-force. At last, the National Government was reversing a bad (stupid) trend by bringing work to the so-called "ragged army" instead of sending the idle workers to far distant areas to find work. This was a kind of Social Revolution.

When told about my green card awaiting collection at the local Labour Exchange, I didn't believe it, for my informant was one Willy Lloyd, (a fellow member of the local Communist Party) who was a notorious wag and leg-puller. However, the characteristic leer was absent from his cynical face, "Honest to God!" he swore, not withstanding we were both Marxist Atheists I believed him. So I pedalled my cronky push-bike to the Labour Exchange. Sure enough, there it was! The clerk strongly advised, "If I were you, I'd get there real soon for you must know jobs there are scarce and it is a great chance for YOU especially!" and he gave me a palpable wink and a nod for he probably knew that I was a Party Member.

So I cycled hard up the steep Gadlys hill and covered the mile or so to the Cable Works in double-quick time. I couldn't help wondering though why they should send for ME: a Communist; a potential or even a probable trouble maker? Passing through the large factory gates after showing my green card, I saw with awe and a rather sickening feeling, my first meaningful factory. This would be my first job in Abertaff for four years and my first factory job - ever. Yes, I was scared!

Soon I was ushered into an office with a few other young men but we were interviewed one by one. I was introduced to the Works Manager, one Bill Crookes, a handsome blonde man with penetrating steel-grey eyes. I soon found, to be confirmed many times subsequently, that Crookes had a hard, cynical nature. On confronting me he positively leered.

"We know all about you," he confided, "a notorious Party member... eh?"

I was on my guard and interrupted with, "I think you mean my elder brother, Ed. HE may be notorious. Anyway, he's far away in Spain fighting in the Civil War."

"Oh well, maybe so," said Crookes with a broad grin. "Anyway, we are going to give you a chance here, but bear in mind, this is a non-union shop so we won't tolerate any hanky-panky union-making here. Furthermore, it's a twelve hour shift, alternate nights and days. No arguments, take it or leave it!"

Crookes concluded his masterful advice (or was it dire warnings!) with, "If you don't want it on my conditions, there's plenty of men idle in Abertaff who do! Understood?! So you start on Monday morning, 6a.m. sharp, OK?"

I didn't like his harsh conditions or his bullying attitude but, naturally, I didn't argue. I simply nodded agreement and cycled home.

As I entered the kitchen, knowing Mother was there with the inevitable teapot on the hob, I started singing George Gershwin's popular song: *Good News*, "Good News! O bring us the good news, do! Tell us the good news; good news!"

"Oh!" said Mother. "You're happy. So what's the good news?"

"I've got a job in the new factory; yes, the cable works!"

"NEVER!" gasped Mother. And it took quite a long time to convince her. And it took a much longer time to persuade other members of my family that I had really landed this unexpected job. However, my sister Ann was doubly delighted for her husband, Ted, was already working in the cable works. In fact, he was in the very first batch to be taken on, one of the first ten!

Alas, my singing of *Good News* soon turned to a bum/falsetto note, even a "miserere!" for I soon detested the work. I was put on the cable paperlapping section. This meant that I had to stand at a complicated machine (no sitting allowed) for twelve hours with only one break for a meal (no tea breaks). I would have to watch - very carefully - the many spools, meticulously spaced out, throwing insulating paper around the bare wire cable. One could not relax as the paper had to lap neatly (not WRAP!) it was agonizingly slow, repetitive, boring work.

I soon realised that if I stayed in this job for long, all my dreams and realistic aspirations for an academic or journalistic career would be doomed. So within a month I decided to get enough money together saving hard to enter university, assuming of course, that I could pass the entrance exams. After all, for six 12 hour shifts I was being paid £5; a lot of money in 1938. And I had already spent an academic year at a non-vocational college in North Wales (The College of the Second Chance!) and had left with a good, if not a glowing, report.

So, telling no one in advance but my mother, of my bold scheme I planned and saved. When I had got together £12, I travelled to Cardiff to the university by day, for I was on the night shift in the works, and forsaking much-needed sleep, I sat the exam (three papers in three days) and duly got the *Good News!* that I had passed the Mature Matriculation Exam. When I told Mr Crookes that I wanted to leave, and why, he grinned and made his typical caustic comment, "OH! I know, you'd rather be a scholar than a worker, eh?"

However I was very surprised at being informed by Crookes that the General Manager wanted to see me. He was one Thomas (Tommy) Elder. Incidentally, Elder had soon been nicknamed by the men "Shnozzle Durante" because he had a huge nose very like the popular film comedian of the time, I soon discovered that Mr Elder was a sentimentalist. I had been summoned to his posh office upstairs. He began by saying, "I have a younger brother very much like you... a radical... joined the I.L.P... but developed academic aspirations, just like you .... went to university ... now an Oxford Don ..... doing very well .... and very happy. So good luck! and we hope you do as well as my brother, eh Bill?"

Crookes was non-commital. All the time Elder was waxing lyrical, Crookes was looking at me with a leering smile. As I left the room I couldn't help considering the contrast in the two men!

I propose to pass lightly over my time in Cardiff University College mainly because my academic efforts there were abortive. The pursuit of my studies in English Literature, History and Philosophy went well enough but, alas, I had to leave after two terms simply because I ran out of money. I had applied to various sources for grants but all in vain. Out of the £12 I had saved for my risky venture, I had to pay £ll in Varsity fees in the first term. I was then stymied! However, my plight became known to various people, some influential. For example: Abertaff's M.P., George Hall, although he had suffered many times from my heckling at his meetings, sent for me. I went to his home. He expressed sympathy and encouragement and he offered me £5. When I hesitated on taking it he said, "Oh! please don't regard this money as a bribe for your silence at my meetings. In fact your interventions make the meetings more lively and swell the crowds. Regard this money as a gift if you prefer?" I accepted it and saw Hall in a new and better light. A month later the Secretary of Abertaff C.W.S. one Bowen, asked me to attend his office and gave me £3 as a help to my fees.

However, instead of being encouraged I felt humiliated, and fearing a long drawn-out struggle for my fees I suddenly quit College. So from March to June (1939), I was unemployed again, and terribly conscious of failure! And even worse, I dreaded the possible, even probable, taunts of those who would exult in my failure.

Meanwhile, I wrote letters of thanks to George Hall and Bowen explaining my action. Hall was kind enough to reply and he even asked me if I would like to return to the cable works, stressing that he had much influence with the management. I replied in the affirmative. And so in the July (a year to the day I had started there) I returned. I was again interviewed by Bill Crookes, but this time I was one of a group being vetted by him.

And I was quietly but terribly enraged when he said to us all (but he seemed to be looking directly at me): "You'll find, lads, that you have to work and work hard for your living, and it's better to be a practical man like an engineer than an unemployed scholar, eh!"

I was seething with suppressed anger as I left the works. So much so that I made a point of hanging around that day to find Crookes to give him a piece of my mind! I even made my way to the street where I knew he lived. At last I saw him get out of his car to make his way to his house. I stopped him in his tracks and harangued him.

I said, "I thought you were very unfair, even rude, in saying what you did to ME especially earlier today!"

He smiled ironically and answered, "Oh! You are touchy, my lad. I was speaking to you all, collectively. If I have hurt your tender feelings, I'm sorry. See you Monday morning early, OK!"

Sometime during the Monday morning I was surprised to be summoned to Mr Elder's managerial office. He was very friendly. He said, "You may as well know that it was your M.P.'s plea got your job back. Mr Hall was very eloquent on your behalf. I'm personally sorry that you couldn't stay in university. However, looking to the immediate future, the same rules apply here. We know quite well of your political affiliation and local record, but as long as you don't start any union making and keep your nose clean in that particular, and work hard, you're welcome to stay here as long as you wish!"

I couldn't help thinking it was odd that George Hall, M.P., who was sponsored by the Miners' Union as our Parliamentary representative, could become a shareholder in this non-union cable works, as was widely rumoured!

What became more odd, even bizarre in fact, was that on my return to the works I was given a new job. Instead of returning to the awful paper-lapping machine I was made a crane-slinger. This meant that I would follow the overhead crane with various slings and hoisting gear. By this job operation I was able to talk to all the workmen and in a grand position to start recruiting for union membership if I wished; if I DARED!

In fact this is what happened. For in September 1939, War broke out, and very soon Joint Production Committees (regular meetings of bosses and workmen to boost War production) proliferated quickly everywhere. And less than a month after the War broke out, I was approached by a union organiser of G. & M.W.U. (The General & Municipal Workers), one Sid Hunt, to start a branch in our works. (In retrospect I realised it was the wrong union for us. We should have opted for the A.E.U. - The Engineers). I also wondered later why Hunt picked on me. But I was young, vain and foolish I guess, and agreed to meet Hunt and a small group of "activists" in a local pub, The Swan.

The following Monday morning I was summoned to the management office yet again! Messrs Elder, Crookes, and one other were there and all looking stern.

"Now Mr Gee, or should I address you as Comrade Gee?" Elder barked. "We have it on good authority that you and some other COMRADES met in the Swan pub last Saturday evening for the purpose of starting a branch of the G. & M.W. Union! Recall that we gave you fair warning when you returned to our employ, that we would not tolerate any union hanky-panky in our works! So what have you got to say for yourself?"

For some esoteric reason I was very calm. Always somewhat romantic and superstitious, I felt I was fulfilling a "destiny"! I answered coolly and slowly, "You know very well sir, that since we last discussed this matter the objective situation has radically altered. You must realise that the War is making all the difference. Joint Production Committees are being created everywhere, especially in factories. And in return for workers' co-operation workers are, naturally, expecting union recognition!"

I did not seem to make any impression on the three bosses who continued to threaten me.

As soon as I got home that evening I wrote a serious letter to George Hall, M.P. (he was now a member of a War-time Coalition Government; in fact, Junior Minister for Colonial Affairs). I asked him to persuade the Managers of the Cable Works to recognise our projected union. Within a week I had a favourable reply. And almost on the same day I was again called to the factory office. My reception was bizarre, fantastic!

The same three members of the Management were present but this time Mr Elder asked me to sit down. He then offered me a cigar and a "choice of drinks" (?). I declined both but I sensed victory - correctly! Elder concluded the session by saying: "We assume that you are the Workers' Shop Steward?" (Not yet confirmed.) "We will meet you and two others you choose once or twice a week as a Joint Production Committee." Meanwhile, I was nearly peeing in my trousers in suppressed mirth!

Within a year we had 450 members in our union branch (90% of total workers), some of these were women, recently recruited by the works for shell-case production. Incidentally these women were the most demanding of my time and energy.

I hurry on to describe the main events leading to my quitting the cable works. In the three and a half years I worked at the factory, I witnessed many incidents: some funny, even hilarious, some serious, even tragic. I recall the funny ones in relation to certain personalities, for there are always "characters" in every work situation. However I only recount here some serious and tragic accidents, and two incidents that probably had a lasting effect on me.

On three occasions, men repairing the semi-glass roof of the high factory fell through. One was very badly injured, and two, falling on to moving machinery, were killed. My brother-in-law, Ted, was witness to another terrible accident when a work-mate on the same wire-drawing machine had his right arm torn off!

One of the incidents affecting myself was, tenuously, connected to the other, and I recount here/now.

In April 1940 I was called up for military service. Initially I had, of course, to pass a strict medical exam. The night before the exam, to prove my fitness to the family, I did a Gopak dance, leaping on to a stout table as a grand finale! The next day I had an awful shock to find I was unable to pass the medical test. Two doctors asked about the nature of my job and when I told them that I was a crane-slinger, walking many miles and man-handling heavy loads from time to time (carrying and stacking pigs of lead; 116lbs each), the doctors advised me to seek easier work or expect a very short life! A subsequent X-ray test revealed evidence of T.B. as shown by partly healed nodes on my lungs.

The irony of all these facts was that few people believed that I was unfit for military service and some cable works men even suggested *sub rosa* that I had got a brother-in-law doctor to wangle a medical certificate so that I could dodge the army.

One of these slanderers was Dai Forward (well named for he was famous locally as a good inside-right footballer). One day on the shop floor I was called simultaneously by two men to bring the crane along to pick up a cable drum. It so happened that one caller was a foreman, the other was Dai Forward. I went to the foreman first. When I got to Forward he met me with a torrent of verbal abuse, alleging that "although a shop steward, I was really a Boss's toady!" etc. Many angry words flowed between us until Forward thought he had given the *coup de grace* by denouncing me as a 'draft-dodger'! Both of us ignoring the fact that he also was not in the army! He then challenged me to fight him. I had no intention of meeting his challenge. But on leaving the factory at the rear end of the works, Forward rushed up and said, "Come on, fight, or show how yellow you are!" He threw off his jacket and squared up to me.

I said, "Look, I am your shop steward, I'm meant to help you not fight you!"

He answered, "Bollocks to that! Come on...!"

I knew he wanted my blood so I caught hold of him in wrestlers' style. I forced him to the ground and sat on his chest, pinning his arm under my knees. I then proceeded to lecture him in a most avuncular way, "You can see," I said, "that I am much stronger than you. I don't want to fight you, so when we get up PLEASE, PLEASE, GO HOME!"

I set him free but he rushed towards me with clenched fists so I hit him hard on the jaw. He fell but was still quite conscious and very angry. He had in fact, fallen on a pile of broken bricks and, as I began to walk away, I noticed with horror that he had picked up a piece of brick rather larger than a cricket ball and, of course, as hard as one! I sensed that he was going to aim it at me. I half turned away, but suddenly felt a terrible blow on the upper side of my head between my right ear and eye. I was almost stunned into unconsciousness. I saw however, that Forward was moving towards me! He was, in fact, running past me for dear life. He must have known that he had really injured me. I gradually came to my senses, if only because I could feel blood running down my right cheek, staggered to the works ambulance room and found a nurse on duty. She asked me what had happened. I told her it was an accident, without mentioning the fight. Strangely, I never did tell anyone about the scrap until many years later. The nurse cleansed my wound and put a large plaster on the injured place. Alas, I have suffered some deafness in my right ear for a long time (but realise there could be other causes). Now in old age I am plagued by giddiness, and often wonder, as I feel the bump and notch on the old injury, if I suffer from a tumour caused by that blow inflicted over 50 years ago!

I turn to happier incidents from my cable works days and one event above all that changed my life completely and for the better. In the winter of 1940-41 my brother Ed came home on army leave. He said to me one evening, "Do you know that you have a new employee in your cable works? A girl, sister of our constant pal, George Davies? I have met her with George and she is a stunning beauty! You should try to meet her." (George Davies was a firm friend we had made through our membership of the Left Book Club since 1936; George was a wagon repairer but was also a considerable intellectual, an authority on Shakespeare, W.B. Yeats, T.S. Eliot, etc.) "Yes," enthused Brother Ed, like all our family, film-struck from an early age, "this sister is the spitting image of Dolores Del Rio. One of your favourite actress-beauties, isn't she?" I didn't take Ed's words too seriously for I knew very well that he was prone to hyperbole.

However, a few days later I was one of a small gang of workmen unloading shell-cases from a railway wagon. In charge of our gang was a friendly, easy-going foreman named Len Whittington. He was called to a nearby phone and I was quick to observe that he was very chatty and bubbly. I approached and asked, "Who are you talking to so merrily?"

He replied, "Oh, it's Miss Davies, the new office girl recently arrived from London."

"Oh!" I broke in. "Can I have a quick word?" and before he could answer I had plucked the phone from his uncertain grasp. "Hello there, Miss Davies," I said and promptly introduced myself. I was pleased when she said, "Oh, yes, I met your brother recently. And my brother, George, knows you very well and thinks very highly of you."

I was bold and asked, "What do you do for entertainment these nights?"

"Oh, nothing in particular. I haven't made friends yet, only newly arrived."

"Do you like dancing?" I urged.

"Er - yes."

"Well... can I pick you up on Thursday evening and escort you to the dance at our Memorial Hall?" And so it was arranged.

On the Thursday evening, dressed in my best with an extra ounce of scented Vaseline on my hair, I went forth on my "blind" date. When I arrived at George Davies House, George apologised for the inordinate number of glasses of alcohol spread around his sitting room.

"We are celebrating our father's pension birthday," he said. The fact was that most of the Davies family had moved to London at the height of the Economic Depression in 1933. They were now living in Neasden, N.W. London, but during the Battle of Britain, with intense air-raids, a land mine had dropped in their street and they sought refuge in safe Abertaff with George and wife and son.

I looked anxiously around the room for a girl like Dolores Del Rio. George divined my concern.

"Oh!" he soothed, "Kate is upstairs completing her toilette. She's quite excited to meet you. I've told her all about you, all favourable, you will appreciate!"

I had decided to impress her with my generous spirit aiming to give young Ralph, her ten-year-old nephew, a shiny new sixpenny piece as she entered the room! And so I did when I beheld this supremely beautiful girl. Brother Ed had not exaggerated. She was tall and slender. She had raven-black hair, blackberry eyes beneath the most striking, gloriously arched eyebrows I had ever seen, in reality or on silver screen! She was dressed in sober black but this was offset by a long gold chain drooping from her beautiful slender neck. I was transfixed. It was LOVE AT FIRST SIGHT!

So we went to the dance and decided to meet again... and again. We seemed to be in complete social and spiritual harmony from the beginning and our mutual liking blossomed into a deep love in a matter of weeks. Every Sunday morning we would meet and climb the Graig mountain and, observing the silver birch trees and the budding of golden daffodils, and the "mewing" of puss-willows and catkins, we thrilled to the rapidly expanding spring (despite the continuance of a terrible War!). I would recite yards of poetry to her, and she would eagerly respond.

Alas! It was altogether too lovely to last. By the April (1941) the Blitz on London had noticeably eased. We did not know it yet but the Nazi armed forces were getting ready for Operation Barbarossa, the invasion of Russia.

So in late April Mr and Mrs Davies and other kin felt safe to return to Neasden, London and naturally there was increasing pressure on Kate to go back home also.

But meanwhile, Kate was becoming a favourite secretary to the managers of the Cable Works. And gradually the news leaked out that Kate and I were courting.

One day I was summoned to Tom Elder's office. (I was there often now as shop steward, and as one of the three workers on the Joint Production Committee.) Elder, however, wanted me on this occasion for quite another purpose. He wanted to make me "a proposition". (I ought to record, in parenthesis, that the cynical Bill Crookes first realised that Kate and I were forming a lover's liaison when he mistook her signal. I was unloading a wagon of shell-cases one day as Crookes stood near by. Kate was leaving work and waved to me. Crookes thought the wave was for him and returned the sweet signal, then Kate shook her head and signalled beyond. Knowing him to be a womaniser I relished that piquant moment.)

A propos the proposition by Elder, he asked me to sit down and then offered me a cigar and "a glass of something". I declined as Crookes looked on with his usual cynical grin.

"We learn," said Elder, "that you and Miss Davies are sweethearts, is that so? Well we think, all of us, very highly of Miss Davies and her secretarial abilities. In fact I would like to make her my own special private secretary, isn't that so, Bill?"

Crookes, still smirking, nodded in agreement. I waited silently and patiently. Elder took his time to elucidate his "proposition"! At last he came to the point.

"What I would like you to do is to plead with her to stay here in Abertaff and not to return to London. If you succeed you will be rewarded. We will offer you a promotion!"

"A promotion?" I queried in great surprise.

"Yes," Elder said with a benign smile. "We are well aware that your job as a crane-slinger is quite arduous and we know that you failed to pass the army medical exam. You may not know that John Rhys James, our storekeeper, is retiring next month, so we are willing to offer you the post of head storekeeper!" (I knew well enough that there was only ONE storekeeper in the entire works.) Elder went on, "It will be a very soft job compared with what you are doing now but we will also give you a rise in wages. What do you say to my proposition?"

I answered, "Will you give me a little time to consider all this?" (I had to wonder, apart from other vital considerations, if the managers were being cunning, taking me off crane-slinging to reduce my influence with the workers).

"Of course," said Elder. "Let us say that we can expect your answer within a fortnight but don't forget to coax Miss Davies to stay with us!"

Kate and I had some hard, hectic and anxious discussions in the following days, for her Mum and Dad and sisters were begging her to join them at home in London.

Soon, it was the Whitsun holiday, a weekend plus two days. Kate went home for the vacation and, on impulse, I followed her. Air raids had ceased, or so we thought. So I sat in the back garden with three of her sisters, who told me that Kate was discussing my accommodation with her mother. (Later I considered that this was a ploy to get me alone.) The eldest sister spoke first, "You must know that we are all very concerned for Katie's future. She tells us that you are trying hard to coax her to stay in Abertaff." I tried to counter this thesis by telling them of the managers' wish.

The sisters could not accept this argument. It was obvious that they had made up their minds to get Kate back home in London. They now exerted all possible pressure with cogent arguments.

"You should realise that Kate has qualifications far beyond the cable works standard. Surely you know that Abertaff is a mean little provincial backwater. London has infinitely more to offer. We know there's a War on now but it can't last forever. Anyone can see that London has unlimited scope for anyone with ability and ambition. In Abertaff it shrivels and dies!"

I began, honestly, to see the logic and force of their arguments, so later that day, and subsequently, Kate and I decided that she should return home for good and I would follow in good time maybe after the War. However, I was soon restless and lovelorn and so in June I quit my job in the cable works and travelled to London to seek work in and around Willesden. There were plenty of vacancies. Meanwhile everybody in the family and among my workmates thought I was mad! For on May 10th 1941, one of the heaviest of German air-raids had caused havoc in London.

However, my decision was sound and of long term great benefit. For instead of ending my working career as head storekeeper in Abertaff Cable Works, I eventually resumed my pursuit of academic honours and ended my professional life as Polytechnic and Open University lecturer and Counsellor, M.A., BSc., Dip-Ed & F.R.G.S. Kate also has held some prestigious posts, apart from helping me!

TEACHER TRAINING

I started my Teacher Training Course in October 1945.

In so doing I began to realise one of my life-long ambitions. I had, since a very early age, a longing to be a Teacher and a "Man of Letters"! I was now past 30. Since age 12 I had been a butcher's boy, newspaper roundsman, coal-miner, navvy, hotel-waiter, cable-maker, crane-driver, munitions maker (electrolytic-parkeriser!) cafe manager, etc. Still I yearned to be a teacher and a writer!

At last, in mid-1944 (with the Second World War still raging and myself polishing lenses at Dallmeyer's Telephoto-Lens Ltd., Willesden, London) my wife, Kate, saw a Ministry of Education notice in the News Chronicle saying that "100,000 new school teachers would be needed when War ended and applications could be forwarded now". I applied the very same day!

I began training on October 3rd 1945. I had been asked if I wanted to wait for a residential college to open at Alnwick in Northumberland or go immediately to attend at a day college at nearby Camden Town, London. I settled on the latter. (I ought to explain that my year's course of study at the non-vocational college at Harlech, Wales in 1937-38, and my two terms at University College, Cardiff, and a few testimonials, were sufficient to convince at interview at London County Hall, that with training I would make a suitable elementary teacher.)

The College at Camden Town had for me, a passionate and romantic proletarian, a very special, illustrious history. It had been founded as "The Working Mens' College" of London, a great pioneering effort inspired by the Christian Socialists led by Charles Kingsley, F.D., Maurice and Tom Hughes, the author of *Tom Brown's School Days*. Everything about the college and its history seemed apt and propitious for a sentimental working-class chap.

The scheme was called "An Emergency Course for the Rapid but Thorough Training of Teachers". It was to run for 54 weeks without holidays.

We met - 600 mature men - (all over 25 years of age, some nearly 50 years old), in the Great Hall of the college. We were first addressed by the Principal, Dr F. Bradley, a 50 year-old wise and kindly gentleman. He was followed by a Dr Swann who gave us more "nitty-gritty" data. Later we broke up into alphabetical groups for tutorials, then into chosen subject groups. (I had opted for History, Geography and English Literature.) We had College lectures and seminars for the first three or four weeks. Then came the exciting day when we were sent out in little groups of two or three to the schools for Teacher Observation.

My companion for this period of training was one Howard Dickson. We couldn't have been more vividly contrasted. I, short, stocky, utterly working-class in origin, in manners and type of dress, and with a pronounced Welsh accent. Howard was very tall, handsome, beautifully attired, of obvious bourgeois upbringing, public school background with a "plummy" Oxford accent to match. He was also brimful of self-confidence; I, invariably nervous and lacking in panache. Although we were mutually cheerful and very polite to each other I think a clash of temperament based on social background was inevitable.

The first school chosen for our Teacher Training Observation was a secondary modern at Haverstock Hill, somewhere between Highgate and Hampstead. As soon as we arrived we were taken to see the Headmaster. He was one Mr Read, about 60 years of age, a skinny, wrinkled, cynical and caustic man. As he concluded his introductory remarks with many words of dubious advice, he warned, "One more thing before you go around the various classes, you may as well know that all the teachers here think that I am MAD! The truth is that THEY are ALL MAD! And I am the only sane person on the staff!" After a long pause with a cynical leer he said, "Oh, by the way, we now go to morning assembly; for under the terms of the new Education Act, in case you don't know, morning assembly is compulsory as is Religious Instruction."

We now accompanied Mr Read and all the teachers to the Main Hall and sat on the platform facing some hundreds of boy students (or were they called pupils?). After some preliminary remarks and the fitful singing of a hymn, the Headmaster began reading a text from the New Testament Bible and specifically, Corinthians; V.1 to 13., in which St Paul enjoins us all to show CHARITY, which suffereth long and is kind, and the greatest of these is CHARITY. But before Read could finish his 'sermon', we were all thrown into utter confusion when he leapt from the platform with the agility of a monkey and held a boy in the front row by the neck of his jersey and punched him hard on the jaw! I was not sure what the effect of this act was on the others present but I was deeply shocked and somewhat sickened. Returning quite calmly to the rostrum, Read said, "I'll deal with any other lout like that if he misbehaves in assembly, for this morning assembly is a very Holy institution! Remember that!"

Dickson and I now made our way to the classrooms and eventually found Classroom no. 6 as advised by Mr Read, to introduce ourselves to a Mr Everard who was to demonstrate a "Crit." lesson for our benefit. I knocked tentatively on the door and a very loud voice barked "ENTER!". We espied a man seated at the teacher's desk marking the attendance register. He was about 50 years of age, balding and with bulging, grey-red rimmed eyes. A bristly brown moustache, we soon discovered, symbolised a bristly temper!

For Mr Everard hailed us with an hysterical shout: "Teacher trainees? Yes? Oh, Yes! Take my serious advice! Avoid this profession if you want to stay sane. Get to hell out of it as soon as you can! No? Not today? Oh well then, sit down. Yes, anywhere if you can squeeze in. I've been asked by the Boss to give you a Crit. lesson to demonstrate the noble art of Teaching. It's English Lit. so I've chosen a bit of poetry (what old Spenser called 'Poesy' don't you know?). So if you're sitting comfortably, I'll begin. Now boys, what season of the year is it?" (It was late October.) We waited a long time for a reasonable answer (giving Dickson and I a scornful Everard leer). At last one boy said, "The football season, sir". Most of the other boys agreed.

"So what was the season before this, before the August hols, I mean?"

"The cricket season, sir!"

"YES!" was chorused by thirty five others.

Everard turned to us with his bleary eyes and weary manner, "Brilliant, aren't they?"

We were, of course, non-committal.

Everard agreed at last, "But if you go to the Heath, towards Hampstead, nowadays, what kind of trees do you see (if you SEE anything at all) which may tell you it is a new season?"

Several boys now answered rapidly and loudly, "Conker trees, sir!".

"Yes," Everard assented, "CONKER trees, as you should say, Chestnut trees! And what has happened to the leaves. What colour are they and what has happened to these leaves?"

"They've turned yellow and brown and some have fallen to the ground, sir!"

"Yes," said the long-suffering teacher. "Now we're getting somewhere," (looking at Dickson and I in mocking triumph). "And what about the weather, eh? Is it warm and dry?"

"No, sir," offered one or two boys brighter than the average. "It's colder and damp, sir."

"Yes, and misty?" urged Everard.

"Yes sir."

At this climactic moment in the lesson, Dickson turned to me and very quietly whispered, "The poem he's chosen is Keats's *Ode to Autumn.*"

I winced in apprehension, for I feared that Everard had overheard Howard. Alas, I was correct. He spun rapidly around in his chair and faced us with his bulging eyes speckled with fiery red spots and saliva dribbling from the corners his mouth; he shouted ever so loudly at Dickson: "YES! It's Keats's *ODE TO BLOODY AUTUMN*! And what about it?" He proffered an old, battered book of verse to Howard. "DO YOU WANT TO READ IT instead of ME? With your posh OXFORD accent you might do better, eh?"

Of course Dickson froze! And we listened to a desultory reading of this lovely poem and a crude analysis in a deafening silence.

We were very glad to leave Room 6 and poor, pathetic Everard, and to move on to Room 7 and Science.

As we left the Haverstock area later that day I said to Dickson, "Well, Howard, what did you think of our very first day of School Observation?"

Howard was very obviously depressed, "Oh my God! It has been a dreadful eye-opener! If this is typical of our schools today and what we are in for, I'm afraid I've made a great mistake. In fact, the Pater advised me against this radical change in vocation. He urged me constantly to stick to Lloyd's Bank and work patiently for promotion as he did so successfully. I must admit that it was a nice, quiet, tranquil life there, though I was terribly bored sometimes. And I thought it would be pleasant to teach English Lit., especially Drama, for I belong to three Drama societies."

A month later we had another spell of Teacher Observation. I was a bit surprised and even sorry to find that Dickson and I were chosen to go together again. For I was not at ease in his company. We had few things in common. His posh Oxford accent and patronising manner irritated me. I feared that there might easily be a clash - an open rift - of personalities. I feared correctly.

As we travelled to our next school, The Robert Blair Secondary Modern, in London's East End, Howard seemed to go out of his way to be rude and to provoke me. (Though I have to say, in long-term retrospect, that he was quite unconscious of verbal injury and I was always prickly in this particular.) Dickson said, "Oh, by the way, you might like to know that I am planning with some other Drama enthusiasts to stage a play in college in the last term, mid-September perhaps. I've already chosen Shakespeare's *Much Ado About Nothing*, fully costumed and I know some talented girls who are willing to join us. I'd like to give you a part but I don't know quite what to do about your Welsh accent."

I was stunned and quite mortified but decided not to show it. I merely said, "Oh, I'm far too busy with my studies to fritter precious time away with drama. I'm determined to make a success of this basic teacher training." (Actually I had been deemed "very promising" at college in North Wales, as an actor for a prominent part in Shaw's *Saint Joan*.) But inwardly, I was seething with suppressed hostility towards Dickson. I thought, "Oh, Howard, with your lordly, haughty attitude, you will sooner or later come a cropper!" I was correct and I didn't have long to wait. Howard would be humbled that very day!

When we arrived at the school - early - we were ushered in to the Headmaster's study and told to await his arrival. At 8:45 he came bustling in. He was the very antithesis of Mr Read. He was short and fat, dressed in an old blue suit topped by an old-fashioned bowler hat. He was rosy in cheeks and very merry in manner. He was exceedingly friendly, seeming so keen to put as at our ease. After preliminary questions and some sound advice, he took us to morning assembly. There, with many other teachers on the platform, we overviewed about five hundred children aged 11 to 14. Unlike harsh, pedantic Read, this Headmaster, Robert Roberts (called BOBS by his devoted staff) disdained to read from the Bible. Instead, after a pleasant, didactic story, he recited a poem which I, incidentally, had learned in Junior School. And I knew it very well by heart. It was called:

TIM, AN IRISH TERRIER

It began:

> It's wonderful dogs they're breeding now,
> As small as a flea, and as large as a cow,
> But my dear lad Tim, he'll never be beat,
> By any other dog he ever ever met
> "Come on!" says he, "I'm not kilt yet."

And ending:

> So I laugh when they try to make it plain,
> That dogs and men never meet again,
> For all their talk, who'd listen to them,
> (With the soul and shining eyes of him)
> Would God be wasting a dog like TIM?

I could sense the sheer joy of the children listening to Roberts' lovely stories, and especially the poem "TIM". I could also tell that Mr Roberts was pleased with himself. He proudly took us back to his study to give us advice about our visits to classes and teachers for the rest of the day.

"Incidentally," he asked, "what did you think of our morning assembly?"

"Excellent!" I said.

"Yes, very good!" conceded Dickson and then added. "Though I couldn't see the point of the poem!"

Roberts blushed and gave Dickson a very hard look. (And I thought: "Oh, Howard! What a pompous bloody fool you are!").

I believe that what followed that day was planned by Roberts as a kind of subtle revenge by him on Dickson for the latter's blatant indiscretion. Roberts informed us that he himself would give a "Crit." lesson for our benefit and that we would receive his summons later on to attend. On receiving the message we found Class 5 and saw that Roberts was already standing before a class of eleven-year-old boys. He had a new long piece of chalk in his hand and a large globe before him. He announced that he was going to give a lesson on the significance of Longitude and Time. He introduced the subject with references to the pioneer work of Newton and started by pointing to the U.K., and London and specifically to the significance of Greenwich in the scheme of things. He then told the eagerly attentive boys how every fifteen degrees of longitude equalled an hour in time, and how Newton calculated the time in Jamaica, etc. Then by spinning the globe and pointing to various well-known places, asked the students to guess the time there. It was exceedingly fascinating but not exactly easy.

However, after about twenty minutes of elucidation, there was a knock on the door and a prefect announced that Mr Roberts was wanted to answer a call on the phone. I believed then, but later found out that this interruption was contrived! Roberts responded immediately, and putting the chalk firmly into Dickson's hand, said, "Please carry on with the lesson!"

Dickson turned ghastly pale and looked stunned. He made no effort to get up. The students looked at him expectantly. But there was no movement from Howard. It was beginning to become embarrassing. At last, I got to my feet and took the chalk from Dickson's paralysed hand, and proceeded with the lesson in my own amateur way until the bell sounded.

Before we left the school that day, Mr Roberts sent for us and asked Dickson how he had got on. Howard was obliged to admit his defeat in the Geography sequence and told how I had managed to finish it. Roberts sympathised but I think I detected a faint smirk of glee on his rosy face.

As we proceeded homeward, Dickson was man enough to admit his humiliation, and added, "I must congratulate you on the way you rose to the occasion. You responded magnificently. I only wish I had your self-confidence, but you see I never did take to Geography and I want to specialise in English."

I assumed an attitude of humility, but tinged with a philosophic air, "Oh, it was nothing; but as new teachers in secondary modern schools we will have to be prepared to muck in and be ready to take more than one subject, be alert for emergencies." But then I decided to tease Dickson, and felt justified in doing so. "Anyway, Howard," I began, "so you think those Cockney boys understood what I was saying? Did I make my points clear?"

"Oh, absolutely," conceded Dickson. "You were excellent! I certainly followed it all, and incidentally, I learned quite a lot myself!" Then he added, "You were very logical, forceful and clear!"

"In spite of my Welsh accent?" I demanded.

He blushed, and giving me a coy look, he concluded, "Oh, yes, and I only wish I had your quick-witted eloquence."

Our third excursion to the schools came after about five months into our college training. But this time we were expected to teach, and to be observed by regular school teachers and by two college tutors. I was assigned to St. Augustine's Church School, Kilburn. On arrival, I was told that I would be expected to take Geography, and that I had two hours (in the school) to prepare. Suddenly I had a happy inspiration to choose "Coal Mining in Great Britain", (the subject was very much in the news. For coal nationalisation was in the offing).

In the allotted time available to me I made some headline notes and drawings on some post-cards. I made thumb-nail sketches of the four major kinds of coal-mines (as a matter of fact I had worked in them all though I was determined not to reveal this to the students and other people present at my lesson). In the classroom, I swiftly translated my drawings to the blackboard while I expatiated without hesitation on the history, geography, geology and working, with all the prevalent dangers of the industry. It seemed I could do no wrong. I felt I had a genuine "captive audience". Everybody seemed to be utterly fascinated by my phrases and my drawings. It was not my vain imaginings. After the lesson in an empty classroom the school-teachers and - more important for me - the college tutors, were eloquent in my praise.

"That was one of the finest lessons I have ever witnessed," rhapsodised the senior tutor.

A week or so later our Principal Bradley, summarising the work of the term and proffering advice for the future, said in the Main Hall to our six hundred trainees: "I urge you all in your teaching practice not to be too rigidly academic. You come from various trades and industries and many of you were, very recently, in the armed forces. So don't be reluctant to draw on your own secular experiences in order to enliven your lessons." He went on, "The best lesson we have had reported in the last term was on coal-mining."

Later that day I bumped into Howard Dickson. He said, "Oh, Helloh! By the way, I have it on the grape vine that it was YOU who gave that much praised lesson on coal mining. Am I correct?"

"I dare say so," I answered. "And do you know, Howard, all the students, as well as the teachers and our tutors, understood every word I uttered - in spite of my Welsh accent!"

He blushed and said, "Oh! I guess you'll never forgive me for that gaffe!"

As Easter approached we had a mini drama festival in the college. Several groups of students, specialising in English Lit. staged scenes from famous plays. Our group - led by College Tutor Glover, decided to put on scenes from Shakespeare's *Henry IV*, and I was persuaded to play the plum part of Fluellen, the brave but fussy patriotic Welshman. The costume was delivered but, alas, my hose (trousers) were missing! Glover begged me to make a rapid visit to the designated West End costumiers while he delayed our performance. My trip was abortive, and I played my part *sans* hose. A subsequent photograph (a very large and intimate picture) showed me forcing the braggart Pistol to eat my leek with the bristling hairs on my legs prominently displayed!

Later Howard Dickson approached me and said how much he had enjoyed my "virile performance" and he begged me to play the part of Borachio in his forthcoming production of *Much Ado About Nothing*. I accepted "as long as I could choose my own style of accent!" though I wasn't exactly flattered to be playing the role of the drunken lout Borachio.

Despite being tempted to tease "Dickey" by showing off I did not, in fact, show him my final reference from Principal Bradley and his team of tutor assessors. For it proved to be a very good report (with a distinction in History and English Literature) and after predicting that I should make "a very competent teacher", it added a rider that I was also "a note-worthy performer in the Drama Festival, as also in the college production of *Much Ado About Nothing*."

After we quit training college I never saw Dickson again; that is to talk to him. But one evening, I attended a performance of *Coriolanus* by a first-class professional cast at the New Theatre in

London's West End.   I simply couldn't help noticing the tall commanding figure of Dickson in a walk-on part (as a soldier). And I had to wonder, "Has dear Howard finally made the grade as a professional actor, and has he now decided that school-teaching is not for him?!

EPILOGUE

I have often pondered the same deep question about myself! Yet I did teach - after my special fashion - for about 35 years in junior and senior schools; at polytechnics; for the Open University; and at summer schools for foreign students at several Oxford University colleges.

But I have not been recognised as a writer - YET. Perhaps "this consummation devoutly wished" will be realised "ere I shuffle off this mortal coil"?!

Yours, in hopeful anticipation,
"Gee-Gee", April 1994.

"MURDER! HE WROTE"

During the period I worked as a school teacher in the plebeian area of Kilburn (Middlesex) in the early 1950's, I taught two boys who became, in greater or lesser degree, involved in famous murder cases. The two boys were students at Percy Road Secondary Modern School. The boys were the same age and in the same class, but they were totally different in appearance and temperament.

Jimmy O'Connor was short, neat, very quiet and never troublesome.

Roy Langdale was very big, slovenly, also quiet - but suspiciously so! He proved to be very troublesome!

Jimmy O'Connor was always pleasant, obedient and very well behaved but never outstanding in any branch of study or games. I always thought, however, that Jimmy was too quiet, too withdrawn. He invariably seemed confused and had an air of sadness.

Langdale, a quite different type, was brought to me by our Headmaster, T.P. Hall, with an earnest plea: "Try to make a man of him, Mr Gee, for he has been in a great deal of trouble already despite his tender age." Langdale, like O'Connor, was eleven plus.

When I asked Mr Hall quietly later, about the kind of trouble Langdale had been involved in, the Headmaster said, "Oh, a lot of petty thieving, nasty bullying of smaller boys, and even girls, and... even... worse."

When I naturally enquired about the "worse", Mr Hall was clearly embarrassed and whispered - very falteringly - "Well... there is even a story... that he has been acting as a kind of Junior *pimp*... for a senior *souteneur*, who has made an air-raid shelter into a very low class brothel to which very young girls are enticed! But mum's the word!"

Far from making a man of Langdale, he threatened to make a nervous wreck of me! I had put him to sit at the rear of the classroom. Like all the other boys he sat at a plain wooden desk which contained a large area inside for books, pens, pencils, etc., and was covered by a movable wooden lid. Occasionally, after the boys had left in the evening, I would inspect the interiors of their desks. I invariably found nothing to worry me, until one evening I came to Langdale's desk. I began to find that he was hoarding very unusual "loot!" So I decided to keep a regular, watchful eye on this particular desk.

I noticed also during lessons whereas I was able to keep most of the lads reasonably interested in the subject, whether History, Geography, Literature (less successful in Maths, which I loathed) I soon discerned that Langdale was usually fidgeting inside his desk.

So occasionally I would stroll with a nonchalant air down the aisle towards Roy but he - always with a sly and cunning scowl - would shut the lid of his desk very quickly ere I got to him. This, naturally, only increased my curiosity.

One day, at 12 noon, as the boys departed for mid-day break (and for many the school dinner), I stopped Langdale and said, "Just a minute, Roy, let's see what you have in your desk!"

Very reluctantly he opened the lid and I was amazed to see hundreds of packets of razor blades inside.

"Where on earth did you get these, Roy?" I asked as I looked hard into his podgy, brutal face and tried to hold his gaze to mine without success. Looking sullen and only slightly furtive, he replied, "Found 'em, sir."

"Oh, really!" I pursued, "REALLY? Where?"

"On an old rubbish dump near Paddington Rec'."

"Oh, I see," but I pressed him. "So why do you keep them here in school?"

"Oh," he faltered, "I can't take them home, 'cos me Mum would be scared... and me Dad might get mad. Anyway I'm hoping to sell them soon... sir."

Actually I was fascinated in a kind of morbid way, so I decided to give Roy only a mild rebuke saying, "Well our school desk is not meant for this!"

Some days later, at mid-day break, I looked into Langdale's desk again, to find it full of packs of playing cards of the gambling kind. These had disappeared after a few days. But within a week or so when I peeped into the "Artful Dodger's" den again, I found it stacked to the brim with electric light bulbs. I began to be amused until one day I found the desk "chokka" with packets of condoms (invariably called, in those days, "French Letters"). I also saw, with some alarm, that the inside lid had a very pornographic poster fixed there, the first I had seen in a school classroom. Recalling what T.P. Hall, our Headmaster, had told me about old air-raid shelters being used for low-class brothels locally, I now got tough with Langdale and told him not to use his school desk for unorthodox purposes.

I revert now to Jimmy O'Connor. Receiving data offering our students a "pen friend" scheme with U.S.A., I decided (as a long-term, dedicated member of the League of Nations; and later United Nations Associations) to persuade the boys to take the idea. I called for a show of hands and to my delight every boy indicated an interest except, that is, Roy Langdale. I was now obliged to fill in cards giving basic data on the boys' ages, hobbies, favourite sports, etc. but also giving fathers' trade or profession. When I came to Jimmy O'Connor, he became distinctly confused and for a time inarticulate especially about his father's trade. Eventually, he mumbled,
"My father is in the merchant navy, sir. So I don't know exactly where he is now."

Jimmy's inadequate answer caused an explosion of ribald laughter, and between subsiding guffaws I heard some boys shout, "His father's in prison, sir!" Some others said, "He's in for life, sir!" and one very cruel boy wailed, "Jimmy will never see his Dad!"

I looked hard at poor Jimmy, and saw that he was now blushing terribly and beginning to cry. I shouted, "SILENCE! The next boy who says anything detrimental to or about Jimmy will be severely punished!"

Naturally, I pondered the case of Jimmy and wondered about the whole truth of the case. I did not have to wait long. Some few weeks later I was called one afternoon to the Headmaster's study. Mr Hall said, "Do sit down, and read this letter carefully."

I noticed with some concern that it was from Dartmoor. It was signed James O'Connor and had obviously been censored. The prisoner explained that he was serving a life sentence (later it was revealed to us that the terrible jail-term was for murder!). The main thrust of the letter, however, was a request. He, O'Connor, (in Dartmoor for the rest of his natural life) had been receiving copies of the local newspaper *The Willesden Chronicle* and over a fairly long period. He said he was now reading, for the last few months especially, about the sporting exploits of "O'CONNOR!" i.e. young O'Connor of Percy School, Kilburn. It seems that he played excellent cricket in the summer and was now a wonderful centre forward in his football team! The letter ended by claiming that the O'Connor

mentioned so often and so well-praised must be his son, and he would
be greatly obliged to have a school photo of him, without causing any
embarrassment to young Jimmy.

"Now," said the Headmaster, looking to me for confirmation, "it
is fairly sure, isn't it, that the star sportsman O'Connor is referring to
is MICHAEL? Both the boys O'Connor are in your class, isn't that
so?"

"Yes," I answered, "Michael O'Connor is outstanding both as a
keen student and a sportsman. In fact, I aim to recommend Michael
for a transfer to the Willesden Grammar School under the new
scheme." I went on to add, "However, Jimmy O'Connor is a nice
lad; not bright, but always pleasant and well-behaved."

After some thought and further discussion, Mr Hall said, "Well,
we both feel sorry for father and son, and it's hard to resist this
poignant request. A school photographer is due soon so will you
arrange to have small GROUP photos, with Jimmy in the middle?"

This was done and, in due course we had a letter of thanks from
Dartmoor.

The saga of O'Connor is bizarre and fascinating, and continues to
amaze to this day (Feb. 15th 1994). He had been accused of murder
while involved in an act of burglary in Kilburn in 1942. He was, in
fact, sentenced to death! He was only reprieved within two or three
hours of execution. He was then told that he would be a prisoner for
life.

In 1952, a famous and handsome lady barrister named Nemone
Lethbridge met James O'Connor in Dartmoor, and became convinced
of his innocence (he had always vehemently insisted on this, saying he
was framed by others). Lethbridge secured his release in the mid-
1950's. She had gradually become emotionally involved with Jimmy,
and she married him. They had a son who was therefore, a half-
brother to the young Jimmy I knew. Later James O'Connor and
Nemone Lethbridge divorced, being "incompatible".

In February 1994, the *Independent On Sunday* newspaper
published a main feature on James O'Connor. It included a photo of
Jimmy re-united with Nemone Lethbridge (or seemingly so?). The
main thrust of the article was that they are still trying to completely
clear his name of all suspicion of the 1942 murder.

123

The feature also reminded older readers (like myself) that O'Connor had high praise and fame for his wonderful plays about Crime and Punishment. His drama *Three Sundays* was about a prisoner awaiting execution and hoping against all the odds for reprieve. In the play it does not come. Whereas the T.V. viewing of this very morbid drama was particularly harrowing, O'Connor's next - *A Tap on The Shoulder* - proved a very comical satire. The T.V. version begins with a hardened criminal being tapped on the shoulder by an arresting policeman. The play ends with a "tap on the shoulder" of the self-same criminal by the Queen's sword at his Knighthood ceremony!

I return now to the bizarre story of Roy Langdale and his strange connection with one of the most famous (some say notorious) murder cases in our modern British legal history. In fact, its tragic denouement featured the last person to be executed in the U.K. This was Michael Hanratty (1962).

This killing became popularly known as the "A6 Murder", wherein a married man, Gregsten, was having an extra-marital affair with his secretary, Valerie Storey. Cuddling in his car in a cornfield, they were "kidnapped" (or abducted) by an armed man, and forced to take a long and horrible ride around the outskirts of North London. Eventually the gunman forced the couple out of the car, shot Gregsten dead, tried to rape the girl, shot her and left her for dead!

Valerie Storey, however, recovered and was eventually called to an identity parade. Strangely, she was given more than one chance to pick out the alleged killer. Her first "choice" had a perfect alibi!

She eventually picked on Hanratty, stressing his "staring eyes" and his "marked Cockney accent".

Hanratty pleaded his complete innocence right up to the morning of his execution, even after his Catholic last rites! He had earlier given an alibi that he was over a hundred miles away in North Wales on the morning of the murder (but admitting that he was passing on stolen goods). Two people in Llandudno, one a landlady of a guest house, supported Hanratty's alibi. But in the dread event, it didn't help him in any way for the most crucial evidence against him came from a fellow prisoner who claimed that he had shared the most intimate confidences with Hanratty while taking exercise with him at Brixton jail.

This other man was ROY LANGDALE!

Langdale swore on oath that Hanratty (who was his main buddy in Brixton) confessed to him - Langdale - that he had killed Gregsten and raped Storey and "tried to finish her off"!

It should be emphasised that Langdale was facing his 12th conviction then (the usual charge being robbery with violence) and was assumed guilty of so many previous crimes, that Roy would surely get a three year jail term. In the event (and could it have been a reward for his "co-operation" in clearing up the A6 Murder Trial? Well, his help anyway?) Roy got a suspended sentence.

A number of books have been written on the A6 Murder Case, for example by Louis Blom-Cooper, Lord Russell of Liverpool, A.C. Hale, Paul Foot, etc. Many famous people including ex-Home Secretaries, have called for a public enquiry; a judicial review, etc. By the way, the claim by Roy Langdale that he was a special pal of Hanratty's at Brixton was later exposed as a blatant lie. Most bizarre of all in this notorious case was the fact that one Louis Alphon confessed to one of our prestigious reporters that he - ALPHON - was the A6 Murderer!

To conclude: I have often wondered, over many years, what I might have done at the time if I had known that Roy Langdale was giving the most crucial and fatal evidence in that trial which ended with the last execution in Britain. Could I have tilted the balance in favour of Hanratty?

A COMMUNIST MENACE!

In spring 1954, I moved school to be nearer home. My wife had got herself a very good job with British European Airways (with the clerical staff) at their base in South Ruislip. However, she was obliged to work full-time. Our children were still of rather tender age: girl 9, boy 7. As the B.E.A. post offered the very pleasant bonus of very cheap foreign travel (only 10% of total fare for us) it was an offer too good to be missed. So I decided to take a teaching post in our own area, or nearly so. I could then arrive home at about the same time as our children who walked home from a school in our street.

The new school I now moved to was in the bourgeois part of Ruislip. I will call it 'Brownfields'. I will give my new Headmaster the pseudonym of 'Mr Richard Howells'. At the outset I have to declare that he was the nastiest Headmaster or College Principal I ever encountered! He became the bane of my life, even to the point of my becoming paranoiac!

I had to travel (by push-bike) to get his approval after a brief interview by the Chief Education Officer, Uxbridge. When I got to Brownfields School it was about 4:15p.m., and all teachers and the junior pupils (aged 7 to 11) had dispersed. I soon found that Mr Howells was a very small man, of about 45 years. He was also very thin and weedy with a heavily wrinkled face. His beady brown eyes flickered nervously as he talked, with eyelids fluttering incessantly. I couldn't help noticing also that he never looked at me directly but seemed to gaze downwards to his hands on his desk. He also sniffed frequently as he spoke. (In fact, inwardly, I had already nicknamed him Mr Pecksniff).

I listened with growing alarm, as he confided that, like myself, he grew up in South Wales, Glamorgan, and specifically Pontypridd. I must explain my growing apprehension: my home town of Abertaff was only twelve miles from Pontypridd. And between the ages of 19 and 26 I had been a very active Communist. My brother Ed was a fanatical Stalinist and we had often been to Pontypridd to speak at open-air meetings during the troubled years of mass unemployment and active resistance to Fascism in 1930-40. What if Howells knew all this!?

It was now 1954 and the Cold War was still in a severe winter. Admittedly we did not have sinister committees openly trying to penalise Communists of present and past vintage, as in the U.S.A., nevertheless, there was a slightly more subtle but still definite anti-Red witch hunt. In fact, our own County Council (Middlesex) with a Tory majority of only three, had just voted to ban Communist headmasters.

One "Red", C.T. Giles, had been appointed Head of Acton Grammar in 1947, and during the 1950's, stories had been spread that he was favouring Communist teachers for his staff, and deliberately chose Literature and History books of a Left Wing trend. The Conservatives, who now had a narrow majority on education committees, were using the name of Giles (and another "Red", Max Morris) to justify their would-be ban!

In spite of being thrilled by the Alliance of the U.K. and U.S.A. with Russia during the War to resist and conquer Fascism, and the glorious victory of the Red Army at Stalingrad (the Year of the "Russian Glory" as Churchill called it), for various compelling reasons I quit the Communist Party in early 1945, and never re-joined.

In 1950 I had embarked in the quest of an extra-mural degree (BSc. Econ.) with London University. As I was a full-time teacher I could pursue this aim by attending a couple of evening classes per week to improve my standard in my weaker subjects, this backed up by a great deal of swotting at home with the willing tolerance of my beloved wife Kate (no shrew, she!). By spring 1954, I was making good progress and my coveted first academic honours were now in sight. What a pity if the anti-Red witch hunt would threaten any prospects of a promotion enhanced by a degree?

So withal, I was uneasy, if not downright worried, when informed by Howells (approximately my own age) that he came from a neighbouring town in south Wales, and might know too much for my own good. What if he were the malevolent anti-Red kind of man? Alas, my fearful presentiment proved all too well imagined.

Apart from my worries in the political sense, I soon found that Howells, in spite of his frail physical appearance, was a tyrant of the worst kind. In fact, the very morning I started work at Brownfields, a male teacher named Jones stealthily approached me and after introduction said quietly, "I'm leaving this week, and you have evidently come to replace me. A great pity that we hadn't met last week... so that I could have warned you!"

Naturally I was worried and asked, "Warn me? Why, whatever do you mean?"

"Alas! you'll soon find out that Headmaster is a real **BASTARD**! A thorough sadist. He delights in setting out to tyrannize and humiliate every member of staff. His favourite ploy with me was to enter my class, ask me a series of seemingly vital questions, and before I could answer, the bastard would walk down the aisle and straighten a picture on the far wall, stroll back, and ask a new series of questions. He did that at least once a week for the last three years until he has forced me out. AM I GLAD TO GO!"

Jones's opinion of Howells and his warning, was conveyed to me surreptitiously again and again by other members of the staff in the ensuing week. Jones also made it clear that Howells preferred lady teachers because they were more likely to be pliant to his will. I soon found that I was only one of two male teachers, and the other, Claude Grall, (of French extraction) was not certificated, and on "supply", which was bound to make him careful and a little servile. I noticed too, that whenever Howells appeared in the staff-room at tea/coffee breaks, a distinct hush was felt. Also one could almost feel the cringing attitude of the cowed ladies, and a kind of frenetic competition as to which one of them would fill his cup!

There was one exception to this attitude, however. This was a Miss Ferrant.

She was a tiny spinster of about 40 years. She was a very plain lady with a parrot beak for a nose, beady little eyes which seemed to survey everything and everybody simultaneously. She was the only teacher I can ever recall who could read and interpret register names and figures upside down, a great asset when doing register returns at the end of term.

Ferrant was always bubbly with constant chatter and she would often end conversation with a malicious sneering *coup de grace*! I also soon learned that, *sotto voce* and *sub rosa*, she was nicknamed "The Ferret". What I liked about her was that she was the only woman on the staff who was not intimidated by Howells and I wondered if she could be my ally in the troubles ahead, which I felt would be inevitable!

It emerged that the most pathetic member of our group was the Deputy Head. She was a Mrs Ward: a big, rather good-looking woman, very pleasant to the rest of us but with a distinctly weary and woeful countenance.

Gradually she confided to me that Headmaster was wearing her down with constant, niggling complaints. "I can't stand much more of it," she said one day. "I might have to find another school, even if it means demotion!"

I now found myself in an increasing dilemma. I was by nature and experience, a constant fighter against tyranny and injustice. (Strange and sad that I could not detect and denounce Stalin's tyranny, 1933-53.) But I wanted to hold on to this new job because my wife had taken this very agreeable full time post with B.E.A., and I had made her a faithful promise that I would be working near home to meet the children from their school. I ought to record (as it assumes importance in this story) that I volunteered to take on the responsibility of N.U.T. correspondent (Union Rep.) after Jones had left, as no-one else wanted this dubious chore.

My first brush with Howells came within the first month of my life in Brownfields School. In retrospect, it was bizarre, even hilarious! I was giving my 10 year-old pupils a so-called History lesson. I had recently seen the film *Marco Polo* (with Gary Cooper in the leading role). So I expatiated on ancient China and featured Polo's tour of this great country and its marvellous civilization. I invariably like to amuse as well as educate, especially with young children. I stressed the fact that though the Chinese were pioneers in the use of gunpowder they did not exploit its use in warfare. To make this sequence of my lesson more lively, I recounted a scene from the film where fire-crackers were thrown at Marco Polo's feet which made him jump in the air. This "tickled the kiddies fancy", and they laughed loudly. So, delighted, I repeated this and made a little mime of it. The children laughed again, somewhat louder. Suddenly I saw the youngsters glance apprehensively towards the door. I turned around and saw the crumpled features of Howells glowering with his nastiest expression (which even in his calmer moods was never pleasant!).

Looking at me obliquely, with eyelids fluttering madly he said, "I heard laughter!?"

"Oh,... Yes..." I replied, wondering what he found wrong in that.

"It was loud laughter," he pursued.

I now looked at him and tried to read the strange thoughts in his face but as usual he looked at his trembling hands. Then he asked, "What lesson is it...?"

"History," I replied.

"Oh! Really! HISTORY! So, what's funny in History?"

I was silent, but I turned to a boy in the front row with an appealing gesture (he was a very bright pupil and ever-ready with an answer).

"Mr Gee was telling us about Marco Polo," the boy said, "and how he jumped when some naughty Chinese threw fire crackers at his feet." The kids laughed loudly again.

"SILENCE!" shouted (or even screamed?) Howells. Then struggling to become calm and sane, he said, "Oh! I see China... Oh, yes... Polo... Marco Polo... Well, now then children ... let us see what Mister Gee... really and seriously, knows about Marco Polo!"

I was absolutely amazed that Howells should so forget a long standing code of teacher's mutual etiquette that one member of the profession should try to correct another before students. In fact National Union of Teachers' rules (rule 11) make it a serious offence. Yet Howells (an N.U.T. member!) was going even further: he was trying to hold me up to ridicule! He persisted, but still looking down, "Let's see if Mr Gee knows when Marco Polo arrived in Peking!"

"Oh, yes," I answered promptly, "1275 A.D."

I was now determined to use Howells's own low-down tactics and try to humiliate him. "Now children, let us see what MISTER HOWELLS knows about Marco Polo and his family, for Marco was first taken to China by his father and MR HOWELLS will now tell you his name."

I looked at him. He was still looking down, with hands trembling and eyelids flapping furiously. He stuttered, and he mumbled, "History is not my strongest subject," and as the children burst into loud laughter, louder than before, Howells hurried out of my classroom.

A few days later I was engaged in P.T. and small games in our playground. Suddenly Miss Ferrant appeared, pretending to pass by. But she paused and whispered, "Don't look now Mr Gee... but our ever vigilant Headmaster is at his study window, and STUDYING YOU, and he has been doing this for at least ten minutes... is he trying to GET SOMETHING on you?"

Before I could essay any answer the "Ferret" had melted away. But I realised, only too well, that she was probably correct.

I was somewhat depressed about my prospects in the late summer of 1955, in view of my situation in Brownfields. However, in the first week of August during the long holidays, I was tremendously elated by the news that I gained the coveted BSc. Econ. degree by London University. We, as a family, celebrated my success by taking an extended holiday in South Wales, including a spell at the sea-side on the Gower near Swansea, and a week at Abertaff among family and old friends. Before leaving Ruislip, however, I had sent notices to certain newspapers about my academic success. I did this partly out of vanity but my main aim was the more practical one of trying to enhance my prospects of promotion.

The day I returned to school after the holidays, the first to congratulate me on my academic success was the redoubtable Miss Ferrant. "I saw the nice notice about you in the local paper," she said. "Very well done! but you know of course that H.R.H. Howells will never forgive you for this. You must be aware that he's only got the bare minimum teaching qualifications. And he dislikes you intensely!"

"Does he like anybody on our staff?" I asked.

Miss Ferrant sniffed scornfully. "Not one of us, in fact he's incapable of liking anyone!"

About a month later an event occurred which made me more apprehensive than ever about the possibilities of evil intentions from Howells. An important N.U.T. meeting was announced for early October (1955). The two main items to be discussed and voted on were:

A. To seek the ending of the oppressively unfair Eleven Plus Examination.

> This ONE DAY exam (devised in 1926, and revised but retained in 1944) blighted the hopes of millions of very young children of academic and professional advancement.

B. To attempt to end the iniquitous Political Tests for teacher promotion, i.e. No Communists to become Headmasters.

I ought to explain that recent elections had returned a narrow majority for the Labour Party in Middlesex; so the chances of these "reforms" (if one saw them as such) were enhanced.

As the N.U.T. Correspondent for our school, it was my duty to inform my colleagues of this important meeting and urge them to attend. (But as an old campaigner for trade union activities, I knew only too well that attendance at evening union meetings was always poor.)

This particular one was better attended than most but I did not see any of my colleagues present. However, I was delighted to witness the success of the two progressive resolutions, both carried with large majorities. What followed next day at school was fantastic but for me, very menacing.

Mr Howells called me to his study; he even arranged for a deputy to take my class. As I entered his room, he said very politely, "Please sit down!" I had to wonder why he was so uncharacteristically gushing. Was it possible that he was belatedly going to compliment me on my academic success? It did not take long to have such grandiose illusion shattered. Never looking straight into my face, and with eyelids flapping even more than usual, he began, "I'm assuming that you were at the N.U.T. meeting last evening?"

"Yes," I answered, "and a very good meeting it was! You should have been there," I added.

"Oh, I never go to these local meetings," he sniffed. Then, as if covering up a prejudice, he mumbled, "I have very little time for evening meetings. Will you please give me a resumé of the main conclusions?"

I did this and stressed that the "progressive/liberalising" resolutions had been passed.

Howells sniffed again and asked me, "Do you know Arthur Horner? Surely yes?"

I was amazed at the seemingly ludicrous question, but I was immediately on my guard for I knew that Horner was a Communist and a prominent leader of the militant Miners' Union. (In fact in the late 1930's I had been a Chairman for Horner in South Wales on one occasion). I answered Howells with a naive question, "Oh! Do you mean Horner the cartoonist?"

"NO! NO!" said Howells irritably. "You were a miner. I mean the Miners' Leader!"

I said with a show of heat, "I never told *you* that I was once a Miner. Anyway, I simply cannot see any connection between last evening's meeting and miners and Arthur Horner."

I thought I could discern a scowl and a leer of triumph in Howell's face and voice.

"Do you know the man Todd, a prominent member of the N.U.T. local committee?"

"John Todd? Of course! Very nice chap and a very able negotiator."

"Oh, perhaps so," Howells sneered, "but did you ever know that he is the son-in-law of Arthur Horner, the COMMUNIST leader of the miners?"

"No, I did not," I replied "but that doesn't make Todd a Communist."

"Oh, but he is you know, furthermore, the entire leadership of the local N.U.T. are nothing but a menacing bunch of REDS, er... I mean Communists!"

I was amazed and deeply worried, and after muttering my disapproval of his reasons for wanting my report, I was glad to quit Howell's room.

From that hour on I became very apprehensive and increasingly depressed, becoming more and more convinced that Howells knew that I had been an active Communist, and possibly still a Party Member. I feared now that he could sabotage, despite my new academic honours, my efforts for promotion.

Soon another event caused me to be even more gloomy. One day Mrs Ward, our Deputy Head, confided, "I will be leaving very soon, Mr Gee."

"Oh," I enthused, "You've got a Headship... elsewhere?"

"Not at all," replied the dear lady with a melancholic air, "I'm demoting myself. I can't stand Mr Howells' tyranny any longer. He may drive me to a mental asylum if I stay here much longer. So I am taking a humble teaching post elsewhere. You can imagine how bitter I feel!"

"Why not stay and fight?" I urged, "And I will help you. This needs to be exposed!"

Mrs Ward shook her head sadly, "No, I won't fight this."

When the news got around the staff we all agreed it was sad and unfair. I said, "Something should be done about this. Howells is driving a lovely person out, I am going to reprimand Howells in open staff meeting at the earliest opportunity."

"Hear! Hear!" I heard, but the agreement was very muffled and I had to wonder how many of the other ladies were just waiting to don the Deputy Head's mantle!?

At the end of term, on the last day (December 1955), Mr Howells summoned us to a staff meeting at 4p.m. After a number of comments about the term's work Howells, looking down as usual, and in mock-mournful tones said, "It is now... my very sad duty to say 'Good-bye' to Mrs Ward who has been such a splendid and valuable member of our team. So sorry to see you go, to show our appreciation of, and for, your great service to the pupils and to us as staff, I now present you with this gift token. Do you wish to respond?"

Mrs Ward - now in tears - shook her head. I could no longer contain my long pent-up anger, "Excuse me! Friends and fellow staff members," I began nervously, but in a stentorian voice. "We all know only too well Mr Howells, why Mrs Ward is leaving. You have DRIVEN HER OUT! She is going because she cannot stand your petty but sadistic tyranny any longer. Can we, the rest of us, now hope that you are going to mend your ways and become more humane?"

There was a deathly silence while I waited for some other member of staff to speak in my support. The profound silence continued. I could feel my heart thumping as I waited in a kind of agony for an allied voice. Surely there was ONE? I took a sly glance at Miss Ferrant. The silence continued.

At last, Mr Howells, stroking his little chin with skinny, trembling fingers, and with a very croaky voice, said, "Our meeting is concluded. Good Evening!"

As we were all moving to the exit door, without looking at me Howells said, "I'll see you in my study, Mr Gee."

As I walked towards his room, little Miss Ferrant passed near me and whispered, "Brave Man!" I thought: a fat lot of good you are 'Ferret'!

As I entered Howell's room he hurried nervously behind his desk, as if he feared that I was going to assault him. As he squirmed into his chair, without looking at me, he barked, "You can sit or stand... as you like... I don't give a damn what you do... you insolent... devil!"

"Oh," I said calmly (and I had to wonder why I was so cool), "this may turn out to be a long session, so I'll make myself comfortable."

Howells, looking down at his spindly fingers which were rattling on his desk. "Oh, you think you are bloody clever don't you!? But you're bloody well not!"

Realising that any pretence was now useless, and the breach in the open, I threw caution to the winds and replied, "Oh, I don't know that I am bloody clever, not diabolically smart, but in view of my recent academic success I am obviously cleverer than you! Something which makes you bloody envious."

He snorted loudly, "OH! YOU may think that, but every evening when you mount your shabby second-hand bike, all you get from other staff members is PITY!"

"Oh!" I answered, "I don't mind that at all. If I can get their pity, there is some hope for me. There's no hope for you, for their sole reaction to you is CONTEMPT!"

Checkmated, and with a baffled aspect he shouted, "Oh yes, you are running true to form, for I was warned about your character before you came here!"

"Oh," I countered, "then you had an advantage over me, for I was not told about your dreadful tyrannical character until I arrived, alas! I've heard plenty since, witness poor Mrs Ward!"

Howells now collapsed and shrieked, "Get out of my sight!"

As I cycled home after the row with Howells, I experienced a glow of something like triumph. I felt like a kind of St. George who had slain a dragon! The confrontation had to come and I felt at that moment that I had won a battle against sadistic tyranny.

However, a few days later, on reflection, and in a more realistic mood, I realised that I was in trouble. After the Christmas holidays I was asked one day to attend a minor meeting in the Headmaster's

Study. I was very surprised to be summoned but I soon noticed that a Mr Sage, a very well respected retired Head of a Middlesex College and now a member of committees was also present and asking me very politely to sit down. He looked at me in a kindly way and said, "Good morning, Mr Gee. Now... I am aware of certain difficulties here... it has been brought to my attention that some friction has occurred between Mr Howells and yourself. I have heard your Headmaster's version of the trouble... perhaps you would like to give me your version?"

"Well now," I protested, "I have not heard what Mr Howells has told you; this seems to be unfair." Mr Sage visibly winced and blushed. I was emboldened and continued. "Perhaps, with all due respect to your office, and to me, and even to Mr Howells, the best course for you to take in this matter is to call a staff meeting, and to find out what my colleagues feel about this. Alternatively, if you have the time to spare, you might see each member of staff to find out what each one thinks as to the rights and wrongs."

Mr Sage looked sad and said, "Oh dear, Mr Gee, let us not be precipitate! I propose a cooling-off period... say... for a few weeks... and if relations between you and Mr Howells do not improve I will offer you a transfer to another school."

I protested. "I do not wish to leave. Perhaps you could transfer Mr Howells? I am pretty sure the vast majority of staff would prefer that!"

Mr Sage raised his arms in a mild gesture of despair and moaned, "Please let it be as I have proposed."

Actually, in spite of my bravado, I was getting more and more depressed. I could not hide my plight from my dear wife and told her I would have to apply for other teaching posts even if they were further afield, hoping also for a promotion. My wife raised the thorny question of a reference from my present Head, and I recognised the problem. In fact I sought out my friend Todd of the N.U.T. He opined, "He has got to give you a reference. Of course, it may not be a glowing one. But if he gives you a bad one our N.U.T. Committee will summon him to explain it (as he is a member), but you may as well face it, Howells can do you a lot of harm on the telephone!"

My gloom deepened, and I now asked my worried wife if she could possibly induce her B.E.A. bosses to allow her to go part time so that I could look further afield for a teaching post, hopefully with a promotion. She promised she would try, but gave me the caveat that B.E.A. usually asked employees to do at least one year of full time work before asking for part time. So desperate was I becoming, however, that I applied for a post "Head of Geography" in a College of Further Education ten miles distant. In my application form I decided not to mention my existing post at Brownfields. I was very elated to be called for interview. However, during my session with the Principal, he asked, "Are you unemployed at present, Mr Gee? That is, after working for your degree? Is it the case that your last full-time job was at Percy Road School, Kilburn?"

I now knew I was going to be in trouble! And I remembered those pregnant lines of Walter Scott: "OH! What a tangled web we weave, when first we practice to deceive!" I had to admit that I was, in fact, working at Brownfields and had been for over a year.

The Principal asked, "Why on earth haven't you put this very relevant fact on your application?"

I need hardly expatiate on the sequel to my quest for this post. Of course, I didn't get it.

A month later, however, I was stimulated with fresh hopes. I had a letter from Willesden Education Committee informing me that I was short-listed for the post of Headship (no less!) of Salisbury School, Kilburn. Great excitement within the family! Alas! Within days I had another letter from the same address with the following cryptic but awesome words, "Before you present yourself for interview on Thursday will you please complete the enclosed form and send it to us by return post?" It read, "Are you, or have you ever been a member of a Fascist or Communist Party!"

I said to my wife, "Of course I could tell a brazen lie, but I fear they would discover the truth. I'm afraid that MI5/MI6 have my name on their Black List!" My next experience of job-hunting only seemed to confirm my deepest suspicions - absolutely !

Getting more and more depressed, I also, paradoxically, became more reckless. I now applied for a post as "Senior History Tutor" at the Queen's School B.A.O.R. (British Army of the Rhine) based at Moenchen Gladbach, in north-west Germany. I tried to rationalize my odd action to my puzzled wife by claiming that B.E.A. also had bases in the area. To my great surprise I was called to interview which was to take place at the War Office, Northumberland Place, near Trafalgar Square.

When I was ushered in to the Interview Room I discerned, with some alarm, that a large, very long, table was occupied by at least ten men in army uniform and all seemed to be of the officer class. At the head of the table facing me (I was sitting at the foot), sat (I was told) Major Reeves. He was resplendent in a superior, light Khaki uniform with pips up and chevrons blazing.

"Well now, Mr Gee..." he began in a pukka Oxford accent, over-laden with a sneer of cold command, "you have applied for this Senior History Post at our excellent Queen's School B.A.O.R. Correct?" (His manner was so sharp and bossy that I wondered if I should stand and salute him!) "We have to assume that you are well qualified in History, eh what, eh?"

"Well," I answered, "I did get a distinction (97%) in training college for History, and I have taught the subject with success for many years."

"Ah yes," barked the Major. "So you don't mind submitting yourself to a little History test now, do you, eh what!?" (I nodded in agreement). "Well... let us see now, eh what... 1066 and ALL THAT, eh what!? Tell us Mr Gee, who in your OBJECTIVE opinion, won the battle of Hastings... was it the REACTIONARIES or the RRREVOLUTIONARIES? Eh what!?"

With the last sentence with the words 'OBJECTIVE', 'REACTIONARIES', 'REVOLUTIONARIES', first I felt sick at heart, then a mood of mounting anger, for I realised that Major Reeves was taunting me with old Communist clichés. I replied as calmly and as coldly as I could, "I do not know what YOU mean. But any schoolboy knows, even if YOU are that ignorant, that the Normans defeated the Anglo-Saxons at the Battle of Hastings."

"OH! OH!" said the major. "I thought it was the bloody Red Army, eh what!?" At that, he burst out laughing and there was a ripple of girlish giggles.

At this, I got up and shouted, "You ought to be bloody well ashamed of yourselves! To think that you could get me to come all this way at some expense in time and money, just to indulge your silly selves in juvenile pranks!" As I left the room I could hear the major still laughing, but I discerned no giggles.

As I travelled back home I was most terribly depressed, and in the following weeks I suffered a profound bout of paranoia, specifically: persecution mania.

I was now 41 years of age and, because of *anno domini*, my prospects of professional advancement would obviously dwindle. I had worked hard all my life in a wide variety of trades including "dirty slog" in coal mines. I had a very good record as a teacher, and had gained a university degree by extra-mural effort. Yet I was being thwarted. I had to guess - dismally - if my trouble was due to the machinations of a malevolent Headmaster, by sinister telephone messages, or was it longer-term?

Was the political "ghost" of long ago (1935-45) still actively working against me, vide MI5?

Meanwhile, the bad news had filtered through from Brownfields School to Education Office, Uxbridge, that the friction between Howells and myself was continuing. So in September 1956, a message from Mr Sage informed me that I would have to start in a new school much further from home, in January '57. My gloom deepened, and the on-coming Christmas vacation threatened to be far less than a festive occasion within our family.

In mid-December, I received a letter from a Middlesex Education Body calling me to an interview at one of their polytechnics (Kilburn). I then recalled that I had applied for a post of Grade B Lecturer in Economics and Cognate Studies. The interview was set for December 22nd.

I went to Kilburn with little or no hope, and when I found five other candidates in the annexe room, any scintilla of hope evaporated. To add to my despondency, the other men gossiped about their existing jobs and it emerged that all were in Further Education already. When I had the temerity to ask why then they were seeking this post, they all laughed and said, "Don't you realise that this job is Grade B?" Suddenly I realised that this was promotion for them. So what price my chances?

Interrogated by College Board members later, I had the pleasant sensation that the Principal of the Polytechnic, Mr James Platt, B.Com., evinced a kindly, fellow feeling towards me. His father and brothers had been coal miners, he said.

"Well, Mr Gee," he continued, "you have had an extraordinary working life so far. It's a great credit that you have become a teacher and gained an extra-mural BSc.Econ., against the odds. You evidently know what hard work is and I have to warn you that there is plenty of hard work here. Are you willing to face it?" I grinned and nodded. I got the job - now a Polytechnic Lecturer - with a salary boost of £500.

I was so elated on returning home that, changing from bus to tube-train at Notting Hill Gate, I nipped into an off-licence and bought a bottle of bubbly. And Kate and I celebrated my success from 10p.m. until well past midnight! And, double bliss! Kate told me with glee that B.E.A. had conceded part-time work!

EPILOGUE

One day during the Christmas break, in Ruislip High Street, I met a Brownhills School colleague. She was Mrs Melding, wife of an Uxbridge Vicar. She seemed genuinely delighted when I told her about my new job. She invited me to the Vicarage "for tea and a chat, on Saturday."

I guessed she wanted to tell me something "out of school" so I went.

After a nice tea, the large lady unbosomed herself.

"You know, Mr Gee," she confided. "Nearly all of us on the Brownfields staff admired you for your brave stand against Mr Howell's awful rule but we were too afraid to say so openly. I'm ashamed to admit that I was too scared to speak out. But please bear in mind, Mr Gee, that my husband's income is not large, and two of our three children are in very expensive boarding schools. So I need my present post. I also have to explain, that I am uncertificated and "on supply".

I remained silent, nodding in sympathetic agreement. Mrs Melding then, with an embarrassed air, more or less concluded with the confession, "And I wonder if you knew that, at every opportunity, Mr Howells would warn us, have nothing to do with Mr Gee if you can help it: HE IS A COMMUNIST MENACE!!"

JESSICA AND THE MOUSE

It was during a family holiday on the Loire (early summer, 1985) that my wife learned, with some consternation, that our daughter Lorna, was pregnant. Our entire nuclear family was enjoying a short stay at a mini-chateau called Domaine-de-la-Rey! Our party consisted of my wife and me; our daughter and son-in-law, Paul; and our son, Frank - over from Canada with his bride-to-be, Kathy.

When my wife told me about Lorna, that she had confided the "big news", we were, in fact, both worried because Lorna, married for nearly 20 years, was now over 40 years of age. We also knew that she had never enjoyed robust health. We agreed, moreover, that she and her husband were now in good jobs and comfortably off, but only after a long period of economic and vocational uncertainty. It was natural that we were worried about the radical change, in domestic and financial concerns, which the prospect of a child would mean. But our over-riding anxiety was the age of Lorna and her health in pregnancy.

On my wife's advice, I did not raise the subject with our daughter during the holiday. On parting in Sussex to return to our respective homes I decided to be quite tight-lipped in the matter, but embracing Lorna in a more than usually firm bear-hug, I had to suppress a sob.

The day my wife and I arrived back home in our beloved Swansea, I was very disturbed to see a little brown mouse in our pantry. I actually squirmed with something approaching horror as I espied its nose and brown silky body and long tail slither down the side of the pantry fridge. Perhaps I should explain that apart from birds (of the feathered variety) I detest all creatures, great and small! I have to admit that I hate all dogs and cats and, especially, rats and mice, slugs, snails, flies, spiders, etc., *ad nauseam*!

When I espied the mouse I cried out in frightened dismay, so loudly that my wife shouted, "What the heck is the matter with you?!"

I replied, somewhat hysterically perhaps, "We have a mouse in the house!"

"Where?"

"Here, in the pantry, behind the fridge."

My wife expressed surprise tinged with some scepticism. But in a mood of panic, I urged her to help me move the fridge, and sundry pots and pans. Very reluctantly, my wife, as we moved objects, big and small, rather frenetically around, said "YES" she had seen "the little bugger!"

Over the next few days, weeks, and even months, we sometimes saw the mouse. And what proved to be very annoying was the definite signs of its continued existence as revealed by nasty contamination of our basic foodstuffs. We began to find tiny, but definite, mouse droppings in our sugar basin, and worse still, in our cornflakes!

After a while, some months later in fact, we saw "the little bugger" in our bathroom and then in our airing cupboards. We consoled ourselves with the proposition, "Well, dear, while it's up here it cannot contaminate our food."

In mid-November, with mouse apparently still in residence, my wife, Kate, bade me a fond farewell. Daughter, Lorna, with pregnancy well advanced, to our continuing concern, alerted us that the fateful hour was very near. My wife was determined to be present at the critical time, always recalling how terribly difficult the birth of our son was in 1947.

Alone in the house on the night of November 21st/22nd, I went to bed at my usual midnight hour. Early in the morning of the 22nd, I awoke abruptly and switched on the light to see the time. As I looked up directly above me, I was amazed and somewhat scared to espy a little brown mouse crawling along the picture rail which runs around the entire bedroom. Fascinated but in a weird/scary way, I crawled very quietly out of my bed, and followed the trail of the "little bugger". I lost sight of it when it passed behind a large wardrobe. When it emerged yet again, it paused above a large picture of little children playing in a street. I recalled with a flash of brilliant intuition (!) that the picture had no glass in its frame. So, arming myself with a long ruler I moved stealthily towards the vital area, and rapidly and frenetically tapped the mouse with the ruler. To my ecstatic joy and relief the "little bugger" fell behind the picture. Frantically, I banged the picture repeatedly against the wall, and I distinctly saw the mouse fall like a stone behind a large book-case.

I then stood in perfect silence, and waited stock still for over five minutes. I heard no sound whatever, and concluded that this St. George had slain his "dragon"! I looked at my alarm clock. It was

5a.m. precisely. Far too early to get up, so I went back to bed with a feeling of some triumph!

Enjoying my breakfast at my usual hour (in easy retirement), 9 to 9:30a.m., the phone rang. It was my dear Kate, calling from our daughter's home in Herefordshire. "You will be pleased to know George," she said with evident emotion, "Lorna had a beautiful baby girl this morning.

"Early this morning?" I queried, with more than usual curiosity.

"YES, at 5 o'clock, precisely." I smiled but said nothing. My wife expatiated with natural pride and grand-motherly emotion, "Yes, a lovely easy birth. A beautiful girl with a lovely head of silky brown hair. Her name is already chosen, it's JESSICA."

About a week later my wife returned home and after rhapsodising about the easy birth of a lovely brown haired, grand-daughter, Jessica, I told Kate about the mouse and how I had conquered the "little bugger"! To my great dismay and disgust, Kate would not accept one word of my account.

"It was exactly as I have described," I insisted hotly. "Why can't you believe me!?" I urged.

Kate replied, with scorn in her face and voice, "You could never have trapped and killed it in the way you describe. It is incredible and utterly impossible! You can't half spin 'em!"

I decided, at last, that I could never convince my wife with my tale, nor anyone else.

Over a year later, the exact date was January 12th 1987, we had a domestic disaster. In common with thousands of other Britons, we suffered a terrible freeze-up, and with the thaw came a flooding of the house. Several rooms in our house were ruined including my beloved study-bedroom. A few weeks later, after the necessary insurance claims, painters and decorators and carpet-layers started re-furbishing the house. Preparing my study-bedroom, Kate and I had to remove a large book-case. As we got it unloaded and moved, Kate said with a gasp, "Good Lord! Here is a little brown mouse!"

"It's dead I should hope!" I asked smiling to myself.

"Oh, yes... quite dead!"

"So you see Kate," I commented, with a hint of cynical triumph in my voice, "I did kill 'the little bugger' after all, and in the very way I described. And by the way, it happened at 5a.m. precisely, on November 22nd 1985, exactly at the same time as Jessica was born!"

Kate smiled, but was non-committal.

TOVARISH GREENIN: BEING COMRADELY WITH RUSSIANS

The first time I was aware of a country called Russia was in 1920, when I was 5 years of age. In junior school we had an urgent appeal from our Headmaster and class teachers, "to help the poor, starving Russians!" I and other young members of our family passed on the news to our parents. My mother (Cordelia), though very poor, was always responsive to such appeals. She gave me, after saying "I'll try to find something", a tin of condensed (skimmed) milk and gave sister Ann a very small tin of corned beef.

Much later as a student of international politics, I learned that the famine in Russia (1919-21) was the long-term result of the 1917 Revolution and the subsequent Civil War, backed by the "intervention" of invading Allied powers.

In January 1924, I learned that Lenin, the famous Bolshevik leader of the U.S.S.R. had died.

However, it was in the 1930's that Russia loomed large in my consciousness and that of my family. In June 1934, I joined my father and brother Ed in the dole queue. We were very poor, and as the Economic Depression had now lasted for three or four years, we simply could not envisage any end to it, we rather expected it to last forever, "as a certain corollary of the inevitable decline and fall of Capitalism", as brother Ed pontificated, quoting those wiseacres, Karl Marx Engels and Lenin.

In fact, Ed joined the Communist Party and urged me to do the same. Religiously, though a militant Atheist, Ed bought *The Daily Worker* (price 2d) and then started reading the illustrated magazine *Russia Today* (also priced 2d). Sometimes Ed would get a loan of a very large and glossy magazine called *Soviet Union*. Meanwhile, by 1938 we were certain that Capitalism in the U.K., and even in the U.S.A., was doomed and Russia became our Utopia.

During the War (1939-45), when working on munitions at B.T.H. London, and an active Communist and A.E.U. committee member, I, like millions of others, thrilled to the exploits of the Red Army, especially its magnificent victory at Stalingrad! Even that age-old enemy of Bolshevism - Winston Churchill - hailed Stalin as a great

"Warrior Hero", and lavishly praised the Red Army "which had torn the guts out of the Wehrmacht" (the German Armed Forces).

By 1945, with other compelling interests, for example, the pressing need to enter a new profession and to get academic success, my interest in Communism waned. I quit the Party, and stopped buying *The Daily Worker*.

In 1956, I was horrified and dismayed when Russian soldiers crushed the Liberation movement in Hungary with great brutality. I experienced the same emotions of revulsion over the cognate Czecho-Slovak tragedy in 1968-69.

However, my interest and fascination in Russia continued unabated for I was always entranced by its music, ballet, and especially its wonderful literature.

In spring of 1972, now a polytechnic lecturer with a good academic and teaching record, I saw an advert for "A Cruise in the Black Sea" in the summer. This "Voyage", starting in Constanza, Rumania, was to last twelve days and the ship would call at Odessa, Yalta, Sochi, etc; and end at Istanbul. All this for £60! The firm offering this "magnificent" cheap cruise was Clarkson's. (In retrospect, small wonder it went bankrupt soon after!).

I discussed the prospects of the trip with my wife but she showed no interest in visiting Russia at that time.

Our plane arrived in Constanza later than scheduled, and we boarded the ship in the early hours of the morning. We, members of the touring party, were amazed to find all the stewards standing at their stations ready to serve us supper at about 2a.m.! We felt very sorry for them. Later that day we docked at Odessa and I had the temerity to take surreptitious camera shots of many ships, including the war variety, in the harbour, this being forbidden I believe. Later on I was bold and enterprising enough to take some splendid photo-slide shots of the famous Richelieu Steps where Eisenstein had filmed his wonderfully dramatic sequences for his epochal film *Battleship Potemkin* (1925).

We were given a very good tour of Odessa: quite an impressive city with a splendid Opera House, a fine Winter Palace, and a striking statue of Alexander Pushkin, Russia's negro Poet Laureate. However I was surprised and disappointed to find all around the city and environs, only women sweeping the streets and parks while soldiers, sailors and male students walked around in ease encumbered by nothing heavier than glossy briefcases! (Not my idea of Communism and Women's Liberation, and I recorded this on camera!)

Most of the time on this cruise we were accompanied by two female guides, Olga and Ludmilla, and I soon made friends with them, ending our association eventually with gifts of books, chocolates, and some silk tights (or were they nylon? Anyway, as advised by my wife).

But it was later in the cruise that I made a long-term friendship with a Russian female which proved to be quite significant (more anon).

Our next main port of call was Yalta, having seen, without staying long at, famous Sebastopol. Yalta is a very picturesque city with lovely parks and splendid winter palaces once exclusive to Tsars and the nobility; now it was claimed "for all the people"! We viewed the lovely Swallow's Nest home of Chekov and also the famous, splendid, Ottoman palace where the "Big Three" - Stalin, Roosevelt and Churchill - had their momentous, epoch-making conference in 1944.

Incidentally, I found a really beautiful Swans' Lake in a Yalta park and my photo-slide picture of it is a gem! While taking the photo, I suddenly discerned a lovely troop of children and/or youths in Pioneer uniform encircling the lake (Pioneers are the Russian equivalent of our Boy Scouts and Girl Guides). There were about thirty boys and girls of ages, say 11 to 15. I took a photo of them which emerged to be a good one.

A few days later at Sochi, a lovely, lush, seaside resort, sitting again in a pleasant park, I espied the same troop of Pioneers. That evening resting in the same park, and minding my own business, a dozen or so of the same youngsters came into the area and walked briskly around singing a Russian song the tune of which I recognised. As I whistled the melody the Pioneers seemed to be encouraged to entertain me. At last I joined in the chorus (I had learned the English in my Party days). In my *lingua franca* it ran:

> "Soviet Land: so dear to every toiler,
> The World's workers pin their hopes on thee.
> There's no other land the whole world over
> where the People walk so proud and free!"

Though now quite sceptical, if not downright cynical, of the veracity of this blatantly propagandist song, I sang the chorus heartily. These young Pioneers seemed momentarily thunderstruck. They came to an abrupt halt and shouted in chorus: "You know it in ENGLISH?!"

"How do you know it is ENGLISH I am singing?" I challenged.

"We are all learning English in our schools," they proudly replied.

Soon they all gathered eagerly around me and plied me with questions. They were so keen to speak English and to talk about the U.K., London, the Scout/Guide movement, etc. They ended by asking me about my trade or profession. (One of them must have asked about my family. I must have mentioned my daughter, Lorna. More anon).

Although proud to be a polytechnic lecturer and counsellor for the Open University, I decided to announce my profession in the simplest terms: "I am a school teacher," I said. This proved to be a tactical blunder.

For several now urged me loudly, even vociferously, to find them pen-friends. I now realised that at Poly and O.U. level, pen-friends would be difficult to arrange. One young raven haired girl with blackberry eyes was very persistent, so much so as to persuade me to give her my address.

Evidently, I gave her my pencil/pen and the name of my daughter (Lorna), failing to explain that she was about 30 years of age. So I had little or no intention of keeping my glib promise (but more anon).

I now proceed to recount my second trip to Russia. This was in 1975, not a cruise; long flights were involved, to Yalta, Sochi, Moscow and Leningrad. My main guide on this trip was a youngish blonde woman named Nona. She was very likeable and we became good friends in quick time. In fact she confided that she had been married and divorced twice already. And she was now enjoying her third sexual relationship and was contemplating marriage again? (I thought, why bother with marital ties for the third time!?).

After three or four days in Sochi, we were due to take the long flight to Moscow. As we waited in the airport lounge, Nona and I discussed aspects of the trip. As we descended from higher topics to

148

trivia I confided that the thing most regretted was the lack of a nice cup, or preferably pot, of strong tea with MILK, not lemon, ENGLISH style.

"Oh! but why didn't you tell me this before?!" said Nona. "I could have arranged it. Come with me now and I will look for an old waiter friend across the way and I feel sure he will oblige!"

Two minutes later Nona was introducing me to Ivan. He was a huge, very fat man of about 55-60 years of age, and very jolly. He reminded me strongly of the comedian Oliver Hardy, of Laurel and Hardy fame.

After Nona explained my wishes she left us and Ivan, with a lovely broad smile said, in perfect English, "So, my dear sir, you desire a nice pot of English-style tea? So, you shall have it!"

Quite soon he brought me the longed-for nectar and it was really tasty. Ivan stood by my table glowing and seemingly sharing my satisfaction. We started conversing very amiably.

"How is it that you speak such good English?" I ventured.

"Ah!" he replied, "I worked many years in England... before the war... You see, I am really Latvian, much nearer England than Georgia..."

"What kind of work did you do in England?" I boldly pursued.

"I was a waiter in the Piccadilly area, of London, I mean."

"Good Lord!" I laughed, as I shouted, "So was I... in the famous Café Royal."

"And I worked, or was it slaved?" he asked with a wink, "at the famous Savoy."

We enjoyed some interesting reminiscent comparisons until I suddenly realised I had to get ready fairly quickly for my flight to Moscow.

"Really excellent tea," I said sincerely. "How much? (I did not need to I ask "*stolka stoeet*?")

"Nothing!" said Ivan. "It's on the House! What's more," invited Ivan very warmly, "have another pot, I can do it in... how do you say in England... in a jiffy!"

I accepted, and said again, "EXCELLENT! Now how much?"

"Same price again!" replied Ivan with a chuckle. "It's on the house!"

Satisfied that Ivan's largesse would not consign either of us to the *Lubiyanka* (notorious prison), I agreed. But he would not accept my proffered tip. "No tipping allowed in Communist Russia," he insisted. "It's bourgeois corruption." I repeated my offer, but he was adamant.

In Moscow I shared a room in Hotel Ukraine with a young Scots teacher named Andy Craig. One night, reminiscing over the day's tourist sights Andy said, "Are you a drrrinking man, Mr Gee?"

I hesitated in answer, considering extra expenditure on rapidly diminishing roubles. But when he produced a large bottle of good whiskey I admitted that I was very keen on alcohol!

"What about a wee dram, then?" Craig invited. I agreed, and after a few more not so wee drams, we became very talkative and increasingly recklessly so. Andy asked, "Have you noticed the appearance and number of prostitutes around the hotel precincts, Mr Gee?"

Although I had spent a few years working in Piccadilly, often wandering around the sleazy streets of Soho, I answered, "NO! And furthermore I would have thought that after Lenin's famous pamphlet and pronouncement on the subject it would have been banned or utterly died out!"

In spite of the fact that I was old enough to be Craig's father, even grandfather, he must have considered me to be bloody innocent, or K.G.B.!

"Well now... Mr Gee," he challenged, "are you willing to put it to the test? Are you agreeable to stepping outside the hotel for a wee while to see what might transpire?"

I agreed. We were both a bit tiddly, but throwing caution to the Siberian winds we went down to the front of the hotel, turned a corner, walked about twenty yards and sat on separate park benches.

Within a very few minutes we were propositioned. The girls knew the universal key-words for sex encounters. They were very pleasant but their kind of "Russian Friendship" we could, or should, do without.

I turn now to my third and most eventful tour of Russia. This time I escorted my wife, now called "Katya". The background impelling our decision to go is worth explaining and recording.

In the summer of 1977, I received an unexpected letter from U.S.S.R., specifically from Yerevan in Soviet Armenia (the southernmost city in all Russia). The forwarding address was: Abovian 20128, flat 44. It was signed Rosalina Baghdasarian, and read:

"Dear George Gee,

I have your address and I now want to correspond with your girl Lorna. You promised a pen-friend. You gave me your address in Sochi and your pencil... "

And a rather poignant repetition: "I want to correspond with your girl."

I found the letter (five years after I met this girl in Sochi) very touching. It pricked my conscience that I had been so cavalier in promising one so urgent and sincere, a pen-friend.

So my wife and I decided then to be Rosalina's pen-friend. I also made a vow to Kate and Rosalina that as soon as an opportunity came we would meet in Yerevan.

A year passed by but one day I got an Intourist brochure advertising a "Tour of European U.S.S.R." including Leningrad, Moscow, Sochi, Baku, Tibilisi, ay... and Yerevan and fortunately in more or less reverse order! (Fortunately because of an accident that befell me. More anon).

So in June 1978, now at ease in retirement, Katya and I started our tour. I need only concentrate on the Caucasian part of our trip to tell of many strange events and bizarre encounters.

I had alerted Rosalina well in advance, and was "on pins" for her reply to give me advice about our meeting in Yerevan. I had to ask myself, "What if the K.G.B. had intercepted letters in the Cold War climate and decided to disrupt it?" Rosalina's reply with vital advice, arrived only in the nick of time! The day before we left U.K. she said that she knew we would be staying at the Iveria Hotel while in Yerevan for this was always Intourist's arrangement. Coincidentally her sister, Gayaneh, worked in the hotel as a Beautician ("How posh!" Kate commented).

We were advised to phone Rosalina at home as soon as we arrived. But I put to my sensible wife that we should have our evening meal before phoning so as not to put the Baghdasarian family to any trouble in trying to feed starving Britons!

We phoned at 8p.m., and to our great surprise, within minutes, Rosalina and her handsome mother, and big brother "John" (Ivan) were warmly greeting us. What immediately followed was embarrassing: for they promptly marched us at a steamy trot to the nearest ice-cream parlour and ordered a large banana-split for each of us. Kate and I agreed by nods that we had to gulp down our portions, though still trying to digest our heavy supper.

Rosalina was the only member of her family who could speak English. We had little or no Russian, so she was kept busy as interpreter. After walking around with the family for about an hour, we pleaded tiredness. We were curious and prepared to see their home as we, like so many tourists from the West, were. But on parting this first night, Rosalina said, "One night we will take you home."

When we returned to our Iveria Hotel, as we boarded the lift, we espied two youngish men. It amused me to see them carrying two bottles of champagne but more so because they also had two tumblers half full of the drink and were trying to avoid spillage. I said to my wife, "Look at these two chaps, Kate, have they been to a party or are they going to one?"

Immediately, one of the men, who looked the spitting image of the young Stalin, (when aged 30) smiled at me broadly and said, "BOTH! We are going to finish the party now. Will you come too?"

Coincidentally, we all got out on the same fourth floor. "Stalin" urged, "Do come along with us, PLEASE!?"

Very decisively, my wife said, "NO! NO!" Then more kindly, she said, "No, thank you all the same but I am tired."

We paused in the corridor, and "Stalin" turned to me imploringly and coaxed, "Do come."

I found him irresistible. "All right, I'll come along after I escort my wife to our room."

"O.K." advised Stalin. "Room 404, in the corner."

Within five minutes, I was in Room 404, and was elated to see four bottles of (Russian?) champagne and several glasses. I wondered who else was coming. "Stalin" was a compulsive talker but in very good English. His pal was silent throughout. The former introduced himself as Vladimir. "At least you can call me that for now. I have to have many other names. My friend is Nikolai; you can call him Nicky, and when you say that, he will nod and give you a nice smile!"

"Are you local people?" I asked.

"Oh, no," said Vladimir. "We are Georgians, from Tibilisi. We are here for three days only?"

152

"Oh," I joked, "I too, am a Georgian!" After a quizzical look, I explained that my name is George. We laughed and began to exchange views about our homes and countries, and culture and customs. After an hour or more of talk, consuming the champers all the time, we naturally got more familiar and boozy and we went on to sing lively songs. I regaled them with some English and Welsh numbers but I was happy to join in with some Russian songs I knew, like, "*Volga, Volga, mat rodnya*", which I translated for Vladimir as: "Vodka, Vodka, lovely liquor, beautiful as thou art strong," and "*Kalinka*", "*Oh chectonya*", etc.

At last, worrying about my wife worrying about me, I prepared to leave. But very curious by nature, I asked Vladimir about his profession, for I had confessed mine early on. "I am a policeman," he answered without a pause.

"You are not in uniform tonight," I ventured.

"I am a policeman," he insisted, "but I NEVER wear uniform!"

"Are you K.G.B?" I challenged.

He laughed loudly. "You may be correct!" He changed the subject, and touching my shoulder in very friendly fashion, he asked, "Where do you go after Yerevan?"

I said, "To Tibilisi."

He smiled and said, "Ah! We too. But you will be staying in Intourist's Iveria. I will be staying in a superior hotel. Now, my friend, Nicky, works in this hotel as a chef. He makes an excellent Crêpe Suzette. So, I invite you, yes, and your wife, to join us on your second day in Tibilisi, and we can all have a superior meal together."

I intended to hold Vladimir to his promised invite. (But more anon!)

Next afternoon, after lunch, my wife and I strolled to a park not far from our hotel. We sat on a long park bench and started discussing our tour, and our reactions to Armenia in particular. Gradually I was aware that about two feet away on the same bench was a man who seemed to be listening intently.

At last, I said to Kate, "You know, my dear, I believe that this gentleman is keen to hear and assess every word we are saying."

The man, of distinct Armenian aspect, said promptly, "Oh! Do you mind?" And after a pause he added, "I find it all very interesting."

"Oh!" I said in apologetic vein. "I sincerely hope we haven't said anything to give offence to you or any Armenian people."

"Not at all," he responded, "But do you mind if I ask you what country you come from; are you Americans?"

When we confessed to being poor Britons, the man moved perceptibly nearer. (Perhaps he was sympathetic to poverty). "What part of the U.K.?" he asked.

When we said "Wales," he moved closer still until we were shoulder to shoulder.

"Do you mind if I ask what city or town?"

When we chorused, "SWANSEA", the man grabbed my arm so that it hurt.

"Did you know DYLAN THOMAS!?" he shouted.

"No," I replied, "but we live in a street only one kilometre away from his birthplace."

He was highly delighted; ecstatic.

It was our turn to ask questions: "Why are you, an Armenian, so keen on our Welsh Thomas...?"

"Oh!" he thrilled. "I love his writings, especially his poems; his short stories too, and his drama. In fact, I am in the process of translating all his works!"

I was sceptical, "Not *Under Milk Wood*, surely not!"

"Well, that is difficult, I must admit," he conceded, "but I'm trying it!"

We now grew very curious, and begged him for some explanation for his rather strange cultural interest. He informed us that he was a Professor of Literature at the local Yerevan University, with special regard for Anglo-American Literature. Towards the end of our strange conversation the Professor asked me if I knew the name of the (or a) most recent book on Dylan Thomas, and I was able to quote *No Man More Magical* by Sinclair. Our Professor then had the temerity to ask me, "Are you willing to send me a copy if I promise to pay you subsequently?"

I agreed and recorded his address, viz: Aztem Naroutunyan (name), c/o Erevan 9; Teryan 59; Fl.12. I duly sent him the book. But, alas, no reply. But I have to wonder if an over-zealous K.G.B. censor confiscated the book? (What if it was Vladimir?)

The last evening in Yerevan, Kate and I met the Baghdasarian family by appointment, again. We had now decided, after three nights, that they were not going to invite us to their home. Kate felt certain (with her feminine intuition) that they were really too poor - like most Russians - to want us to witness the sordidness of their domestic and culinary state.

However, when we did meet them, they were insistent that we accompany them home. We surrendered, only to find that we soon stood before a very shabby tower block. It looked very depressing, seeming only to confirm our worst suspicions. Furthermore, there seemed to be no lift and we had to climb bare stone steps up to the fourth floor. However, as we entered the apartment we were agreeably surprised to find it brilliantly lit by a central chandelier. We quickly noted a large television but we were far more impressed on seeing a brightly polished baby-grand piano, with music sheet in place. We also, cautiously, espied a large, sparkingly clean bathroom, and a spacious kitchen with a very large fridge (much bigger than ours).

After the usual preliminaries, Mrs Baghdasarian and her two daughters led us on to a very pleasant balcony, "from where one could see on a clear day," Rosalina assured us, "the famous Mount Ararat", though this was really fifteen miles away, just over the border in Turkey. (We confirmed this the next day as we left. I should also record that in the main Yerevan museum a Communist/Atheist guide showed us parts of Noah's Ark!).

We were now to sample the famed Armenian Hospitality (and how!). The mother helped by the two girls, brother "John", and Aunt Annya opened up a huge folding table on the (Ararat) balcony and started loading it with delectable viands: many kinds of cold meats; chicken drum-sticks, yum-yum; etceteras. And the sumptuous meal concluded with huge strawberries and ice cream. What followed the supper was truly amazing and deeply touching; we were given a present for every single member of our nuclear family. And the *piece de resistance*, which we couldn't resist, was a handsome, large "silver" samovar, in full working order! (When we showed envious members of our touring party next day, they all vowed, "Oh, you'll never get THAT through customs". But we did!). Of course, my wife and I had taken the precaution to have presents ready to please the Baghdasarians, but they proved to be so paltry in comparison with theirs for us, that I dare not list ours!

Next day we left Yerevan by plane for Tibilisi, but I ought to mention that two days before we departed we discovered (through many photos garlanded with laurel wreaths) that the great Armenian composer, Katchaturian, had just died. I beg the reader to believe me when I swear that my wife and I had no part in his death. In fact, I dote on his music, especially *Spartacus*.

The first day in Tibilisi, a visit to the home of Stalin was scheduled, but significantly, did not ensue.

On our second day in Tibilisi, we were due to meet Vladimir and Nicky and "enjoy a superior meal with them!?" We never met them, for that morning disaster struck! I should explain at the outset that my wife worked in a Swansea hospital. When I retired in 1977, she urged me to adopt a new regimen of health ("get rid of the tum", etc). Part of the course involved exercises. One of the exercises was very strenuous. It involved touching the toes with knees held rigid! I was game to risk this.

I went out on to the balcony of our Tibilisi Iveria hotel. It was a glorious morning, and as I looked across the snaking river and up towards the steep cable car mountains, I felt very well indeed. I began my exercises but when I essayed the toe-touching operation I heard a distinct "crack!" and felt a dreadful pain in my lower back. I could not get up off the floor. My poor (long-suffering) wife urged me repeatedly to be "bold and brave. You've simply got to get up!" No use! I lay on the floor for a long time in a crumpled heap.

Eventually, we both remembered that we were due that morning to visit the famous Tibilisi Turkish baths. With a Herculean effort, and with a great deal of "tut-tutting" help from my wife, eventually from a steward as well, I managed to dress. Soon a taxi took us to the Turkish baths. It was a lush, plush Ottoman affair. One was encouraged to lie in warm sulphur water which spurted and/or gushed all around from beautifully tiled (golden and brown) walls. With a cautious look around as I lay in the refreshing (but strong-smelling!) water, I noticed it was mixed bathing with many nude bodies; some grotesque, some fascinating. After a couple of hours in the water espying the more fascinating bodies, I began to feel better. And I was even able to dress myself much to my wife's relief.

We left the Bath precincts and started to walk - quite briskly - back to our hotel. Alas! I stumbled off a badly cracked pavement, and "Ouch!", there it was again: that dreadful pain in the lumbar region! I stopped walking and started to crawl (like a crab?). Wife said, "Yes?" Kate was now quite exasperated. "Oh George! We simply can't go on like this! We're only half way through our itinerary!"

We stood stock-still on the pavement, feeling very miserable, until my enterprising wife suddenly looked up at a very large new building and, touching my shoulder, she cried, "Oh LOOK! Can you see that nurse on the third floor? See her standing by the large window?"

I did not, but realising that my wife had hospital connections, I didn't contradict but asked her, "So what do you intend?"

She said, "I'm taking you into that hospital right away!"

Very soon we had talked our way in. At least Kate did. With only a little, very little trouble, we got into a large, newly decorated room. In the centre of the room was a big table covered with telephones of various colours together with small cabinets and files. Behind the impressive display of office "O & M", sat a large, handsome and altogether impressive man. As soon as I had exhausted my pathetic Russian: "*Doobray ootra*," and "*Ya ochen rat ponakov meetsa*," etc., the man shook his head and pressed a button. Before one could say "*Da*", a pretty young lady came in. She told us she was an interpreter and that the handsome man behind his desk was the Director. I turned to my wife to explain my problem and plead - woman to woman - for help.

"But why have you come here?" asked the young lady.

"My husband needs hospital treatment!" urged Kate.

The interpreter smiled, but sadly, and said, "Oh, but this is not a hospital. This building, still under construction, is being prepared as a centre for the Olympic Games in 1980."

My wife echoed my audible groans. In my desperation I suddenly wondered if I had an ace up my sleeve that would do the trick! I took out of my wallet a card to prove that I was a fully paid-up member of the British Soviet Friendship Society. Whether our new hosts were now motivated by politics or by genuine sympathy (I prefer to think the latter), the nice fact was that after a few words between her and the Director, the girl turned to us with a sweet smile and consoled, "Please don't worry, when you leave here you will find a motor-car waiting at the door to take you to a very fine hospital."

And indeed, so it was: in fact a chauffeur-driven limousine as fine as any I had seen in Labour-controlled cities in South Wales (Mayoral!).

The most compelling, persistent memory of this hospital in Tibilisi was that it was run entirely by women: from Director to cleaners. I must record also, and above all else, that the efficiency was absolutely first class. However, I could be blinded by self-interest: for I was slightly embarrassed, as a passionate egalitarian and former Communist, when on arrival (and not dead!) I was put at the head of a long queue of patients. I was also very glad to have the services of a pretty girl interpreter. Soon I was interviewed by a mature handsome woman. After having an account of my condition and needs translated I was taken on a trolley to a room where, for the very first time in my life, I received a massage. A huge, muscular (Georgian?) woman kneaded her thumbs and fingers into the small of my back and lumbar region. Though painful, I began to feel some relaxation of tension. To my great surprise I was then wheeled into another room and received similar treatment but with the variation of warm wet cloths and a few gentle slaps on back. Later I was taken, again by trolley, to an imposing Physio-Therapy room.

I was now placed on a long table, on my stomach, where incidentally, I could see the recording dials (registering effects?). I was interested to observe that this intricate machine was a gift (*etant donné-*) from the Joliot Curie Institute, Paris. (I recalled that this famous married couple - she a daughter of Marie - and that Nobel Prize winners were not allowed to travel to Russia during the long Cold War because they were Communists!)

While I was receiving the physiotherapy treatment with my dear wife sitting on one side and a pretty interpreter on the other, I was being asked repeatedly, if the needles being applied to my back were too hot or too sharp. After this further relaxing session I was offered tablets and an injection. My wife approved the pills but dissuaded me from taking the injection. When I asked her why later on, she merely said, "It could have been a TRUTH drug, and you know what a shocking fibber you are!"

In summary, I received marvellous treatment at this hospital. Furthermore I was cordially invited to return the following day to continue the cure. I accepted the kind offer. (Thus I missed the arranged meeting with Vladimir and Nikolai.) I was so grateful for the wonderful treatment I had enjoyed in Georgia that when back home, I wrote a warm and sincere letter of thanks to "The Director and Staff (Dr Kavkasidze) Hospital No 4, Chavchavadze Avenue, 4 Tibilisi, Georgia!"

EPILOGUE

The rest of our Russian Tour (1978) was rather quiet and uneventful, contrasted with the excitement, trials and tribulations, experienced in the "deep south" (with "Georgia on my mind"!). Our pleasant relationship with Rosalina Baghdasarian lasted for about ten years more to 1988. We exchanged cards and gifts, especially for birthdays and around Christmas time. Such cards from her were sent for the "Feast of Father Frost", January 7th to 9th, i.e. the original historic time of Western Christendom. The last message we had from Rosalina was in answer to our anxious query assuring us that she and family had survived the terrible earthquake. But all were affected and worried by the savage war between Armenians and Azeris. Rosalina was now married and had two children. And my wife and I agreed that her "romantic juvenile urge to correspond with Britons" had waned to extinction!

However, I am happy to record that we have made many more Russian friends without needing to travel to their country. A mutual love of music has provided the means of this pleasant liaison, viz: in 1991-93 Russian choirs have come to South Wales, including Swansea. The first of these was the Vilati from Moscow. It had a joint concert with one of our local male voice choirs: 'Cor Meibion Ystrad'. One of the "old-timers" of this group is Ken Evans, a former college colleague/friend of mine. A day before the concert, Ken and his wife Beti, came home to introduce two of the Vilati singers: Tamara and Galina, delightful Muscovite personalities and lovely sopranos. Correspondence with them continues.

Other singers came to Swansea: this time (1992-93) from Estonia. These included a family: Nikolai, Ludmilla (Luda) and daughter, Maria. We got so friendly in Autumn 1992, that I invited them to "our" Lawrence House, 2 Polstead Road, and from there I escorted them around Oxford. In the same month (October) we had two spontaneous concerts in my home. We tape-recorded this and it emerged very well. We can be heard singing English, Welsh and Russian songs. Luda has a particularly lovely voice. I have only a creditable one (?) and I made a special effort to impress our Russian guests with my renditions of *"Volga, Volga, mat rodnaya"*, *"Kalinka"*, *"Pretty Minka"*, and especially *"Ochi-cheonia; ochi guichia...* ("Oh! Those dark eyes!" etc)!

Correspondence with all these new Russian friends continues and I sincerely hope it goes on.

So I end for the time being with my favourite Russian salutations: *"Khorosho!"* and *"Ya ochen rat: poznakov meetsa"* - "Welcome! I'm so pleased to meet you..

However, the use of *"Tovarish"*, "Comrades" is frowned on since 1989 and the collapse of the U.S.S.R. I think this is a pity: I LIKE TOVARISH!

ON THE TRAIL OF LAWRENCE OF ARABIA

My sister, Elinor and her son, my nephew Terence Phillips, bought a house (2 Polstead Road) in Oxford in 1969 which caused many changes in my lifestyle.

This was no ordinary dwelling. It was a large, splendid house of sixteen rooms in delectable North Oxford. There is also a lovely large bungalow in a very spacious back garden. But its main claim to fame is that it was the home of T.E. Lawrence (of Arabia) and family for 25 years, 1896 to 1921.

My eldest sister, Elinor, was a most unlikely person to become the owner of this historic house. For "Nelly", born and reared in Abertaff in industrial South Wales, had lived in dire poverty as a miner's daughter and miner's wife until she was 61 years of age. She was widowed at 43 with four children. She was never out of Abertaff except for a very short and occasional holiday in all those years.

So how did it transpire that she became the owner of Lawrence of Arabia's house? The clue to this strange event is bound up with the story of her eldest son, Terence (born in 1921). After very poor and obscure beginnings after service in the R.A.F. in War-time, he was able to get to a university college in late 1945. He obtained a B.A. degree in French and after a very short period of teaching, he migrated to U.S.A. In New York he met a very enterprising lady who, very coincidentally, had also migrated from Abertaff; in fact she had been a friend of Nelly. Terence now helped her to run her boarding house and observed how this shrewd woman was making a lot of money!

Terence returned to the U.K. in the early 1960's, and after a while he got a job teaching French at the Oxford Polytechnic. He had to go into digs and soon evolved the bright idea that he and his mother could run a better guest house than he suffered, based on his New York experience .

He persuaded Elinor, now in her mid-sixties, to move to Oxford. They set up a boarding house, first in a run-down area of this famous city. They made a go of it. They moved to a better suburb and made a profit. In 1969 they learned that 2 Polstead Road was on the market for £50,000. They worked fast and secured the lease (later they got the freehold). Soon they were able to accommodate fifteen lodgers for "B & B", most of them students.

One of the exciting finds in the huge house, apart from the famous Lawrence Bungalow, was the discovery that much of the Lawrences furniture and sundry items had been left in the main house since 1921.

The explanation for this is necessary: in 1921 the shrunken Lawrence family (two sons killed in the Great War, and father recently dead, etc.) moved out. Mother, Sarah, together with her son Robert, went as missionaries to China. T.E., after All Souls, moved to London, and the youngest son, Arnold, also moved out.

The next occupants of Polstead Road soon moved elsewhere, and the third owner, a Mrs Brodie, died there but intestate. Apart from a lot of solid Victorian furniture, Terence Phillips found in the very large attic many books, two swords, some ornamental daggers, a fascinating vase, an expensive Victorian gold watch, a black and white drawing of T.E. reminiscent of Augustus John's, and, most interesting to myself, Mrs Lawrence's shopping book. This book had entrances dating from the week the family moved in (Sept. 15th 1896) and running on to 1900.

I first visited this famous house in 1970 and soon realized that its potential as a quasi-Museum was considerable, as yet unrecognised. In the same period (Autumn 1970), I happened to see an obituary notice in *The Times* followed by a bequest, wherein a certain M/s Laidlaw had left £70,000 to a Lawrence Memorial Fund. All the money was to go to T.E's last house - Cloud's Hill, Dorset. This spurred me to write a letter to the Ministry of Works (now Ministry of Environment) putting a strong case for diverting some of the Laidlaw moneys to Polstead Road. I pointed out that whereas Lawrence had resided, off and on, in Cloud's Hill for nine years he had his more intimate family contacts with the Oxford house for 25 years. Alas, my only answer from the Ministry of Works was "dusty" negative.

At this period (circa 1970-75) I was busy in a full-time teaching job in South Wales. I was even more committed to a much loved part-time post with the newly-formed Open University. Meanwhile also, Terence Phillips was busy in a full-time teaching post in a college in Newcastle. My aged sister, now past 70 and afflicted with

162

increasing deafness, was struggling to maintain the guest house in Polstead Road.

In 1977 I retired from full-time work. In the meantime, my nephew had persuaded me to join him in creating a school of English for foreigners in Oxford using 2 Polstead Road as our base and calling it The Lawrence School of English (see illustrated headed note-paper overleaf). In launching the school I assumed the mantle (or should I say academic gown) of Principal. I was now able to put after my name some useful titles. My nephew assumed the role of Director of Studies. We also discovered that we had seventeen teachers in our extended family, although in the event, owing to full-time commitments elsewhere, only one or two of our relatives joined us. However, we found plenty of staff members by advertising among recently qualified (but unemployed) Oxford graduates.

After advertising abroad (through, for example, a relative in Geneva and another in Rome) we opened our first school in St. Anne's College in July 1975. We got seven students only. The next year we had thirty students. In 1977 we were beginning to achieve success in welcoming fifty five students. I should explain (with some pride) that we were able to hire Oxford colleges together with their halls of residence, if able to give sufficient notice and meet the fees promptly. For instance: in our second year we were able to rent Somerville; next Brasenose, with its ancient annexe in Frewin Hall. Another year we were privileged to have the most beautiful college in Oxford, St. Edmunds, (called, endearingly, by regular students "Teddy Hall"). In 1980 we enjoyed the use of a substantial part of the second biggest college, Magdalen, with its extensive and splendid gardens and its easy access to the Isis river and the glamorous punts. One can easily imagine the effect of all this on the foreign students. They began to grow in number and diversity. Over the years most of these were French, then Italian, then German, some Spanish, a few Arabs, some from Latin America, three from Hong Kong, and a very colourful man from St. Catherine's Monastery, Mount Sinai. He was a native of Austria and kept asking me, "Why is the word *fahrt* vulgar (voolgar) in English, since in German it merely means the "route" or "way"?"

In summary I should emphasise with pride that every student was delighted to receive an impressive certificate (with a red seal attached) verifying that one had completed a "Course of Study, in the Lawrence School of English" in prestigious Oxford!

Meanwhile, visitors to our Lawrence House came, first in a steady trickle, then in a fuller stream. Let us recall that the first biographer of T.E. Lawrence was the American journalist Lowell Thomas. His study, however, was almost sheer hagiography. In fact it was Thomas who created the Lawrence of Arabia legend. The next biographer was Robert Graves, who had a Fellowship at All Souls at the same time as T.E.L. and they became friendly, after a fashion. Strange that Graves, a shrewd man, could swallow whole a lot of the tall-tall stories pedalled by Lawrence!

B. Liddell-Hart was the third writer to try to unravel the enigma that the life of Lawrence presented. True, he did spot some whoppers that T.E.L. had palmed off on Thomas and Graves, but his study is also too adulatory. It took many years for the bubble of the Lawrence Legend to be pricked by Richard Aldington (1955). Incidentally, it was Aldington who first mentioned 2 Polstead Road, and several times, and more importantly, revealed the truth of Lawrence's father's real name (Chapman), and of his living in sin with his house-servant, Sarah Madden. These sordid facts may provide the clue to Ned's romancing and his persistent propensity to changing his name (!?).

The next period of the spate of Lawrence biographies was, no doubt, stimulated by the tremendous boost given to the legend by David Lean's spectacular film (1962). Our house in Polstead Road also had a new lease of life as a spin-off from the film. Many new biographers came at regular intervals, as revealed subsequently by the dates of the books and the inclusion of many photographs. One of the earliest after 1962 was almost entirely pictorial. This was by Percival Graves (nephew of Robert). Then came Desmond Stewart with his carefully crafted and critical biography. For example: Stewart rejected the sensational story of T.E.L's. torture (including a sodomy attack by several Turkish soldiers) at Deraa.

By contrast, a very small life by one Victoria Ocampi is very sickly in its adulation. It was acclaimed by Lawrence's youngest brother, Arnold, as "the very best biography". (One is tempted to comment, "He would say that, wouldn't he!?"). The first of the later biographers I actually met was Paul Marriott who concentrated on the young Ned growing up in Polstead Road; going to his first school, etc. We were able to show Marriott the inside of the cupboard door in the front room wherein father Chapman measured the height of the boys as they grew up, Ned never exceeding 5ft 5 inches (perhaps another clue to his tendency to boasting and telling TALL stories). Marriott's book includes some useful photos and data on the Bungalow. *A propos*: Desmond Stewart suggests that the chalet was built for Ned in a preference over the other brothers, because he had discovered his father and mother in sexual embrace; knowing that they had never married he had run away from home and joined the army under age and vowing he would never live in the main house again!

In 1969 Knightley and Simpson published their sensational *The Secret Lives Of Lawrence Of Arabia* with the shocking revelations of T.E.L.'s sado-masochistic relationship (regular flagellations) with Jock Bruce. John Mack (Professor of Psychiatry at Harvard) brought out a massive biography of Lawrence in 1976 under the bizarre title *A Prince Of Our Disorder*.

Incidentally, what I especially have to grumble at, at this juncture, is that few of the later biographers, from 1969 on, acknowledge their moral debt to my sister, Elinor, for so many pictures she allowed them to take. She gave them almost unlimited access to all rooms, bungalow, garden etc., usually without monetary reward. The pity is that Nelly was increasingly frail and deaf, and she was vulnerable to smooth-talking pedants bent on milking the esoteric story of Lawrence. In the run-up to ceremonies (of which more anon) I wrote to many of the later biographers asking for a donation, reminding them of the pictures they got with willing co-operation here but the only ones I recall responding were Marriott and Stewart.

During the period of our Lawrence School of English, we also had a lot of student visitors and a large number of obscure devotees of T.E.L. From 1982 onwards I made new efforts to arouse more positive (and profitable interest) in "Our House". Why 1982? In that year my nephew and I had both retired from full-time work, we also decided to close our school. In June (1982) I had an impressive blue plaque installed on the front of the house. I chose the legend: "This house was the home of T.E. Lawrence (Lawrence of Arabia) 1896-1921". And on the perimeter the message reads: "This plaque was installed by Elinor Phillips and G. Greening, jointly with Jesus and

All Souls colleges". The plaque was unveiled by Sir Patrick Neill Warden of All Souls (later Vice-Chancellor of Oxon. University). Several other dignitaries were present and they appreciated the best sherry (pale and dark) I had laid on in the front room! I may as well jump on six years, and in the same vein mention the commemoration ceremony I arranged for the 100th anniversary of Lawrence's birth. This was in August 1988. I had a very fine stained glass panel inserted into a bungalow window, with the famous T.E.L. portrait by James McBey. Before a large group of famous, and semi-famous, Oxford personalities, some members of the Phillips family etc. the portrait was unveiled by Dr North, Principal of Jesus College. Something that aroused especial interest, which I had arranged well in advance, was the placing of a ninety-year old man, one Jack Easton, who was a very proud comrade in arms of Lawrence in Miranshah on the North West Frontier of India in 1926-8, to sit in front of the portrait. Many photos were taken of dear old Jack, who obviously worshipped Lawrence!

Meanwhile, visitors - famous, notorious and obscure - continued arriving at Lawrence House in growing numbers. I should also mention especially, T.V. ventures. I was present when three of these took place, two under my supervision. The first was in Spring 1985. A small company of B.B.C. experts, or so-called, came to prepare a "definitive study" of Lawrence for the prestigious Omnibus series. This team was led by Julia Cave (a book by her was an extra "spin-off" in 1988). Terence Cave and I, and one other, signed a joint declaration on details, for example, our fee, etc., one clause of which said, "Any breakages due to filming activities would be compensated." However, an over zealous camera-man who wanted to photograph the bungalow from above, (i.e. from the top rear window of the main house) in struggling to open the window wider knocked some ornaments belonging to a student-lodger flying disastrously to the stone floor below. Our subsequent claim to the B.B.C. was, to my disgust, disallowed. Another T.V. company (H.T.V.?) from Cardiff, led by one Z. Pawelko, came in 1986, and he asked me to introduce the film. With pride and great gusto I began (assuming my best Oxford accent) only to be asked abruptly, "In Welsh, please." Unable so to do, I had to decline and so lost my big chance for screen immortality!

But later, in 1988, another chance came when a Director of an Italian T.V. Company, an ebullient Franco Bucarelli, stood in Polstead Road with two cameramen awaiting my return from a shopping spree. Bucarelli explained that, "Meester Filippo says that we are not to start filming until you arrive. It seems, Meester Gee, that you are-a the bossa!?"

When I nipped in the house to ask my nephew to clarify, he said "Discuss terms first, we won't let them film for less than £50 for the hour."

Bucarelli said that one hour was enough (he had just come from Jesus and All Souls colleges). I started bargaining: he interrupted with his move, "I can offera you 50 Eengleesh Bobs - sterling-a," he said.

I shouted, "BOBS!?"

"I mean-a 50 Eengleesh Shillings - Sterlinga," he explained.

I answered, "Don't you realise, Signor," (I felt like the Merchant of Venice) "that 50 English Bobs, or shillings, is only equal to piccolo peanuts?"

After a little further argument, Franco saw that we both meant £50 sterling. Eventually, I received a copy of Bucarelli's film. It is quite good. I am well photographed in front of the main house and before the bungalow, introducing the film. Alas, the commentary is translated into Italian and I no-speaka di-lingo. However, a translator (Terence's sister Geraldine Battista, who lives in Rome) tells me that my suggestion that T.E. Lawrence was murdered by MI5 is rejected later in the film by Jeremy Wilson, who is the author of the authorised *Life of Lawrence* (1988).

Visitors to the Lawrence House now increased in number and variety. There were scores from many regions of the U.K. Many from the continent, few from Japan, three from Israel (!), and several from the U.S.A. and Canada. What amazes and amuses me is the fact that among all the soppy devotees of T.E.L., the dottiest of all are WOMEN. I find this doubly odd, because Lawrence was never a ladies man, quite the reverse. One of the most dotty of the Ned lovers, was one Barbara X, a big, formidable headmistress from Kent. She arrived at our house while my nephew was away. I was tolerant enough to allow her a good inspection of the place. But I was somewhat incautious in taking her to the top floor and pointing to the attic where Terence had found much T.E.L. memorabilia. I

confessed that I had only peeped in once. Barbara was utterly
convinced that she could find more. She begged me for a ladder and I
found it hard to restrain her!

Another case of the Lawrentian soppy worshippers was Mary
Ann Vynyl of Columbus, Ohio, U.S.A. (now deceased). After two
visits to Lawrence House during which I acted a very willing host and
guide, "and acting archivist", in a letter from America she asked me
to become her amanuensis for "a definitive study of Lawrence". I
declined the "honour" stressing how busy I was with more important
humanitarian work like U.N.A., U.N.I.C.E.F., Amnesty
International, etc. When I next met Ms Vynyl at a Lawrence 'do' in
London (1988) she refused to acknowledge me!

A more reasonable devotee but also an ardent disciple was/still is
Professor Rebecca Richards of Santa Clara University College
California. She came twice to our House and apart from showing her
everything possible in Polstead Road, I escorted her and her husband
around Oxford to see all the most famous colleges, libraries, etc. She
was good enough to reciprocate my goodwill by giving hospitality to
me and my son in a splendid hall of residence in the beautiful Santa
Clara University in 1986.

So much for female Lawrence Lovers! But even with men (and I
do include mature males, even up to old age) I find it strange and
amusing to what extent big strong men can be so love-sick with their
hero. More than one member of the Lawrence Society (U.K.) have
gone into raptures before me in recording their emotion in having the
privilege of touching the handlebars of their hero's motor bike! When
I remonstrate very gently and offer them a list of worthier
contemporaries of Lawrence, such as G.B. Shaw, Gilbert Murray,
Churchill, Charlie Chaplin, Irving Berlin, the Pankhursts, most of
whom did good or even great work (and not dubious dealing at the
expense of underprivileged people like the Arabs) the Lawrence
devotees remain unmoved in their utter intoxication!

It is high time that I come now to those visitors who came to our
House and stimulated me (albeit a Lawrentian sceptic cum cynic) to
follow the Lawrence Trail; and I mean in a Geographic context.

In Summer 1987, we received a few visitors to our house who
aroused a new interest, i.e that I might even do a trip to the Levant.

The least important of these people in this context was a little
Hebrew gentleman I espied one day studying the Lawrence plaque. I

soon found he was very interested so I invited him inside and showed him around. He surprised me in more ways than one. For example, he confided that he was a Professor in Arabic Studies at Jerusalem University. When I cautiously deplored the treatment of the Palestine Arabs by the Israeli authorities he replied, "I couldn't agree with you more!" Towards the end of our conversation, he urged me to make the Levant trip and he gave me his address: Dov Rappel, Professor at Bar Ilian University, Bar Ilian, Romat Gan, Israel.

More specifically in the same period, there called at the house a Major Middlemiss and a young friend. It was only by a stroke of good fortune (and my propensity to hospitality) that we met. My nephew - in a bad mood - was almost driving a couple of fellows from the front door, saying, "Very sorry, far too busy." I intervened and soon discovered that the Major lived in Jerusalem, was staying awhile in Oxfordshire, and as an enthusiast for anything Lawrentian, as was his young friend, they "would appreciate a look around". I tried to show them everything of interest. While sitting in the bungalow, and after a long conversation, the Major revealed that he had been one of the military advisers to David Lean in the making of his very famous film on Lawrence. In conclusion he asked me, "Have you by chance been out there to follow the Lawrence trail?" He evidently supposed that I was an enthusiast. He had shown such eagerness that I felt I couldn't disappoint, so I mumbled something to the effect of "No... not yet... but... I am... considering it."

The Major responded warmly: "Look... I am staying long term at St. Andrews Hospice, in a strategic part of Jerusalem. If you do decide to come out, you can be my guest and I'll show you everything you want to see as you have shown me today!"

Naturally I was quite touched, but still cautious, "Well... many thanks... but I very much want to see the three main countries i.e. Israel, Jordan and Syria."

"Oh!" said the Major in a pained expression, "that would be difficult! For... in my scheme you would fly into Tel-Aviv and once leaving Israel you wouldn't be allowed in again!"

I was still pondering Major Middlemiss's offer and considering its restrictions when, about a week later, a very tall, handsome young man appeared in our back garden (the little side door having been left ajar). Suddenly I saw my nephew, in an irate mood, rushing into the garden shouting to the stranger: "Private Property! OUT! OUT!"

I hurried around the front of the House and found that the stranger was one Kenneth Parkes. He was a Yorkshireman of about 30 years. He was now on holiday from Japan where he was employed as a lecturer in English in Kyoto University. He said that he and his Japanese wife had booked into a guest house in Polstead Road, in fact, right opposite our Lawrence House. He admitted that he was "a considerable fan of T.E.L." and he very much hoped, in the few days he could manage to remain in Oxford, that he "could see as much as possible".

I urged him to return to the house in late afternoon when I knew that my erstwhile nephew would be out. Parkes brought his pretty Japanese wife in the afternoon and I gave them an extensive, and very intensive, tour of the place. I found Kenneth so keen and polite, and withal so charming that I invited them to accompany me on a tour of inner Oxford the next day, and starting early I showed all the main colleges, and especially the three with Lawrentian connections: Jesus, Magdalen and All Souls. I was also able to show the building where T.E.L. and his brothers went to High School. I did not neglect Folly Bridge at the exit of the underground river where Lawrence ended his hazardous canoe trip when an undergraduate, etc. It was a long tour, especially for me (aged 72), so we had lunch at the famous old Turf Tavern and a later dinner at the even older Bear Inn. We had even found time to see the beautiful Library at Merton College; possibly the oldest library in U.K.

Ken Parkes was hugely delighted with our tour. In another meeting at more leisure, he asked me if I had any plans to "follow the Lawrence Trail"? When I told him of my tentative consideration of Middlemiss's offer, he responded without pause, "Oh, you can do better than that. You CAN see all three countries (less troubled Lebanon) in the Levant. All you have to do is: A, contact the H.Q. of Royal Jordanian Airlines at Regent Street, London, and: B, also contact 'Lotus Tours', Herts." (I have used a pseudonym of the latter.) "You might well contact as well, an old friend of mine: Bill Warren, who is mad on Lawrence and has followed the Trail, and now runs a little museum in Yorks."

I now hurry on to report that I wrote to Warren who replied with detailed hints, including how best to ride and feed a camel on a long desert trek, how to pitch a tent in a sand-storm, and how to ward off snakes and scorpions or other deadly insects! I wrote a letter of thanks to Warren, but of course, never once did I intend to emulate his Spartan-Desert regime!

In late September, I booked the desired tour with R.J.A. and the firm I will call 'Lotus'. When I arrived at London Airport, I was immediately approached by a representative of Lotus, and given a hundred U.S. dollars. When I expressed surprise and asked "Why this gift?" I was told, "All will be revealed in Damascus!"

Starting the tour I was surprised and somewhat disappointed to find so few fellow-tourists. To begin with, we were only three. The other two introduced themselves as Clive and Heather, husband and wife, from Wycombe. (Clive confided that he too had received a "bonus" of a hundred dollars at the airport and was as nonplussed as I.) In Amman, our first stop, we were joined by a couple from Sheffield: George and Ivy. But within two days of the tour they got a dramatic and sad message that Ivy's Mum had suddenly died, so they returned home. This lead to complications for the rest of us (more anon).

We spent the first free day viewing the city of Amman, its palaces and mosques, etc. The second day we drove out to Jerash, acclaimed as "the biggest Roman City in the world!" Of course we were duly impressed. We had to observe, with mixed emotions, that we were travelling in motor cars like taxis because we were so very few. (We wondered if the shaky political situation in Israel and environs was the cause of low numbers.) We were further reduced when George and Ivy left and the problems that followed were connected and proved awkward! For our main driver left us to attend to the suddenly bereaved couple. We soon found that our new Arab driver could not speak a word of English and, unbeknownst to us, was to drive us all the way to Damascus! (But would St. Paul deliver us safely there?)

We discovered, to our chagrin and cost, too late that he had taken us to the wrong hotel, in fact, the grandest accommodation in this "the oldest city in the world" (so says the guide book!).

Just as we had finished a luscious dinner washed down with delectable wines and rounded off with a tasty Courvoisier, a very fat man came bustling up to our table full of apologies. He introduced himself as Yasser Arrafin (his size suggested his namesake - Arrafat!). He said he was the Lotus representative for Syria. He explained the awful mistake, begged us to pay the "splendid Hotel" extra money and, amid our strong protests he promised that Lotus, U.K. would put things right for us.

We had already paid Visa fees at the border contrary to Tour brochure firm promises. Then a pleasant idea struck me! The hundred dollars bonus was to cover these exigencies! We asked Arrafin about this. He didn't have a clue. He said that he knew nothing whatever about a hundred dollars.

Next day doing the round of Damascus we saw in a deep souk the window where, according to the Bible, St. Paul made a famous escape. In the same bazaar I recklessly spent most of the hundred dollar bonus on expensive presents: Damascus linen for my wife and an ornamental dagger similar to one found in Lawrence House by nephew Terence. No Pauline Light stopped my extravagance.

One day we drove north and we saw Deraa. I took some photos of a grim looking building which might have been the very one where Lawrence was held in captivity and tortured and sodomised (of course my imagination was being coloured by desire, yet I still doubted the veracity of T.E.L's lurid tale!). After Deraa we moved north-east into a very large area of desert. Eventually we reached the great and fabulous, classical Graeco-Roman city of Palmyra. Here is a vast complex of impressive temples and tombs but, alas, for the most part in ruins. On leaving the immense cemetery area around (and I couldn't help reciting Shelley's *Ozimandias* poem to myself) an occurrence we greatly feared befell us: our car suffered a burst tyre. It seemed to take our driver a long, long time to get us moving again. I started musing to Clive about our prospects as the sun seemed to scorch us. Clive philosophically commented, "Oh yes, it is somewhat scary, but imagine Lawrence in a similar plight but not with a car but a collapsed camel - 70 years ago!" A sobering thought.

The last night in Damascus I got a nasty shock. Arrafin knocked on my door and, after reminding me to get ready for early departure next day he said calmly, "Oh by the way, I've just had a message from H.Q. London saying that I am to collect one hundred U.S. dollars or equivalent from you." I tried to argue, grumbled, but in the end paid up. But I now realised that I was going to be very hard pressed to meet sundry cash demands for the rest of the tour.

Next day, after a long drive through surprisingly picturesque country we reached the famous Allenby Bridge. This led into Israel and I was amazed to find how small the historic River Jordan is! There was a long delay on the Bridge and the wily Clive advised me to take my cassette film out of my camera in case, he said, Israeli border soldiers spoiled the contents by rough handling. These latter took our baggage and told us to follow them into the Border station. They then asked us to take a couple of camera shots of the ceiling! I wondered why but hazarded the guess that cameras can be guns!? Now we were detained for a few hours and found the delay annoying. When we saw our baggage again we were told to empty the contents (as if they hadn't inspected them already!). Incidentally, I plead guilty to delaying proceedings in trying to pass through the electronic barriers while several items on my person set alarm bells ringing. The last "culprit" to be revealed was a tiny harmonica which I tend to carry around. (Perhaps I should have told the soldiers that the organ case had been autographed by Larry Adler but they didn't seem to be in the mood for humour. By the way, the autograph is genuine).

On leaving the Allenby Bridge (at last!) we were taken by a charming Israeli chauffeuse on a long ride towards Jerusalem. On the way to the Holy City we came to Jericho. We got out for the young lady was keen to show us in the far distance the remains of the famous Wall (that was allegedly blown down by the trumpets).

"Do you really believe that happened?" I asked.

"Of course," she replied hotly. "Don't you?"

I confessed, "NO!"

She asked, "Are you British?"

"Yes."

"Well then, I assume you are a Christian? And if so you believe the Holy Scriptures as we do!"

I decided it was useless to explain that I was an agnostic!

We spent several days in and around Jerusalem and we were fortunate in having a transcendental and panoramic view of the city and its environs from the strategically placed Mount Scopus Hotel. We did the usual sights: The Dome of the Rock, Al-Aqsa Mosque, the Wailing Wall. We joined in part of the long walk Via Dolorosa. We looked at the Mount of Olives from the Garden of Gethsemane, and so on. In a wider context we made a trip to the Dead Sea and saw Qumran, where the celebrated Scrolls were found (still a hot subject of controversy). I should report that I saw the St. Andrew Hospice but, short of time, I didn't call on Major Middlemiss.

Taking a wider geographic ambit, we were taken one day to Mount Nebo and were shown on the top the great stone that commemorates the spot where Moses allegedly was shown the Promised Land. As I peered into the desolate distance I couldn't help murmuring to Clive, "Moses didn't miss much!" And I repeated a story I heard a Jewish lecturer (of Geography, Swansea University) tell after a Tour of Israel. He said, "If the Israelites on entering the Promised Land, had turned right instead of left they would have found the oil instead of the bloody oranges!"

The night before we were due to leave Jerusalem we had a visit from an Israeli agent of Lotus Travel! He had the imposing name of Solomon. He reminded us that we would be leaving next morning for the visit to the fabulous site PETRA. He also stressed that he was now to collect our cash for this "optional extra". I told him bluntly I could not afford it. He was astounded. He then pressed me hard.

"Why?" he urged, "Don't you realise this is the *piece de resistance* of the whole tour?!" I simply repeated that I was nearly broke.

Solomon, in all his wisdom, could not have been more persuasive: "Have you got an American Express Card?"

"NO."

"What about a Barclaycard?"

"NO."

"Don't you have a credit card of any sort?"

"NO."

"You surely must carry a cheque book?"

"Yes."

"Please let me see it!"

I showed him my Swansea Bank cheque book.

"Will you please write out a cheque for £35. I know how to cash it."

I couldn't help reflecting that my Solomon epitomised the financial enterprise and expertise that made his Race produce so many successful bankers - like Rothschild, Baring, et al!

Reverting to my conspicuous lack of financial skills, I now realised that dire shortage of cash would reduce my "optional extra" trips to ONE! I had to choose between Aqaba and Petra. To strictly follow the Lawrence Trail Aqaba was the obvious one but I decided on Petra for these reasons:

A. Every tourist of the Levant I ever met rhapsodized about Petra. By contrast Aqaba was very dull, they all said. (T.E.L. himself was wonderfully impressed by Petra).

B. I have to reiterate and emphasise, I am not a Lawrence devotee.

C. Lawrence's claim to have "taken Aqaba!" (as, so dramatically, in Lean's film hagiography detailed) was somewhat bogus. The truth seems to be that in the final frenetic charge on the Turkish positions Lawrence, with a blood-curdling cry of "CHARGE!" shot his own camel in the head and was thrown so violently as to be knocked out! The final victory was secured by warrior Auda and his men.

Petra is a miniature Grand Canyon (Colorado). I have seen both. The Petra Gorge is, of course, much narrower, thus much more difficult to clamber down into. In fact I didn't realise until the very last moment (and too late!) on leaving the nearby Petra Hotel that the only way down to see the Saiq Treasure House, magnificently carved out of the solid rock, is by horse! I had never, ever, sat astride a horse before in my life and I was now over 72 years of age. As I sat, very nervously, on what seemed an enormous animal with me very high up in the world (!) I held on like grim death as the descent on the rickety-rackety goat-track began. I had to hold on with both hands to the saddle-pommel and was therefore quite unable to swat the flies that kept settling on my nose. The ride proved so hazardous for me that after viewing the main sights at the bottom of the gorge I decided to walk the long, strenuous, uphill journey back. When I eventually reached the hotel, sweaty, dusty and exhausted, I soon plunged into the lovely cool water of the large swimming pool.

After Petra we returned to Amman for the flight home.

POSTSCRIPT REALISTIC

Within weeks of my return to U.K. (Oxford then Swansea) I wrote to Lotus Travel and, whereas I praised the tour in general, I grumbled at the extra expense incurred by lack of clear information or misleading brochure data. I was pleased to receive soon after, a cheque for £50 in compensation.

In the following spring, I had a letter from Japan. It was from Kenneth Parkes and it included a photo of a tiny Japanese baby. Ken said with great pride that the baby was his son, conceived in Polstead Road, Oxford, and therefore named LAWRENCE.

EPILOGUE FANTASTIC

Ere I conclude I should mention two lodgers particularly, who I met over many years in Lawrence House.

The first is Mr N. Knight who has occupied a room on the top floor underneath the attic. Coincidentally, despite his elder years he resembles T.E. Lawrence. He is very short ("five feet and a fart"), he has very blue eyes and he has a persistent giggle. The top floor of the house is very badly lit. On several occasions I have encountered Mr Knight in the gloaming and with a scary feeling I have often shouted, "Is that you LAWRENCE?!" and Knight mumbles, with a giggle, "No, no, it's only ME!"

The other man I refer to is one Joe Clarke who occupied the bungalow for about ten years (1970-80). I once asked Joe, "In all those years you lived and slept in the Bungalow, did you, by chance, ever see Lawrence's ghost?"

Without hesitation Joe replied, "I really think he walked over me one night as I lay in bed!"

"Good God!" I said. "How did you recognise him, and didn't his boots hurt you?"

"Oh," answered Joe, "I felt the hem of his Arab robe. He had no boots on and I saw the sand between his toes!"

I feel certain that had Lawrence heard these two (first-hand) tales, he would have giggled in appreciation.

1

76

MAKING FRIENDS IN CHINA

I was always fascinated by China even as a school-boy. I well recall reading in a History of Napoleon and France (aged 11) how Bonaparte warned his ambitious generals, looking to the far east, "Let that Giant sleep!" But later I learned how that Giant was awakened, roughly, first by Britain then by France, and later by at least ten other Imperialist powers between 1840 and 1900.

Nevertheless, as a boy I was also frightened to dare enter a Chinese laundry (and there were quite a few in our town) because, like many other kids, we had been sub-consciously indoctrinated, badly/sadly, to fear the Chinese by long-running cinema serials like *The Mystery Of Fu Manchu*. Actually the author of these horror stories, Sax Rohmer, had never been anywhere near China!

By the late 1930's as a young "idealist-Communist" I was deeply moved by the long-drawn-out sufferings of the Chinese people and especially when horribly brutalized by Japanese air-raids and subsequent invasions by that 'new' rampaging, Imperialist power.

Later (1949) I was genuinely heartened by the Communist triumph, not foreseeing the nastiness of the Cultural Revolution which followed. However, by 1980 with the end of that turmoil, the death of Mao-Tse Tung and the jailing of the Gang Of Four, etc., I felt that, given the necessary cash, it would be safe for me to venture into a tour of China. Most of the required money in winter 1980-81 came from my sister and nephew who decided to repay me for my unrewarded and decisive help in creating and sustaining the Lawrence School of English in Oxford (1975 *et seq*).

So on the first of June 1981 I set out on my long-desired big adventure to explore some of the mighty, but still mysterious, land of China. The tour was arranged by the Jules Verne Company and was to last for thirty days. The flight was made under the auspices of Cathay Pacific and it provided a wonderful service. We were about twenty five tourists so we had plenty of room on board, and food and drink were delectable and plentiful. It was an eighteen hour flight to Hong Kong via Dubai. We were to have our first optional trip on landing in Hong Kong: to view the great city from the wonderful panorama provided by the top of the High Peak. Alas, it was raining slightly which made a nasty mist. We saw little, if anything. Next day was Sunday and a rest day. In our Li Gardens Hotel I had already made friends with Sally Yao, a delightful and beautiful receptionist. Subsequently, she told me that she had fairly recently come from Shanghai and that her parents still lived there. I promised her that I would send her a nice postcard from her native city.

Determined to see the much vaunted view of Hong Kong from the Peak, I set out alone on the Sunday morning. I waited for ages at the bus (or tram?) stop. At last, asking a young couple about the frequency of public transport, they told me that it was more restricted on Sundays and I was waiting at the wrong place. When I told them I wanted to go to the top of the Peak, they said they were also headed for the same place and would be delighted to accompany me. Not only so but they insisted on paying my fare for the two stages of the journey, the final part being the steep funicular. When I protested at their generosity, they said, "Oh, it's O.K., you can buy us an ice cream cone when we reach the top?" They were a delightful pair: Roy Chen and Anna May Wong. I took a careful photo-slide picture of them on the top-most point of the Peak overlooking the immense buildings of Hong Kong.

Before leaving this great city I made a visit to the famous Tiger Balm Temple and bought a tin of its magic ointment. The sign on the tin's cover claims that the ointment can cure everything. On the reverse side it warns 'Don't apply it to the eyes'!

Another trip I made was by night to see the notorious Suzy Wong Theatre in sleazy Wanchai. I failed to find it. When I told Sally Yao she smiled and said the building had been demolished some time ago because of its bad reputation.

I should mention ere I leave the subjects of Hong Kong and Sally that she taught me some useful words and terms of Cantonese which would come in handy in, especially, southern China. For example:

Nee Hao?	=	How d'ye Do?
Ch'ing	=	Please
Wo ch'ing wu hsiang	=	Pleased to meet you
Hao	=	Good
Chieh kuan	=	Excuse me
To hsieh	=	Many thanks

and most important:

To shao?	=	How much! (What does it cost?
Si-chien	=	Goodbye, for now

and if wanting companionship this phrase might be useful:

Wo-iko-jen	=	I am alone

and if very bold with ladies and girls:

Wo-ai-nee	=	I love you!"

After three days in Hong Kong we left by ferry-boat via Soochow for Canton (now called Guangdon). This is a very large city, the biggest port in south China, of several million people. And it seemed that every one over 5 years of age rode a bicycle for pleasure or transporting the heaviest loads imaginable. After three days there we moved north by aeroplane to the wonderful city of Guilin.

Guilin is a township of incredible beauty. Something out of this world! A place that might have been invented by Walt Disney in his most inspired mood; certainly the most picturesque place I have ever seen!

It is surrounded and interwoven by small pyramid-shaped mountains and hills around which winds the beautiful Liang river.

Guilin also has tremendous caves all of which merit prolonged visits! It was in this beautiful city that I met a delightful Chinese man with whom I still correspond, even after thirteen years! He was the chief guide for our party while we stayed in that area. I evolved a special relationship with him in the space of a very few days. Fortunately he spoke excellent English. His name is Wang-Guo-Hui. He was very skinny with a long bony face but always with an engaging kindly smile. We soon discovered that we had a mutual love for poetry. His favourite British poet was Robert Burns and his favourite poem was *My Love Is Like A Red, Red Rose*. I had developed a strong liking for Chinese poetry over a long period (in English translation, of course). While working as a commis-waiter at the Café Royal in 1935, (aged 20) I joined the Middlesex Library in Orange Street, just off Leicester Square. In precious leisure time (two hours off between 2 and 4p.m.) I would read voraciously in the tiny park there. I began to read Chinese poetry in translations by Arthur Waley and R. Payne. One poem that I found most fascinating and committed to memory was a little ditty which a commentator traced back to 200 B.C. It is obviously an anti-war poem and runs:

"The beans and the peas were together in the pot
With a view to a nice meal of porridge, all hot
The stalks, in the fire: a fierce heat were begetting
So the beans and the peas start fuming and fretting
Now the stalks and the beans/peas were not meant to be foes,
So why should these try to finish off those?!"

I was very proud to recite these lines to Wang and I was pleased to see that he was expressing his delight in recognising them by laughing loudly.

"Yes," he agreed, "this is a famous and very ancient Chinese poem, and as you say, it is meant to condemn War!"

"I would very much like to have these lines translated - say - into Cantonese so that I could show off by reciting them to my British relatives and friends when I get back home. Can you do it for me...?" I asked him.

At first he laughed then he frowned, "Oh," he said, "It will be rather difficult, for first I will have to put it in Mandarin, then into Cantonese, then into phonetics so that you will be able to pronounce the words fairly clearly. I'll see what I can do with the help of some clever student friends."

I apologised and told Wang to forget it and I dropped the idea.

One afternoon Wang surprised me by asking "Do you like cinema? And do you like Chinese films?"

I answered that I was certain about the first part of his question but had little or no experience of the latter.

"Well," said Wang, "tonight there is a very good film showing at our local cinema. We recommend it highly. I wonder would you and some of your party friends like to see it if I provide interpreters?"

"I'll ask around at dinner-time," I promised.

"Please let me know the numbers," Wang said, "for all seats have to be booked in advance."

It transpired that thirteen of us decided to go. I was greatly amused to find later that night when the film show was over that twelve of our party were asked to go upstairs with only ONE interpreter (with hilarious results), whereas I had Wang and two friends, presumably two extra interpreters, sitting behind me. It was a long film with much action about "baddies" and "goodies", and with one handsome "goody" getting the lovely girl! As we were leaving with the cinema lights up, Wang re-introduced me to his two friends and said proudly, "We have translated your poem!"

With an embarrassed air I asked, "When?"

Wang said, "Now!"

I enquired, in some mystification, "Do you mean during the film?"

"Yes."

"Oh!" I complained. "It must have spoiled the film for you surely!"

They all laughed loudly and Wang explained, "Oh, it doesn't matter, we have seen that film many times!"

After thanking them profusely, I hurried to my hotel room to read the Cantonese version of the poem rendered in phonetics, thus:

> Zhu dou jan doe ji
> Dou zhai fou zhang li;
> Ben shi tong gjan sjeng
> Zhiang jian ni tai ji.   (etc.)

I have the Mandarin version as well but, of course, cannot print it here.

The friendship between Wang and myself grew so rapidly and intensely that we vowed to keep contact. And thirteen years later so it is. We exchange Christmas cards and even birthday cards! When I arrived home I started sending Wang poetry books. By leaving the ends of the book packages open for inspection by suspicious customs officers, they would go very cheaply. To reciprocate Wang has sent me some of his exquisite paintings. He is something of a polymath: artist, printer, musician, poet, interpreter, etc. Wang moved to Australia in 1986, at the beginning he had a very promising post with the Chinese Embassy at Sydney. But then, for reasons obscure to me, he branched out in Brisbane as a freelance printer; he also told me he had just got married. Alas, in 1990, he gave me bad news: his printing business had failed; likewise his marriage! He then moved to the awesomely named Fortitude Valley (!). In 1993 he moved again to Kedron, Queensland. Naturally, I sincerely hope that he will thrive and prosper.

I revert to my tour of China and recount further interesting experiences. After Guilin, we flew north to Shanghai and toured a lot of other old and interesting smaller cities, in relatively easy reach of that great megapolis. By the way: in 1981 Shanghai already had over 12 million people and about 5 million bicycles. Before recounting my "friendship-making" there, I ought to mention briefly a trip to Soochow (otherwise known as Wuhsien) which was the ancient head-city of China's Great Canal: probably the first and greatest before the 19th century and featured especially in Marco Polo's travel records as far back as 1265 AD. By contrast with the friendship I enjoyed in every other part of China, here in Soochow I suffered the first sign of hostility. Strangely, this was displayed by a small group of young children who tried to pick my pockets. They were driven off by our guide who dismissed them angrily as "outcasts!"

From Shanghai we also did a long trip up-river to the splendid city of Nanking where we saw the magnificent bridge built in record time by the Chinese after the Russian engineers abandoned it following the rift in Sino-Soviet relations (including bitter border fighting in 1975). From this bridge also, we were shown the place where H.M.S. Amethyst was pounded by Communist heavy guns (1949) wherein the British fought their last battle in China. At Nanking also, we were very impressed in viewing the beautiful memorial building to Dr Sun-Yat-Sen, the founder of modern Republican China (1911).

Meanwhile, in our Nanking hotel I got very friendly with a charming young Chinese girl who waited on tables, but I soon discovered she was a very intelligent and cultured student who spoke excellent English. She also had a delightful sense of humour. Before we left Nanking I gave her a useful little book on English Literature.

Returning to Shanghai, en route we paid a visit to a large Commune. We were greeted by the leader who insisted that we take tea with him, and "some comrades" before "doing the rounds". This was really my first serious experience of taking tea in the strict Chinese manner. Ever an eager beaver I was soon in difficulties swallowing the brew (which looked like a lot of thick parsley in the hot water!). I had not given it enough time to mash and nearly choked as I struggled with the thick green herbs!

Within the city of Shanghai itself I had several experiences of "friendship", some comic, even hilarious. I will expatiate on two or three of these, the first was in an ideal location in this context, namely The Shanghai Friendship Store. The one I refer to was on the Bund waterfront.

I went in one evening with a view to buying some gifts for taking home. For example: a traditional China (porcelain) set, - a small bowl, spoon and chopsticks. However, as soon as I stepped inside I was surrounded by a host of young people. I had found that on average one in four or five could speak English. I was wearing a favourite seaman's cap and one of the young, friendly, youths asked, "What are you, sir?"

In a foolishly flippant mood, I answered, "Oh... a sea-captain."

"Where is your ship, sir?"

I pointed vaguely down stream. Some of the eager youths craned a neck to look out. So I quickly improvised, "Oh... a long way down the river... (and I should have made clear before now - the Yangste)".

"What sort of a ship?" they persisted.

"Oh, an oil tanker," I lied.

I was so pressed in conversation thereafter that I never got to the shop counter where a pretty little girl was waiting to serve me.

Early the next day, determined to get my gifts, I returned to the same Friendship Store. It was empty so I walked up to the (same) girl on duty. I peered at the display of goods behind her and started asking about quality and prices ("*To shao*; *Chia-chien*?", etc.) However, she spoke perfect English and after a little while, looking at me very intently, she asked me: "What are you sir,... what is your profession?"

Without any hesitation I replied, "I am a teacher... Well, I mean a retired lecturer."

She gave me a rather stern look and with the hint of a sneer in her soft voice she said, "Oh! I don't know how I can believe you, for last evening you told everybody present that you are a SEA CAPTAIN!"

Suddenly I felt dreadfully ashamed of myself. I realised that one should not try to fool intelligent people who have over 6,000 years of civilization behind them and an immense cultural heritage! I apologised to the lovely young girl for my utter foolishness and before I quit the store I took some relevant cards from my wallet to verify that I had been an academic. And I bought more goods from her than originally intended.

Another encounter in the context of making friends in China was in glaring contrast. This was also in Shanghai:

A visit to a major museum had been arranged. I always tire quickly in such places. This was no exception. After half an hour I wandered into the nearby park and sat on a long bench. I placed a Pan-Am travelling bag at my side. Soon a young Chinese fellow came by. I noticed that he looked like Wang-Guo-Hui (tall, skinny, bony-faced but with a ready smile). His demeanour seemed so friendly and benign that I called out "*Ni-Hao!*".

"Ah!" he responded with a broad grin, "*To-hsieh*: *Ni-Hao, Ni-Hao*... May I sit here also?"

"Of course," I agreed.

He looked at my travelling bag. "Are you an American?" he asked with much enthusiasm.

"No, British," I confessed apologetically, "but I can speak American," I hurried to console him. We both enjoyed my joke.

"I wonder can you help me to translate some parts of my magazine?" he asked. And he proffered a large white brochure, obviously well produced. On close inspection of the cover I was impressed by its title. It read: FOR SINO-AMERICAN CULTURAL EXCHANGE.

"This is an impressive title!" I said. "Where did you get it?"

"My Aunt sent it to me... She lives in New Jersey, U.S.A."

I turned to the title page and had to laugh when I read 'Hollywood Songs of the Thirties' (the 1930's). (Some CULTURAL EXCHANGE! I had to wonder what the "Yanks" were getting in return?). As I laughed the young man giggled, and as I read the song titles he asked, "Do you know any of them?"

I replied, "Oh, yes, all of them." As I flicked over each page I had to notice that in all the right-hand margins the young man, or an alter-ego, had scribbled Chinese/Mandarin characters which I presumed to be translations of the songs.

"But it seems to me that you have translated all of the songs!?"

"Oh, no," he protested, "not all. For example, I cannot understand the meaning of the one on page 17!"

I turned to that page and couldn't help bursting out with loud laughter. The title was *Toot, Toot, Tootsie, Goodbye.*

"You know it?" he asked with great expectations.

"Oh, yes!" I enthused. "It was always one of my firm favourites."

"But... What does it mean?" he begged.

"Oh, well now..." I improvised. "It is about a man named Al Jolson. He is leaving his home-town and his sweetheart. He tells her that he has to travel around for some time. But he promises faithfully that he will write to her everyday. He urges her to "Watch for the mail", i.e. to look out for his letters, and he cautions her, "If you don't get my letter, then you'll know I'm in jail."

"In jail?" repeated the earnest young man. "What is JAIL?"

I answered, "PRISON!"

He looked terribly cast down and commented in the most mournful tone imaginable, "OH, I thought it was a very happy song. But now you make me VERY SAD!"

I almost detected tears in his eyes. For my part I didn't know whether to laugh or to cry!

I must now record that in Shanghai our tourist party was made very comfortable in the luxurious Jing-Jang Hotel. A steward on the 4th floor where I shared a large room with one Albert Jenks from Lancashire proudly told me that President Nixon (U.S.A.) had stayed in the hotel a few years before. So I was quick to advise and warn, "I hope his rooms have been well fumigated in the event that I shall have to use any of them!"

But to be serious! I have to report a very strange occurrence that involved me on the very first night we stayed in the Jing-Jang Hotel. I said I was sharing a large room with Albert Jenks. After about fifteen minutes of desultory conversation we agreed to dim the lights preparatory to settling down to sleep. Within five minutes there was a nervous, but persistent, knocking on the door. I opened it to find an hotel steward with an unusually tall and broad Chinese gentleman. He was dressed immaculately in a splendid grey suit. Speaking good English he said he was looking for a Doctor Kissinger (I hasten to add no relation to the U.S. Politician). I had already made friends with the Doctor and had gleaned that he had practised medicine over many, many years in South Africa. He also confided that he had left that troubled area because he could no longer tolerate the Apartheid system. This interrupted night I had in fact bade him *au revoir* on the floor below, immediately underneath my room. I grabbed a dressing gown and offered to check out the veracity of my hunch. It was correct; we located Dr Kissinger.

Next morning at breakfast I asked the Doctor if his meeting with the impressive-looking Chinese gentleman had gone well.

"Oh, yes, very well indeed! He is Dr Chen-Tsung-Wei of Shanghai Hospital No 6, and he has invited me to see him operate today."

I expressed some curiosity. Kissinger said with great enthusiasm, "Do you know that Dr Chen is an acknowledged expert on amputations; I mean restoring amputated limbs so that they can function again?" Although rather ignorant in medical matters I expressed my keen interest. Dr Kissinger waxed eloquent on another aspect of Dr Chen's greatness.

"You see I had already written to him for the favour of some data and the possibility of an interview, for I too am working in the same field and I am trying to learn and to improve this intricate technique. I was highly honoured last night for, instead of sending a messenger, the great Doctor, a wonderful surgeon, came himself to welcome me to Shanghai and to see him operate tomorrow. The Chinese never fail to fill me with awe and respect. Oh, and incidentally, Dr Chen particularly wants me to thank you, on his behalf, for helping to locate me so late in the night!"

This strange, even bizarre, event was verified for me when some little time after returning home I read in chapter 5, page 80, of Alain Peyrefitte's impressive book *The Chinese*, that many facts are recorded of Dr Chen.

After four days in Shanghai we boarded a train for Peking (Beijing). This was an eighteen hour journey northwards but we were very comfortable in our "soft-class". After about four hours of the passage one of our party came to my sleeping berth and begged me to help make a foursome in a game of Bridge. I conceded that I knew how to play but I stressed that I prefer that he would find another, for I had learned that there is an element of sadism in it. After fifteen minutes or so this Bridge fanatic returned saying he could find no one else and urged me to join his little group. He also offered the bribe of a large bottle of *Mo-Tai* (Chinese brandy or is it whisky?) for the winners.

I found to my surprise and pleasure, that my partner in the game was Dr Kissinger. I knew that in the event of my mistakes he would never grumble or bully. However, I soon found that Atkins, the fanatical originator of our game, was not only a very reckless bidder, but, true to the type, was ever ready to blame his very young and frightened wife who was his partner. At last, I could not stand this any more, and shouted, "Atkins! If you continue to blame and bully your quiet wife, I'll quit!"

His spouse smiled in gratitude and whispered, "Oh, many thanks. You're a real friend!"

Dr Kissinger winked at me approvingly and we continued to slaughter our very amateur opponents. At last Atkins surrendered and gave the bottle of *Mo-Tai* to Kissinger. The good Doctor handed it to me saying, "I never touch the stuff!" and with another wink to me he added, "Neither does Dr Chen who always needs a steady hand!"

We were in Peking for four days and saw the favourite sights, especially the vast and splendid Forbidden City. With a natural, somewhat morbid, human curiosity we wanted to see the Mausoleum of Mao-Tse-Tung and his preserved body. Incidentally, I had seen Lenin's and swore it was a wax model! The Mausoleum was a special feature of our itinerary, however, the visit was cancelled at the last minute and the rumour was whispered around our party that "the corpse of dear old Mao had collapsed!" We were then offered a hurried *ad hoc* substitute visit, to witness the lying-in-state of Madame Sun-Yat-Sen (aged widow of the founder of the Republic of China). In fact, we were taken to the head of the long and solemn queue in the Great Hall of the People.

On the penultimate day of our tour we made a visit to that ancient and long-term marvel - the Great Wall of China and we were truly very impressed! And my very last photo-slide shows me fraternising with a young, good-looking soldier of the Liberation Army on the wall.

I find, in retrospect, that I have several photos of Tien-an-Men Square, little realising in early June 1981 that, eight years later, it would become the dread place of that horrible massacre.

But I propose to end this story on a pleasanter note.

For example: my photos of Roy Chen and Anna Wong came out very well and I was able to send them copies for which they were "very grateful".

I still correspond with Wang Guo Hui, even after 13 years and I hope to continue for some time yet!

In summary: I can find no more fitting epilogue than to quote from China's ancient and greatest sage Kung-Fu-Tse, alias Confucius:

"The essence of true friendship is RECIPROCITY,"
Do unto others as you would have them do unto you.

(This was good for 500 B.C. It is still good for today!).

I feel I must add a few lines culled from China's greatest Poet Li Po, (700-762 A.D). These were sent to me for my birthday by Wang-Guo-Hui:

SAYING FAREWELL TO A FRIEND

The green mountain lies beyond the city wall:
Where the clear white water winds in the east.
Here we must part!
A solitary sail will try a flight of a thousand li,
The flowing clouds are the dreams of a roving man.
The setting sun: the affection of an old friend.
So: you go - waving your hands.
Please come back again !

SOME STRANGE ADVENTURES IN MEXICO

On a Friday in mid-September, 1985 I booked for a mini-tour of Mexico. When I got home my wife with a very anxious look, asked me, "Did you book for the tour?"

"Yes," I answered.

She said, "You CAN'T GO!"

I said, rather angrily: "Why ever NOT!?"

"Haven't you heard the news? There's been a terrible earthquake in Mexico City - today!"

I looked sternly at her, "Are you pulling my leg?"

My wife was equally stern, even sombre: "NO! The news has just come through, terrible devastation! thousands feared dead! You can hardly go now!"

The six o'clock news revealed the bitter truth of my wife's sad report. That evening, by coincidence, I was due to attend an important meeting of U.N.I.C.E.F. in Neath. The meeting was an inaugural one for the purpose of creating a West Glamorgan Regional Branch. The Chairman for the evening was to be the famous Lord Tonypandy, until recently Speaker of the House of Commons. The Guest Speaker was announced as a Lady leader of U.N.I.C.E.F., U.K. coming down from London. Her main subject was to be: "The Progress of the Campaign for Massive Aid to Ethiopia". (I should explain that I have been a very active worker for UNICEF ever since its inception so I felt it a bounden duty to attend this meeting.)

I waited for Lady Guest Speaker to finish her address and, during the interval, I told her about my booking the Mexican Tour. I added, "You have probably heard about the terrible earthquake and the devastation of Mexico City?"

"Will you go nevertheless?" she asked.

"Naturally, I'm not so sure now!" I replied.

"When are you due to go?"

"Early in December."

"Oh," the Lady opined, "then yes, you should go. Furthermore you might act as a kind of emissary for U.N.I.C.E.F. and try to make contact with the Lady in charge of our Movement in Mexico. I have met her. She is very able, dedicated and charming and I feel sure (if she is still alive and well) that she will give you a warm welcome.

She will also, no doubt, give you a first hand appraisal of what will be needed to help the poor children of Mexico City."

When I got home I told my wife that I was determined to go to Mexico. I felt I now had a sense of Mission in the trip! I had asked my wife early on if she wanted to join me on the tour. Characteristically she said that these long trips "to far-away, exotic places were too risky." Before my departure she tried once again to persuade me to call it off for she had met a woman who had told her that a cousin had been murdered in Mexico City recently. But I was adamant, as usual, in my determination to go. Seeing I was firm in my resolve my wife, also characteristically, helped me to pack and was meticulous in doing so. She also reminded me that I disliked highly spiced food and that Mexico was famous for this. I then suggested to her that I could take some English food to last me, if only for a few days, until I got acclimatised to a new regime in diet, etc. So, as ever with her customary care and diligence, my wife provided me with some very small tins of corned beef, some sandwiches of ham, and twenty thin, cooked sausages!

At London Airport, ready for the take-off for Mexico City (the sole passenger destined for that stricken city), I was advised that I would have to change at Houston, U.S.A., but that my baggage would clear customs there without trouble (i.e. no examination). Alas, I was deluded! At Houston, Texas, whereas my main suitcase was cleared without trouble, the small black bag I always carried for emergencies on foreign travel was pounced on by a huge negress in airport uniform.

"What have we here?" she demanded as she rifled busily in my bag.

Before I could answer she held up, for close inspection, my sandwiches, and my "beloved sausages".

"These go straight into our fumigator!" she bawled.

I was naturally incensed. "Hold on a minute there! I am going on to Mexico City directly and this food will be my safe diet for several days."

She bellowed, "NO WAY! This stuff is damned dangerous! It goes straight in our trash bin!"

"What the HELL are you doing?" I yelled. "I am going to MEXICO! I am not staying in Texas, least of all in your GOD-DAMNED DUMP of HOUSTON!"

190

It was no use. My protests were in vain. The negress confiscated my food (apart from my tinned stuff) and I was raving bloody mad!

To add insult to injury, I was delayed over three hours in Houston by poor flight connection and I did not arrive in my hotel in Mexico City until well after midnight!

My courier, however, had waited for me. He explained that as I was the only tourist he would be my driver and guide while in the city. He introduced himself as Leo. Leo was a large man, not very ethnic in the Mexique manner. He had a huge, beefy face with a wicked smile. In fact, he reminded me of the famous film actor, Wallace Beery, who, incidentally, had played many Mexican character parts (including Pancho Villa). Like Beery, Leo had a sinister smile and a rumbustious laugh but with a chilling ring to it also. I felt immediately that I would have to be on my guard with Leo; my hunch was well founded!

On the first day out with me as his sole passenger, Leo showed me some of the basic sights of Mexico City and he was a good and interesting guide. But on concluding our trip, he confided, "Alas! my good friend, my car battery has conked out. I don't have the money for re-charging or replacement until I get paid which is at the end of the week and I may not be able to escort you for a couple of days. So, can you lend me X thousand pesos? (The sum he asked for amounted to about £15). Reluctantly I gave him the money but thought, "I'll have to watch this BUGGER!"

As it happened I had already told Leo that I had to visit UNICEF House next day. I had made a preliminary phone call and had been given directions as to its location. It is located on the Avenida Presidente Masaryk, which runs off on the right hand side of the main Avenida Reforma. Incidentally, my Hotel was also on the Avenida Reforma (opposite the large Columbus statue). This Avenue is regarded as one of the main thoroughfares of Mexico and is reputed to run for fifteen miles to the north. I discovered by map and advice, that I could walk to my goal. I found it with little difficulty.

I was greeted with great enthusiasm by the Lady Director. She was a Yugoslav named Vesna Bosnjiak. She made me feel very important by telling me that I was the first Britisher to appear there after the earthquake. I affected to be more important than I really was by asking her how UNICEF could best help the suffering children of Mexico City. After a long, animated discussion Madame Bosnjiak inflated my new sense of importance by telling me that she was arranging for a chauffeured limousine to escort me around Mexico City so that I could see the worst areas of earthquake devastation for myself. As we drove around I was struck by the strange aberrations in the geological effects. Some buildings were utterly flattened. Others, which had apparently stood "next door", were still standing upright. For example: the hotel in which I was lodged on the 12th floor, was absolutely intact and a mere twenty yards away from a mass of rubble which, I was told, had been a handsome theatre or cinema! I know little or nothing about civil engineering so I cannot give any scientific reason for these contrasts other than the guess that some edifices were solidly built, others "jerry"-built.

One of the very large structures that had been destroyed was pointed to by my chauffeur as of major interest and drawn to my attention for it had received T.V. coverage every day and night worldwide. For it was the maternity hospital where many scores of post-natal mothers had died but where scores of tiny babies had been "miraculously" saved!

The T.V. international exposure had shown us, very dramatically over many days, the frantic scrambling over and even under, the broken piles of concrete slabs. Among the rescuers we saw the famous Spanish-American singer, Placido Domingo, who apparently had relatives buried in the ruins.

Later, my chauffeur took me to a working-class district ("very poor," he said) and terribly destroyed by the disaster. (In parenthesis I feel bound to pose the pregnant question: Why in such calamities is it always the proletarian areas that suffer most? Does it necessarily imply that the houses in these areas are more shoddily built? I am also reminded of the story that was much repeated during World War II in the U.K. A bomb fell in the yard of Buckingham Palace. The King and Queen decided to visit the badly blitzed areas of the East-end of London the same day. Consoling the homeless cockney folk the gracious Queen said, "Our house has been bombed too, you know!" Several people are supposed to have then chorused: "Oh! Which one of your houses, your Majesty?".

In this same devastated area I was taken to the edge of a huge camping site where, I was informed, many thousands of homeless people were now in temporary accommodation. My informant advised me that they would remain there, suffering impure water and awful sanitation, until new houses could be built for them. "This might well take a very long time!"

After many hours of riding around to observe the terrible effects of the earthquake I was driven back to Avenida Masaryk where I had another serious conversation with Madame Bosnjiak. I told her sincerely how moved I was by my harrowing experience and I promised that on return to the U.K. I would do everything in my power to publicise the plight of the stricken Mexicans, especially the poor children and do my very best to raise funds through UNICEF for amelioration.

Madame Bosnjiak then surprised me by giving me two packages. One, she told me, contained a long video giving a vivid record of the earthquake, the other was a hundred page report on the disaster. (Alas, on checking both at home some weeks later I found that the video was made by an American technique not found in Britain, and the report was in Spanish. I passed the video to "experts" and got the report translated by an unemployed student, which cost me £40).

On my third day in Mexico City I met the roguish Leo again and, at his suggestion, spent the early morning at a supermarket where he showed me how to get bargains in gifts and souvenirs. Among other things, I got a lovely colourful poncho and a fine large sombrero. Later we paid a visit to the wonderful Archaeological Museum on the edge of Mexico City. I marvelled at the endless and splendid "strata" of Mexican civilizations, from Mayan to Olmec, through Tolmec, Tetechacuan to Aztec, which last was swamped by the Spanish Conquistadores.

Another day, we drove to the southern end of the City where I observed, among other memorable sights, the impressive memorial to Benito Juarez, the saviour of the Mexican Nation. Later I visited the opulent Cathedral and finished the day at the great Royal Palace. The most compelling sight at the Palace over which I lingered long, are the magnificent murals of Diego Rivera. They seem to encircle the entire area of the external walls of the Palace and trace, in great detail and life-size, the entire history of Mexican civilization from ancient Mayan times to the present day. I was so impressed by this gigantic and beautiful work of art that I bought a very expensive album representing it.

Another day Leo, who proved to be a very fine guide (despite his sinister demeanour) took me to see the wonderful Canal of Flowers at Xocimilco (pronounced Shochee-milko). The flowers were very abundant and blazing in their glory. I took some very good picture-slides of this visit (and find it diary-recorded on December 10th). I have a very fine photo of Leo and myself (in a hired, fantastic sombrero) in a gondola with sunshade - the boat was named "Rosita".

The biggest trip in distance and importance with Leo, however, was to the Pyramids, about twenty five to thirty miles out of the city. On the way we called at Mexico University, reputed to have the biggest student population in the World and with some striking buildings with gorgeous murals painted by disciples of Diego Rivera. On the journey to the Pyramids later, we picked up another passenger. He was from San Antonio in Texas and he told me he was making a sentimental pilgrimage to his ancestors birth-place. He was enormously fat, very slow talking and, as I found to my cost, slow moving. We now began to observe in the distance the two Pyramids. One is called the Pyramid of the Sun, the other called the Moon. Leo stopped the car about half a mile before reaching the Pyramids saying that the best approach for a spectacular view was to walk the rest of the way and said he would meet us on the other side of the ancient erections. (It was possible, I thought later, that Leo was too tired or lazy to walk with us!) His leaving us to our own devices caused me to be involved in a rather bad encounter!

After plodding for some distance in the hot sun with my companion stopping too often to examine different things, I suddenly found myself alone at the base of the Pyramid of the Sun. There were no other tourists but suddenly I was accosted by four sinister looking men.

They were about 20 years of age, rough and very unkempt, dirty and withal, to my frightened eyes, menacing. (I couldn't help thinking back to my wife's warning about a murder in Mexico City!). These ugly looking men seemed bent on harassing me. They started bargaining in pidgin English. They were trying to sell me awful junk. When I pleaded lack of money they began man-handling my shoulder bag and trying to pull my camera from my hand. I found it very expedient to hurry away. They followed me, trying to intimidate me into a very poor exchange. Feeling increasingly scared, I hurried frantically to the top of the Pyramid, arriving sweaty and breathless!

Feeling more secure now I looked down to see the four men trying on the same tactics with my fat companion. I wondered if I dare go down to help him but I was genuinely scared. I was greatly relieved when I saw him climb up to join me without being followed. I was then calm enough to take some photo-slides of both Pyramids. In retrospect, I am glad to record that this incident was the only scary one I suffered throughout my tour of Mexico.

That night Leo reminded me that we would be ending our association and a minibus would be at the hotel front early in the morning to take me on the next stage of the tour. As I shook hands with Leo and bade him "Adios", he held my hand a long time and at last asked me for a tip. I was quick to remind him that he still owed me £15. He argued as long as I allowed him and then I warned him strongly that if he still expected a tip without repaying my loan I would report him to my National Travel World agent and ABTA, and get him blacklisted. He scowled but remained silent.

About twelve of us in a comfortable minibus with a voluble young courier now set out for the next stage of my journey which would take us through the high sierras and, incidentally, to the towns of Guernavaca and Taxco among others. The courier was a real Radical in the Mexique manner for, while he was adamant in drawing our attention to the many slum areas on the way, he was also eloquent in contrasting the palatial mansions of the rich, adding, "These are where the ex-Presidents live!"

The scenery became steadily more spectacular as we journeyed onward. Our minibus was eventually travelling at a height of over 11,000 feet and we caught many glimpses of Popocatapetl, the volcanic summit rising to over 20,000 feet! We then spent two or three days at Guernavaca, visiting its imposing Cathedral as well as a palace dating from Conquistador times (circa 1520-50). In the main square we saw a fine equestrian statue of Emelyan Zapata, one of the outstanding heroes of the Revolution (1910).

After Guernavaca, we moved on to even higher land and reached the very picturesque town of Taxco (pronounced Tash-co). Taxco is the main centre of the silver mining industry. Actually by now, I had lost most of the other travellers and I was accommodated alone at a delightful old Ranchero-style inn, this in a mountainous area with a lovely view. One day I ventured to a silver-smith's store to look at some possible silver presents (at bargain prices of course). Apart from my purchase of one cheap bracelet I was given (gratis) some silver coins and many pieces of silver pyrites which seemed to be very plentiful.

During a long walk to my hotel, feeling thirsty, I called at a wayside cafe or inn. There was only one other person as a customer. He was a handsome and very well dressed man. As I sat near him he greeted me with a friendly salutation. We soon got into a very animated conversation. He asked about my family I told him about my wife, daughter and son living and working in Canada and of his frequent trips to the U.S.A. When I reciprocated his friendly interest asking about his family, he looked stern and grew quite sombre, and told me a very sad, if not horrendous, story. He said that he had owned a very thriving business in Colombia. This was a large store, he explained. One day when his only son, aged 25, was in charge of the store a number of bandits entered the store to rob goods and money. "My son, naturally, tried to stop them and the bandits shot him dead."

My informant gulped hard with emotion, I could hear the sob in his voice. I said nothing for I felt that he had more to say. I was correct. After a long pause he continued (but obviously struggling to keep calm). "My poor wife was so terribly shocked by our son's sudden and untimely death that she also died only a few days later, seemingly from awful grief."

After a long silence I asked, "How long ago did the tragedies occur?"

"Quite recently," the sad man replied, "and - alas - I can no longer find rest or peace in my home, or town ... certainly not in my store which. I have closed. So ... I am going far away to try to find solace elsewhere."

"Are you going to Acapulco, as I am?" I enquired tentatively.

"Oh, no Senōr," he answered. "I am going the opposite way to you. I leave for Mexico City tomorrow. Later I will take a plane to Europe. My ultimate destination is Madrid, the home-town of my ancestors, and I still have relatives there."

I mumbled some platitudes of sympathy and *bon voyage* but realised that any words I could muster would be totally inadequate!

Two days later I was up very early boarding a new minibus with new travelling companions. After going through many scenically beautiful mountain passes, we made the long descent south-west to Acapulco on the Pacific coast. I was booked into the huge Grand Plaza Hotel. I soon found it much too big for me, far too commercialized and far too noisy. It seemed that all the time I was there a large band on the first floor was playing loud pop music which seemed to be relayed to every floor (I was on the 12th) night and day! I also found to my cost that I was only allowed one free meal a day and hotel food was very expensive. Always enterprising in tight financial situations I soon decided to dine out when necessary. I found within a couple of hundred yards many shops and modest cafes. I could get a delicious Lobster Thermidor locally for a fraction of the hotel price. I was also able to buy good food in plentiful nearby shops cheaply, and easily "smuggle" it into my room.

Around the base of this huge hotel, almost encircling it like a snake, were many lovely swimming pools, shallow enough for me to take a dip without danger (for I am an indifferent swimmer). There were not many people in the pools for, no doubt, the recent Mexican earthquakes had scared tourists off. However, one pleasant couple I made friends with were from Canada. The husband (if so he was?) was a very handsome, dark Latin type but the "wife" was exceedingly blonde. When I had the temerity to ask her if she was a native of Canada she readily answered, "No, I was born in Lithuania." And she went on to tell me a rather dramatic story with sad undertones. She confided that after 22 years that her parents had enjoyed in freedom (1918-1940 circa) the Russians returned to re-conquer Lithuania and because her father had reason to be very fearful of this, the family, with her as a young child, had to hide in a forest for many weeks until they were able to escape and eventually migrate to Canada.

On the morning of my last day in Acapulco, I began to have an uneasy feeling that my travel agent in South Wales had given me the wrong time for departure from Acapulco to the U.K., via the U.S.A. I enquired at the reception desk at the hotel, and was told, "You must see our main hostess. She is Jacqueline Evans and she knows EVERYTHING!"

I found Miss Evans to be a large blonde woman of 50 to 55 years, exceptionally bright and cheerful with obvious *bon hommie*.

"How pleasant to hear an English accent after many many months," she said.

"Well, Welsh actually," I corrected.

"Oh," she beamed, "all the better! My Father, Dai Evans, was Welsh though I was born in Surrey."

After Miss Evans had confirmed my time of departure which was two hours earlier than I had been told, I asked her, "How long have you been living here in Acapulco?"

She said, "Oh, only three years though I have been in America a long time, mainly California."

"Oh, where in California?"

"Most of the time in Hollywood."

An incorrigible film buff, I exclaimed, "Hollywood! How exciting! You must have seen a few film stars in your time there!?"

"Oh many; not only seen but mingled with."

"Really!" I nearly shouted with a hint of incredulity.

"Oh, I can see you don't believe me. Tell you what, while I dash to my room for something, please order a gin and tonic for me and anything you may like for yourself, tell the steward to charge it to my account, and before you can say Kirk Douglas I'll be back to show you something."

When she returned she was carrying two large albums. They contained, as I soon discovered, scores if not hundreds of photos of the most famous Hollywood stars of the period 1940-1985. The crucial point that Miss Evans wanted to emphasise was the big number of photos which showed her standing or sitting cheek by jowl with the most famous of those, i.e. "house-hold" names: Bette Davis, Crawford, Rogers among the ladies; and James Stewart, Wayne, Douglas, Lancaster, etc. And many of her with Katy Durado and Anthony Quinn (and she reminded me that the latter two are of Mexican origin).

"Were you ever in films yourself?" I tentatively asked.

With pleasant modesty, she replied, "Oh, only in walking-on parts, hardly better than an extra, you'd hardly notice me!"

She later paid me a compliment. She showed me a picture of a broad-faced, moustachioed man and asked me to identify him. I said, "I'm not quite sure but he looks a bit like Omar Sharif!?"

"Many people have said the same thing," she answered, "but that is not correct. You can be forgiven for not knowing this one, you have probably not even heard of him. He is Sergei Bondortchuk."

"On the contrary," I boasted, "he made the epic nine hour film of Tolstoy's War and Peace, and he - himself - played Pierre Bezukhov."

"Wonderful!" Miss Evans enthused. "You are the first ever to answer with all the details correctly!"

We had a very pleasant hour together and as I moved to leave she said, "Lovely to meet you and to have such a lively conversation on a topic of mutual interest. Don't forget me, and any time you are in Acapulco, DO look me up." She then gave me her card which reads:

Jacqueline Evans;
Presidente: La Torre De Papel; S.A.:
Periodicos De Los Estados.
Filomeno Mata 6-A, 06000,
Mexico. D.F.

Two hours later I was at Acapulco Airport but facing an unexpected crisis. As customary in my foreign travels I had got rid of all my "alien" coin and I only had sterling left in my pocket and wallet. When I went around the various exchange desks in the airport I found to my surprise and chagrin that nobody would accept my sterling. "I must tell Mrs Thatcher about this," I thought, but on a deeper level I was getting quite worried. Before I dare board the plane I would have to pay 10 dollars or equivalent in airport tax. Only U.S. dollars or pesos were acceptable. I began to experience a sense of panic when suddenly I seemed to be surrounded by a large body of American tourists obviously preparing to get the same flight as myself. I decided to be bold and loudly vocal. In my best stentorian Public Town-Crier's voice I shouted, "Can one of you Americans please come to my rescue!? I have no dollars nor pesos. I have enough sterling for the airport tax but nobody here will accept it! Can anybody please help me?"

There was a long pause which seemed endless. At last, a tall, rugged man, rather like Walter Matthau, the actor, turned to a middle-aged lady and said, "I say, Mame, you've got a fistful of bucks, can you help this poor Limey in distress?"

She passed him some notes and he handed them to me. I pulled out my wallet to give him the sterling equivalent. "Oh, no thanks," he said, "sterling's no use to me. Consider it a gift."

"NO! NO!" I protested. "I only want a loan. So I must ask you for your address so that I can repay you when I return home."

Reluctantly, he gave me a card which I still have and reads:

Carl T. Russ, Realtor Associate,
416 Englewood Isles Parkway,
Englewood, Florida 33533.

"Oh, by the way," he asked, "what part of U.K. d'ye live in?"

"Swansea, Wales!"

"Oh," he enthused, "I've heard about Wales. Lovely little country they tell me: mountains and sea. Land of Song, etc. How about doing an exchange next year?"

"O.K.," I replied with more politeness than enthusiasm.

"I have a nice house near the sea," he gloated.

"Same here," I said.

"What kind of automobile d'ye have? Mine's a Chevvy." (Alas, I have no car but quoted a rich relative's favourite Volvo, realising that no exchange with Florida was likely!). However, I did return Russ's ten dollars with a lame excuse about the proposed swap of houses.

I arrived back home in Wales a couple of days before Christmas and after a reasonable interval I contacted the new head of U.N.I.C.E.F., U.K., the very able and dedicated Chris Bunting (no baby he!). I told him about my promises of help in Mexico City and begged him to start a big campaign for the relief of the children's suffering there. It took two years to realise but with constant propaganda and persistent pressure by myself and others a sum of £25,000 was sent to Vera Bosnjiak for which I also got a letter of thanks.

GEORGIE GEE, ENTERTAINER

I sometimes think that for the greater part of my long life I have been a Public Entertainer Manque. At age 11 I acted in Shakespearean plays in school-produced drama, despite my tender age, acting Shylock! At a working men's college in North Wales (aged 23) I was cast as Robert de Baudricourt in our production of Shaw's *St Joan*. In 1940 I was asked to play, though young, the old crotchety and intemperate Sir Anthony Absolute in *The Rivals*. So I was able to boast to members of my family, especially my children, that I had played Shakespeare, Sheridan and Shaw, the three great S's of British Drama! However, I had never acted solo (unless one considers teaching at school and college and/or preaching the "Gospel à la St. Marx" as acting) until the ripe old age of 76!

When my wife found out that I was on stage in solo performance at 76 she was shocked and could hardly believe it! My relatives and friends could hardly believe it! What's more even now I can hardly believe it!

It is a strange story, worth telling and, I hope, worth reading.

In 1990, aged 75, I suffered a terrible heart attack. It was touch and go! I lay on my sick bed for many weeks. Recuperation was long, painful and depressing. In fact, I have never truly recovered. But I was determined to try to shake off my lethargy; I have always had a strong will to live. A year passed and one day I saw an advert in our local newspaper, *The South Wales Evening Post*, asking for volunteers to enter the Swansea Senior Citizens Talent Competition to be held at the prestigious Patti Pavilion, Swansea. This pavilion was built with moneys provided by Adelina Patti herself.

Apparently this Talent Competition for "The Oldies" had been running for some years but this was the first time that I was aware of it. I now wondered, "Would I be a devil and enter my name?" The only condition as stated in the advert was that contestants must be 65 plus for the men and 60 plus for women. My biggest problem, however, was to keep the fact of my projected entry secret from my dear wife, for she was only too well aware of the reality of my illness and would have tried hard to stop me entering! Another, and possibly a more cogent, reason for my secrecy was the fact that over many

years I had often given lectures with illustrations to various groups
and my wife had the awkward habit of sitting in the front of my
audience, to gesticulate with a revolving forefinger and whispering,
"Faster! Faster!" So I considered it expedient, if not vital, to keep
my project secret lest my wife come to the show and try to "enhance
my speed"!

So I entered my name for the competition in secret and prepared
for it in secret. The show was to take place in the last week of May
(1991). I decided to try to be original and make my own script and
then to work hard to memorise. Here it is in draft:

"Yes folks: I'm Georgie Gee, I'm 76! But look at me - I'm full
of tricks! No! Confidentially, I need two crutches and two walking
sticks! So you must realise (and I tell no lies) I have to fantasise! In
spite of my old rattling bones I like to imagine that I'm Tom Jones!
Don't laugh at that, it's not so daft. For Tom and I have things in
common... apart from both being chased by women. For example:
we're both Welsh, both from the valleys; we both like to sing and
above all, we both SWEAT like HELL! But, as regards my sweating,
have no fear dear ladies, I won't be asking you to pass up your
scanties or panties, to mop up MY sweating (I think that habit is
AWFUL, don't you? As Iago said when he smelt Desdemona's
hanky: "uch-y-fi... DISGUSTING!"). No, dear ladies, I won't even
expect you to pass me your hankies. No, I find - after much
experience and a lot of experimenting - that I can mop up my sweat
very nicely thank you, with a thick paper pad of several £10 notes,
wrapped inside many, many £20 notes. So, dear Ladies (and Gents if
you will) as soon as you see me sweating, don't hesitate to send up
your £10 and £20 notes! O.K.?"

"One other thing: I must confess that I cannot swing my hips -
sensually or otherwise - as Tom Jones does. The fact is I've recently
had a hip joint operation and without much success. In fact (to
paraphrase Shakespeare again i.e. Hamlet, recall "The time is out of
joint; O' cursed spite; that ever I was born to set it right!"). And I
have to say, "My hip is out of joint, O' cursed spite! The bloody
doctors never set it right!" However, my wife consoles me by
assuring me that there is one part of my body that is still sexy!
Despite those whistles and dirty laughs it isn't THAT! (I now wiggle
my knee vigorously and repeatedly.) "Look at this, ladies: it's my

KNEE!... Doesn't that put all you ladies in a rapture of ecstasy?!
...Well, if I continue this sexy knee movement for much longer I
might end up with a RUPTURE of AGONY!"

"So, enough said. I'll now prefer to sing you a song: one of the
Golden Oldies. As I remember, this pleasant song was first featured
in that musical extravaganza Paul Whiteman's *King of Jazz* way back
in 1930. It was then sung by a young male quartet. One of the
singers became very famous, he was Bing Crosby. Now, I'm giving
you two versions of this song, one clean, one dirty." To the pianist:
"Are you ready, Maestro?"

Herewith the song: *Happy Feet* (lst. Version - Clean)

Happy feet, I've got those happy feet!
Give them the low down beat
And they begin dancing.
I've got those ten hap-happy toes,
And when they hear the beat,
I can't control my dancing feet to save my soul/sole,
Breezy blues: they get inside my shoes,
And then my shoes refuse
To ever grow weary!
I go cheerful on a earful, of music sweet;
'Cos I've got those
Hap- hap- happy feet!

And now folks, I feel bound to give you my dirty version. So I
give fair warning to all canine campaigners and doggy devotees,
depart now if you prefer.

Herewith: *Dirty Feet*!

Dirty feet, I've got those dirty feet:
For I am in the street,
Where poodles been pooping.
I've never found a constipated hound;
For all around the ground,
Dogs dollops are found:
Collies' curds and terriers' turds.
Alsatian asses are dropping mess in masses,
Where a poor pedestrian passes.

I'm harried and harassed,
I go careful, and bewareful and try to tip-toe through;
Still I get that DOG SHIT on my shoe!
OH YES! Still I get that DOG-SHIT ON MY SHOE!"

I decided that if I got a good audience response (dare I predict prolonged applause!?) then I would essay an encore for which I had chosen *Whoopee!* made famous by the goggle-eyed comedian, Eddie Cantor.

So my patter for introduction would be as follows:

"And now, Ladies and Gentlemen, I offer you another song, another Golden Oldie. But this is a quite different kind of song. In fact, it is a rather doleful ditty, a sad saga about marriage à la mode, 1930. In fact, if my memory serves me well, it was first sung and made famous by the goggle-eyed little comedian, Eddie Cantor. Do you remember him? It is rather sad but I hope more comi-tragic than tragi-comic. In any case, please remember: it describes the marital state in the "Bad Old Days" of about 60 years ago - when marriage could be a nasty life sentence! In those days divorces were very rare, about 5,000 a year in U.K. and usually only the rich people indulged! Compare this with the modern trend in Britain of 150,000 a year. Then, average British families had five or six kids. Now the average is two and a half kids. Yes, that's right, two and a half! Makes you think, doesn't it?

In those dark old days, a man could regard his wife as a ball and chain and the wife could regard a demanding husband as a combination of Jack the Ripper and Dracula! In those days also, the slogan was very often, "Men must work and women must weep". Usually women stayed home to mind the many kids. Now, in this age of Female Emancipation the new slogan is: "Men must work and women must weep, but not if they've got a husband to keep!"

Anyway, now for the song: *Whoopee!* N.B. Many verses are my own.

Every time I hear that dear old (!) Wedding March,
I'm darned glad I've got a nasty broken arch.
I have heard some people say that marriage means romance!
but at my age (and with my experience) I prefer a picnic,
a game of bridge, or golf, or even a dance!

It's another day in sunny June; another sunny honeymoon
For this is the season; another reason for makin' WHOOPEE!
The choir sings: Here Comes The Bride;
another victim is by her side!
He's lost his reason;
for this is the season for makin' WHOOPEE.

Down through the countless ages, and you'll find it everywhere,
Somebody makes good wages but somebody wants to grab a
share.
She calls him Toodles, and rolls her eyes!
She makes him stroodles, and bakes him pies.
But what is it all for? So that he'll fall for her kind of
WHOOPEE!

But very soon they are marrying; but a baby son she's carrying
A shot-gun wedding is what they're getting
for making WHOOPEE too soon!
Nevertheless, in that first year
It's "Oh, my love" and "Yes, my dear";
The marital bliss is full of kisses and makin' WHOOPEE.

But, a decade on, what do we find?
There's no contentment nor peace of mind.
There's growing doubts now and finding faults,
and far less WHOOPEE,

Now picture a dubious love-nest somewhere on the wrong side
of town.
He's in a shabby old vest; she's in a dowdy dressing gown.
And she grows FAT (again!), but he gets thin;
The kids are making a shocking din.
They're in a prison now
and there's no reason now for makin' WHOOPEE!

Another year, or maybe less;
What's this I hear? Oh, can't you guess?
She feels neglected, and he's suspected

of makin' WHOOPEE elsewhere!
She sits alone most every night;
he doesn't phone, or even write!
He says he's busy, but she asks, "is he?"
I bet he's makin' WHOOPEE! elsewhere

He doesn't make much money: £3,000 per year.
A judge, who thinks it funny, says "You pay 5 thou' to her!"
"Now," he says, "Judge, suppose I fail?"
The Judge says, "Oh, you budge into jail.
You better keep her; You'll find it's cheaper
than makin' WHOOPEE! elsewhere!"

I then add a rider (my own extra quatrain):

This ends my story, this ends my song;
of course there 's a moral, don't get it wrong:
Be careful, sonny, when with your honey,
'bout makin' WHOOPEE too soon!

I must recount now certain other problems of preparation for my would-be rather ambitious, and ever daring, act as Entertainer. Having rehearsed my script in secret in my bedroom many times, and blandly assuming that it was word perfect and not to exceed twelve or so minutes, I then needed, ideally, the sheet music of my two songs so as to be accompanied suitably by the pianist. Alas! We have only two music shops selling sheet-music in Swansea. And they both said they could not get the numbers I sought in the limited time available. I phoned my (always busy) nephew in Oxford and he asked his sister - Geraldine, on vacation from Italy - to search the Oxford music stores. But now "Time was of the quintessence"!

Under duress for a solution I suddenly had a minor brain-wave. I 'phoned the organiser of the venture; she gave me the details (address and telephone number) of the accompanist for the show. He was one Robert Jenkins and he had a very fine reputation as a versatile pianist, etc. I told him of my problem concerning sheet-music and asked him if he would accept my taped cassette of my script and songs if I sent it to him in good time. To my delight he readily agreed. A few days later he was kind enough to tell me that he not only enjoyed my tape (with many laughs) but had already mastered the melodies of the two songs.

And so "the Great Day dawned!" Still keeping my daring act a secret (I had told my dear wife that I was meeting some old college colleagues), I dressed up in my best grey suit (I only have one anyway!), and put on a large bow tie and a straw hat - both bought for the occasion at an Oxfam charity shop for £1.50 for both items together! Competitors had been requested to be at the Patti Pavilion by 11:30a.m. for rehearsals. With the show due to start at 2:30p.m. I considered the waiting time outrageously long, especially for nervous contestants. So I arrived at one o'clock. I had left a note for my wife that I expected to be back home at around 5p.m.

When I arrived at the Concert Pavilion, I noticed that all the artistes were converging at the same time (as if by mutual arrangement). Now a kind of raffle took place to determine one's position on the programme and I was greatly relieved to find myself last out of sixteen. The M.C. then suggested that we would go on in the same order for the rehearsal. The first artiste to ascend the stage steps was a very buxom, handsome woman with a big bust, a big personality and a big but melodious voice!

She had the impressive name of Simone Watts-Williams. When she started singing, *Who Will Buy My Wonderful Day?* (from Oliver), I turned to a man sitting beside me and said, "My God! She's terrific! And I'd better go home! I can't possibly compete with that!"

He, an old-stager of 70 plus years (not competing), replied, "Oh, yes, she's very good! She has won First Prize many times. She's really in the professional class. She will win again, no doubt! But don't go home. You never know your luck; you might be second or third."

Mrs Watts-Williams was followed by a Jolson impersonator. And my word, he had a voice as rich and resonant as Al himself! I moaned and groaned and said to my new-found companion: "He's terrific too! I'm out of my depth here in this competition. Why, he's as good as Jolson himself!"

"Well, he bloody well ought to be! Don't you realise that he is playing a Jolson cassette and he is only miming?"

The third contestant to go up for rehearsal gave me some hope for he was helped on stage (carried on in fact) and laid gently on a sofa. I suddenly realised with a strong wince of painful emotion that this man had only one leg. And as he thrust the stump of a limb forward, he started singing: "All of me! Why not take all of me?" I didn't know whether to laugh or to cry! But his voice was so melodiously poignant that I groaned inwardly.

The next artiste restored my confidence further as to a possibility of a prize. She was a woman of well over 80 years of age. She was also carried on stage and then gently positioned alongside a Zimmer frame! She held on to this frame like grim death. If she had then sung a sad song like *I'm Only A Bird In A Gilded Cage* or something similar, it might have been tolerably suitable. In fact, she jigged up and down holding the frame precariously and frenetically screeching: *Let's All Go Down The Strand (And Have A Banana!)*.

"You see," consoled my companion. "Don't despair. With competition like that you certainly have a chance. Don't go home yet!"

However, the next contestant was a far better artiste. He was Jerry Ormonde (a veritable polymath of Palladium pantos perchance!?). He cracked jokes, he mimicked many famous comedians with a great variety of false noses, then he played the trumpet (very well) but ended his act with a very sentimental song - *Danny Boy* - with a mournful tone that vitiated his comedy.

My companion opined, "Now, he is talented but he can't make up his mind what kind of act he wants."

I agreed. So the rehearsals continued for an hour or so, and I noted with some sly satisfaction that Ormonde and I were the only comedians and my comedy was more consistent than Ormonde's. I was also pleased when I went up on the stage for my try out to find that Robert Jenkins had mastered the melody of my chosen songs without the music sheets.

Rehearsals completed we artistes (!?) were now asked to go to male or female dressing rooms to rest and prepare and await our respective calls. I noted that "Al Jolson" was busily blacking his face and crooning *Mammy* whilst Jerry Ormonde was trying his infinite variety of noses and making W.C. Fields and Groucho Marx wisecracks. I sat beside a handsome old man, immaculately dressed but not seen in rehearsals. He immediately asked me: "Are you competing for The Best-Dressed Man Prize?"

"No," I confessed, with a blush, "I'm competing as an artiste."

"Oh," he observed, "so that's alright then but anyway, I should win First Prize, I usually do. Won it four years running."

"May I ask how old you are?" I ventured.

He beamed all over his impressively ruddy face: "I'm 91, pushing 92. I don't look it do I?!"

"Not at all," I agreed, and added, "What was your trade or profession, and how long have you been retired?"

"Let's see now," he calculated, "about... 28, 29 years I was a railwayman and was a collector and organiser for the N.U.R, but my best, most enjoyable job came after my retirement..."

"AFTER your retirement!" I almost shouted. "What the Dickens was that?"

"Oh, yes," and he beamed again and chuckled, "I was called up for twenty years running by David Evans Department Store to be Santa Claus every Christmas!"

Meanwhile, the senior contestants were being called to the stage wings and returning to our dressing room with various comments of pleasure or regret; mainly of regret.

"Hit a bum note in the second verse, damn it!" Or "Al Jolson" would moan, "My curly wig kept slipping and I sweat like hell!" Ormonde grumbled that he had put on the wrong nose for Groucho.

At last I was paged: "Georgie Gee - on stage soon! Get ready!"

Of course I had butterflies in the tummy but consoled myself by recalling the old adage that without nervous tension the performance is mediocre or dull or bad. However, with my opening lines - a combination of false heroics and self denigration - I could hear the distinct giggles blossom into belly-laughs. Encouraged by this positive reaction I gave a pretty good burlesque and/or satire of the sexy-sweating Tom Jones. And when I tried to wiggle my hips in hopeless imitation and ended wiggling my knee (the only sexy part of my body still operative) I really felt that I had brought the house down! Greatly encouraged I essayed a rapid and rhythmical tap-dance after my two versions of *Happy Feet* and dared to give my encore (taking too much of the stipulated time) but being rewarded with loud and prolonged applause.

Mine was the last act and awaiting the judges' decision, I went down into the Hall and mingled with members of the audience. I had many congratulations but I was greatly amused by two ladies who were adamant that I was exactly like Maurice Chevalier (because, I guessed, of my straw hat and bow tie).

"Oh, dear me," I sighed in mock sadness.

One asked, "Why are you disappointed?"

"Well, you see," I replied, "I was trying to impersonate Tom Jones and Eddie Cantor."

In a far more serious mood I was now getting worried because it was 5:15 and I had left a note to assure my wife that I ought to be home at 5p.m! I sought out the compere and expressed my concern.

"If I were you," he advised, "I'd hang on a while and wait for the judges' summing up about the winners."

Somewhat reluctantly, I sat backstage and continually looked at my watch. At last I heard the Lord Mayor of Swansea make a nice short speech of congratulations: "for all the wonderful talent displayed by our Senior Citizens today!" Then he asked one of the judges to announce the winners: ONE, TWO, THREE. With much pleasure I heard my name called last of the three. I hurried on stage only to discover that the names were read out in reverse order. I was being awarded the FIRST PRIZE! I was thunderstruck! And what followed caused some embarrassment for I was presented with a handsome silver cup, a bottle of champagne, a huge be-ribboned certificate with red seal and, biggest of all, an enormous basket of fruit! All this together with a prize I could slip into my pocket - a cheque for £25.

Now, realising I had no car, I wondered how I could get a taxi from a place I never frequented?! Eventually a Patti Pavilion steward phoned for me and at 5:45 I was homeward bound. On arriving at my garden gate trying to organise my diverse and large prize bundles, my wife, Kate, came out to analyse the commotion I engendered. She was completely surprised and so overwhelmed as she helped to sort my winner's largesse! And she even decided to forgive my truant trespasses!

Two or three days later we travelled to Hereford to stay awhile with my daughter and family and the huge basket of my prize fruit helped to feed us well for several days.

I should now record that the Senior Citizens Talent Competition got good publicity from local and regional press and with fine photos. Our local *South Wales Evening Post* had a banner heading about my act which made me wince because of its raw crudity. It proclaimed (with photo underneath) 'LADIES: THROW £20 NOTES, NOT YOUR KNICKERS!', the detailed report read:

> Georgie Gee, over 76 years of age, described himself as The Pensioner's TOM JONES! Georgie describing himself as the "Jovial Joking Joyeur" was one of several of over 60 year olds competing at the local heat of the Senior Citizens Talent Competition at the Patti Pavilion. Although some entrants even needed Zimmer frames to get on stage, they amply proved that old age can't diminish enthusiasm. Georgie Gee for instance, confessed that a recent hip operation prevented him from "swinging his hips in the sensual fashion of Tom Jones". However he compensated with a quick, nifty tap-dance in an exuberant rendition of *Happy Feet*. Georgie's raunchy stage act paid off with the judges; the Pensioner's Tom Jones won!

The Western Mail, the main newspaper of Wales, also had a banner headline, viz: 'PACKED PATTI PAVILION FILLED WITH LAUGHTER!', and the article ran:

> Swansea Pensioner - Georgie Gee (a Jovial Joking Joyeur) delighted a packed audience at the annual Senior Citizens Talent Competition yesterday. The singing comedian [my comment in parenthesis, "Ye Gods!"] beat all other hopefuls to take First Prize. He had the crowds at the Patti Pavilion rolling around with laughter. "He was wicked; a bit risqué but very funny!" said the contest organiser, Anita Thomas.

Now I must describe the sequel to my totally unexpected success, if only briefly. I was asked if I wanted to proceed to (Whitbread's sponsored, therefore well financed!) the Senior Citizens Competition, the All Wales round, to be held at the Ebbw Vale Leisure Centre in mid-June. I was now excited at the prospects, not for money or cognate prizes, but for the fun (and fame!?) of it But now I was advised and warned that there would be so many more contestants this time round that no act must exceed eight minutes (in the event so many artistes protested at the limitation on their genius that the time allowed was spun out to ten minutes). Now, alas, bad luck dogged my *Happy Feet* footsteps! I had been convinced by Anita Thomas that I would enjoy the services of the same expert accompanist, Robert Jenkins, for I still had not managed to get the song sheets in time. But when I arrived at the venue of the show I was told that I had a new, and very young, inexperienced pianist. And after a few trials he told me bluntly that he found it quite impossible to accompany me. So I sang my lively song with no musical background. Worse still, I also discovered to my acute dismay that the stage was so thickly carpeted that my "lively tap dance" would be silent! (Imagine!)

However (small compensation), I was to go on last and I was the only comedian (singers galore again!). So I could possibly have an outside chance of a third prize!

Despite the many handicaps mentioned, I was placed joint third by the judges and later asked if I wanted to proceed to the All British Finals to be held in Southport, Lancs. in mid-July. (Of this, more anon).

Taking a broad philosophical view of my brief career as a Public Entertainer, it occurs to me that I have had more laughs off-stage than on! For example: between rehearsals and the live show a lady singer, (prize-winner many times) asked me one day, "Do you have false teeth, Georgie?"

Coyly I admitted, "Yes."

"Oh," she commented. "And do you have to take them out when you sing?"

"Oh, no!" I protested firmly.

"Oh!" she admitted, so very candidly, "I have to take both sets out, for I have found, by awkward experience, that when I strain on the top notes they tend to pop out and one sad day they bloody did!"

Sure enough when I studied the detailed video of the Ebbw Vale filmed record I saw all too clearly our "call me Callas", on reaching her high C in her rendition of *One Fine Day* perfectly achieved - no falsetto note - her mouth was wide open, *sans* dentures!

Another example of unconscious humour: I said I was to go on last in the All Wales Concert. Immediately before my act was a magician. Incidentally he flagrantly abused the ten minute rule imposed on all of us. True to his stage-craft, he conjures up not only yards of ribbon but doves and the *tour de force*, a white rabbit. After the use of the latter, an aide put the rabbit on a handy shelf in the wings where I was waiting anxiously to go on. Alas, also on the same shelf, a bouquet of flowers had been placed to be delivered at the show's end to the Lord Mayor's wife. I was utterly convulsed (and too paralysed with shock and "artiste's" raw nerves to act) when I saw the rabbit nibbling at the flowers!

I had to consider carefully, my condition, especially my health, and some other commitments when getting the invite to go to the British Finals. But I must now admit that vanity and the "call of the boards à la theatre" prevailed. However, the arrangements for the trip to Southport, Lancs. were far from ideal and the journey and timing proved to be very arduous (for a man of 76 plus and in frail health). Instead of travelling the day before the show and resting a night before the act, Anita Thomas asked me to meet her on a strategic corner where she and a car driver would be waiting. However, this meant that I had to get up at 4a.m. to get to the car by 5! (I had to remember also to keep my three tablets handy!) We were then taken by a very uncertain driver, "guided" by a very tentative navigator (Anita) to Southport. The journey took all of seven hours and we arrived in an awfully tired state, especially the "artistes".

I was surprised and somewhat angered to find that all the other contestants had arrived the day beforehand, and therefore, presumably had got a good night's sleep and were now refreshed for the rigours of the day! Under the circumstances, I was the last to have a rehearsal and tired as I was, I was obliged to get on stage for what was now something of an ordeal. A small compensatory factor was that I now had the song sheet of *Happy Feet*.

At 2:30p.m. the curtain went up for the start of the show. There was a huge audience (I was reliably told later about 2,000 people) and we were twenty-five artistes. I was late on so I watched some of the performers from the wings. The one who impressed me most was a lithe little lady (aged 70 we were informed) who did three solo dances of completely different styles and ending in a most delightful tap-dance.

She got no prize. The winner, First Prize, was a local hero, a negro, giving a very good impersonation of Nat King Cole. Although I can admit being guilty of some natural bias, my strong impression remains that the winners were chosen by audience acclamation or/and sentiment. For "Nat King Cole" (a local boy) got the loudest applause when the compere asked the people in the Hall for their opinion. A far better singer got little acclaim but he was from Glasgow! The second prize went to a Lancashire man playing a guitar not terribly well but we were told twice that he was nearly blind. And the third prize was given to an old lady of 91 years who simply recited several humorous poems.

Concerning my own act, my first impression on stage was being momentarily blinded by a tremendous light focussed too strongly on my face and over-awed by a very loud four-piece band. In fact "Nat-King Cole's" personal piano accompanist consoled me later saying, "The band was much too loud for you and your very promising nifty tap dance was drowned out by the silly drummer using coconut shells to try to match your taps!"

However, there were compensations, for Whitbreads - who sponsored the show - presented every performer, good, average and bad, with a bumper of champagne and a £50 note. I also stayed that night in a luxurious guest house facing the sea. At breakfast I met the Lord Mayor of a Welsh city and his wife and his chauffeur who told me that they had enjoyed three nights there! I couldn't help wondering why I, an artiste, had had ONE night only?!